# THE SUTRA OF THE HOUSEHOLDER UNCOUTH

## A TEACHING OF THE BUDDHA SHOWING ALL-KNOWING WISDOM AND THE HOUSEHOLDER'S WAY

BY TONY DUFF AND TAMÁS AGÓCS
PADMA KARPO TRANSLATION COMMITTEE

First edition, February 2013
ISBN paper book : 978-9937-572-56-9
ISBN e-book: 978-9937-572-57-6

Janson typeface with diacritical marks and
Tibetan Classic Chogyal typeface
designed and created by Tony Duff,
http://www.pktc.org/pktc/

Produced, Printed, and Published by
Padma Karpo Translation Committee
P.O. Box 4957
Kathmandu
NEPAL

Committee members for this book: translation and composition, Lama Tony Duff; translation, Agócs Tamás; cover design, Christopher Duff.

Web-site and e-mail contact through:
http://www.pktc.org/pktc
or search Padma Karpo Translation Committee on the web.

# CONTENTS


INTRODUCTION ..... v

About *The Noble Great Stack of Jewels* ..... v

Authoritative Statement ..... vii

The Sūtra Petitioned by the Householder Uncouth ..... ix

The Main Themes of the Sutra ..... ix

The Householder Theme of the Sutra ..... xi

Modern Parallels ..... xiv

Learning to Read the Sutras and Honouring the Master who Teaches Them ..... xv

The Non-Dual Wisdom Theme of the Sutra ..... xvi

Modern Parallels ..... xix

Other Emptiness and This Sutra ..... xx

Related Matters ..... xxv

Sources ..... xxv

Sanskrit and Diacriticals ..... xxv

Supports for Study ..... xxvi

THE NINETEENTH CHAPTER OF *THE NOBLE ONE, THE GREAT STACK OF JEWELS'* DHARMA ENUMERATIONS IN A HUNDRED THOUSAND CHAPTERS: THE ONE PETITIONED BY THE HOUSEHOLDER UNCOUTH ..... 1

# INTRODUCTION

This book presents a Great Vehicle sūtra called "The Sūtra Petitioned by the Householder Uncouth". It is part of a very large collection of Great Vehicle sūtras named the *Ārya Mahāratnakūṭa* or *Noble Great Stack of Jewels.*

## 1. About the *Noble Great Stack of Jewels*

The use of the word *ārya*, meaning *noble*, at the beginning of the name is a convention that was settled on when the Buddhist sūtras were originally compiled. Placed at the beginning of a sutra's name, it shows that the sūtra is a Great Vehicle sūtra as opposed to a Lesser Vehicle sūtra. In this context, *ārya* has sometimes been translated into English as "sublime" which is not the meaning at all. Sublime in its true sense means that which is so deep that it *sub* goes below *lime* the level at which the normal mind can access it. However, *ārya* in this context means that the teachings of the Great Vehicle are superior and special compared to those of the Lesser Vehicle and sit high above them in the same way as the *nobility* of a country have a special position above the common people.

The *Stack of Jewels* in the name means that the collection houses a great *stack* or pile *of* the Buddha's teachings and that those teachings encompass all of the Three *Jewels*—buddha, dharma, and saṅgha.

*The Great Stack of Jewels* is comprised of forty-nine chapters, each one being a separate sūtra of the Great Vehicle. These forty-nine chapters begin and end with the words

> "Chapter such and such of *The Noble One, The Great Stack of Jewels'* dharma enumerations in a hundred thousand chapters."

If there are only forty-nine chapters in *The Great Stack of Jewels*, why does each chapter begin and end with the statement that it has one hundred thousand chapters of dharma enumerations? It is because each of the forty-nine chapters contains many smaller teachings in which specific classifications of the dharma are enumerated by the Buddha, so that *The Great Stack of Jewels* contains an enormous number—a hundred thousand, so to speak—of these little sections or chapters of teaching in which classifications of dharma are shown or enumerated. You will clearly see this style of presentation in the sūtra presented in this book.

The sūtras comprising the *Great Stack of Jewels* are records of discourses given by the Buddha and the events surrounding them.

The sūtras always begin with "I heard these words at one time" to indicate that what follows is a written record of something that was heard in person by one of the Buddha's followers. A key point here is that the followers who later recalled what they had heard all were people with extreme powers of recollection because of which it is possible to believe that the written record is highly accurate.

That is followed by a description of the circumstances in which the discourse was given, with information about where it was given, who was present, and so on. Discourses came about because someone would come before the Buddha and petition him for an opportunity to present his concerns. The description of the circumstances of the discourse would include the details of the petitioner and his petition.

Note the use of the word "petition". The atmosphere of the teachings was highly respectful and much honorific language was used. Thus, the sūtras do not merely say that someone came before the Buddha and immediately blurted out their concerns to him but say that someone came and at first *petitioned* the Buddha just to have the opportunity to speak. The Buddha would provide an opportunity and then the petitioner would have the chance to present his concerns. The Buddha would then give a discourse in response.

Towards the end of the discourse, someone would ask the Buddha what name or names should be given to the discourse so that it could be retained in future. The person often was Ānanda, the Buddha's personal attendant who heard every one of his discourses and who committed them all to memory with what is said to be perfect recall. The Buddha would reply with a number of names, one of which would usually indicate the name of the petitioner of the discourse, and the others of which would present one or more main themes of the discourse. Most of the sūtras in the *Great Stack of Jewels*, including the sūtra in this book, were titled with the name of the discourse that showed the petitioner of the discourse.

## 1.a. Authoritative Statement

Authoritative statement is a verbal statement given to others by someone who is a true authority. Authoritative statement was and still is an important point in the transmission of the Buddha's teaching.

The importance of this term cannot be understated. Many of the forty-nine chapters of *The Great Stack of Jewels* are entitled "the authoritative statement petitioned by such and such" where such and such was a person who came before the Buddha and petitioned him for his authoritative statement on some matter. For example, the forty-first and forty-second chapters of *The Great Stack of Jewels* are sūtras petitioned by Maitreya, called "An Authoritative Statement Petitioned by Maitreya" and "An Authoritative Statement

Concerning Eight Dharmas Petitioned by Maitreya" respectively. The Buddha was a person who had total and unimpeded knowledge of all things both in terms of their reality and their surface appearances. Thus, his statements always would be correct and exactly applicable to the situation; they were authoritative statements given at the highest level. The petitioners could have gone elsewhere in the search to have their questions answered. However, by coming into the presence of a truly complete buddha, whatever statements they might hear would be guaranteed to be authentic statements made by a person who had the ultimate capacity to inform his listeners. Remember that in India, at the time of the Buddha, there were many teachers who had founded religious movements. Each of them claimed to be the one who had authentic statement. When you have investigated carefully and come to understand what a buddha actually is, you will understand that only a buddha[1]—whoever that might be—can give the ultimate authentic statement to his listeners.

**Figure 1.** Buddha Śhākyamuni, the source of the transmission of dharma in our era

There are a number of ramifications of the Buddha being someone who provides the ultimate authoritative statement. One of them is that the contents of the sūtras cannot simply be passed off, even when they run quite contrary to our own ideas. They are worthy of careful examination precisely because they come from someone

---

[1] The Buddha's own explanations of what a buddha is are excellent. You will find them in the book *Unending Auspiciousness, the Sutra of the Recollection of the Noble Three Jewels*; see note 20.

who has the authority of total knowledge. Such statements are intended to open us up to further levels of insight, and this can happen especially when they run contrary to our own ideas. The sūtra in this book has many authoritative statements that will run counter to modern ideas but, in every case, careful consideration of the intended meaning will reveal something which is true in one way or another!

## 2. The Sutra Petitioned by the Householder Uncouth

### 2.a. The Main Themes of the Sutra

In the conclusion of this sūtra, Ānanda asks the Buddha how it should be retained and in reply the Buddha instructs,

> Ānanda, for that, retain this enumeration of dharma as 'Petitioned by Uncouth'! Also, retain it as 'Accomplishing the Householders' and Ordained Ones' Trainings'! Also retain it as 'The Chapter on Performing Service and Honour for the Guru Through the Special Intention'.

The first title shows the petitioner of the discourse, a man named "Uncouth" who was a bodhisatva living the life of a householder. This title was used to make the title of the sutra: *The Sūtra Petitioned by the Householder Uncouth*.

The second and third titles show important themes of the discourse. The second shows the main theme of the discourse, the way that a householder should train in the ways of a bodhisatva. The third shows one of the many sub-themes of the discourse, that a householder bodhisatva should, based of course in the enlightenment mind[2] which is also known as the special intention, show the highest respect to his gurus—meaning his spiritual teachers in general—in order to engage them and receive the teaching from

[2] Skt. bodhichitta, see the glossary under enlightenment mind.

them. There could be many other titles, each corresponding to one of the many other sub-themes present in the discourse.

There is a second main theme of this sūtra which is not mentioned in the titles given to it by the Buddha. The theme is the teaching of non-dual wisdom. This teaching appears in the sūtra without fanfare, with the Buddha simply mentioning many times that a householder bodhisatva should do his training within "all-knowing wisdom" or "equalness", in other words, within non-dual wisdom. The absence of verbal fanfare around the teaching of non-dual wisdom can easily obscure for a reader the fact that the Buddha was presenting that very wisdom to his followers not only with his words but with his presence in much the same way as is done in the tantras[3]. Thus, this teaching on non-dual wisdom is there as a main theme of the discourse but, because it is mainly taught through the Buddha's presence rather than through words, this theme is not usually obvious except to those who are extremely knowledgeable of the Buddha's teaching.

Non-dual wisdom taught in the very understated way of the sūtras is the pinnacle or final teaching of all the sūtra teachings. It is the sūtra equivalent of the very highest teachings of tantra, the teachings of Mahāmudrā and Mahasaṅdhi[4]. This teaching is found only in certain sūtras of the third turning of the wheel of dharma, such as the one here, and is not the same as the teaching on emptiness which is the pinnacle teaching of the second turning of the wheel

---

[3] The main difference between the direct presentation of non-dual wisdom in the sūtras and tantras is that in the sūtras it comes without fanfare and is presented in a very understated way whereas in the tantras it comes with considerable fanfare and is presented very explicitly.

[4] … or Dzogchen as it was known in Tibet …

of dharma[5]. The essence of this sūtra is that a householder bodhisatva can practise at the highest level, even though living in a household, by always taking recourse to non-dual wisdom.

## 2.b. The Householder Theme of the Sutra

This sūtra was petitioned by Uncouth who was a Buddhist layman. However, the "householder" in the name of the sūtra does not simply refer to the fact that Uncouth was a layman. The word "householder" is used in the title specifically to show that this sūtra is about being a householder bodhisatva as opposed to an ordained bodhisatva.

As a bodhisatva, Uncouth had two concerns. Firstly, he specifically did not want "to come forth from the life of a householder", as it is called, and live his life as a mendicant, nor did he want to take the step which usually followed that of being ordained as a monk. Secondly, he specifically wanted to ensure that the training he was undertaking as a householder bodhisatva was at the highest level and that he was not being relegated to a lesser level of training because of his choice not to become ordained. His second concern was especially valid and important—in his time, the life of a fully-ordained monk was regarded as the only way to pursue spirituality at the highest level because of which the commonly-held view was that only those who had taken ordination could be practising at the highest level. Thus, Uncouth had come to the Buddha seeking his authoritative statements on how householders should engage in the trainings of a bodhisatva and, moreover, how they could do so while practising at the highest level.

Uncouth begins by requesting the Buddha "to give a good explanation of ... the trainings of the householder bodhisatvas" but does it

---

[5] Although the Buddha does give some teaching in this sūtra on how a bodhisatva is to apply himself to the emptiness of a personal self and self of dharmas, it is only a minor aspect of the sūtra.

in a way that conveys both of the issues mentioned in the preceding paragraph. To make his request he first paints a picture of bodhisatvas in general as ones needy of instruction on the path to enlightenment. He continues by pointing out that those bodhisatvas consist of sons and daughters of the family who have become ordained as monks and nuns. He then pointedly states that those bodhisatvas also consist of "everyone who is staying in a household and who is truly and correctly accomplishing the dharmas of the side of enlightenment". He then asks the Buddha to teach for the sake of those bodhisatvas in general but to do so in such a way that the householder bodhisatvas among them who are practising seriously within the household environment will not be excluded. Finally, he makes the request mentioned just above, for teaching on the trainings of bodhisatva householders.

The Buddha gives a long discourse in reply, covering all the concerns which Uncouth has initially raised. You might be surprised when you first read the Buddha's reply, for it will seem that he is stating that one has to leave the life of a householder in order to progress spiritually. In regard to this, it is very important to remember that in India of that time it was generally accepted that it was not possible to stay in a household and progress spiritually, that the only way for anyone to progress spiritually was to leave life in the household, become a mendicant, and then on top of that to become ordained as a monk or nun. It is necessary to read the entire sūtra while keeping that in mind and also while paying close attention to the details in order to see the actual answers to Uncouth's concerns.

The Buddha had, as he explains in many other discourses, a primary obligation to speak in a way that would suit the ordained members of the audience, in a way that would not disturb their convictions about the path of renunciation and ordination that they had undertaken. He keeps that obligation and it comes across very clearly as the literal meaning of the sūtra that being ordained or at least following the conduct of someone who is ordained is crucial to being a bodhisatva.

The Buddha also had an obligation to speak to Uncouth's situation. He keeps that obligation, but to understand the fullness of what he says about the householder bodhisatva's way we have to look past the literal meaning of the sūtra and look at the details of the discourse and events surrounding it. For example, it was pointed out in the preceding paragraph that a few seemingly insignificant words in Uncouth's initial request for teaching are crucial to understanding the full import of his request for teaching. An important event following that appears in the middle of the sūtra when what one assumes is the entire assembly of many thousands of householders hear the Buddha's very extensive and intensely motivational explanation of the faults of living as a householder and the benefits of being ordained immediately then immediately ask to become fully-ordained monks. It seems that Uncouth has also done the same and become a monk, with the implication being that the only way to truly practise as a bodhisatva is to give up the life of a householder and be ordained, just as the Buddha seems to have been saying. However, it turns out that Uncouth has not given in to the literal meaning and has remained firm in his commitment to being a householder bodhisatva. We see that he knows that there is something about being a householder bodhisatva that is very useful and we see his strength of determination. This is then verified in full by the Buddha in the concluding remarks of the discourse where the Buddha points out that the bodhisatva Uncouth is a much more powerful person in his life of staying in a household whilst conducting his bodhisatva journey than are many of the bodhisatvas who have left the household for an ordained life. Again, the words are few and can easily be glossed over but the import is enormous—the Buddha concludes his whole discourse by clearly stating that the spirituality of ordained bodhisatvas is nothing in comparison to that of a householder bodhisatva like Uncouth:

> Ānanda, this householder Uncouth in this good kalpa will, due to staying in the place of a household, engage in the entire ripening of utterly many sentient beings; an ordained bodhisatva would not be capable of such in even a thousand kalpas or many hundreds of thousands of kalpas. Why is that? Ānanda, it is that the good qualities had by this bodhisatva do not exist in even one thousand of the ordained bodhisatvas.

### 2.b.1. *Modern Parallels*

Uncouth's situation fits very closely with the situation of today's Western Buddhists, most of whom do not wish to leave home and become mendicants and most of whom are equally determined that this should not mean that they are relegated to a life which has been officially stamped as lesser than that of an ordained life. These have become prominent issues for Western Buddhists at this time, and in my mind a careful consideration of the actual meaning embodied in this sūtra could be a very fruitful exercise for today's Western Buddhists. I have found that investigating the sūtra carefully raises issues of great relevance and interest to today's Western Buddhists. Moreover, the sūtra shows those issues in the context of the Buddha giving his authoritative statements about them. I have found the sūtra to be very provocative and equally rich.

The sūtra not only fits with the concerns of today's householder bodhisatvas, but there is a message in the Buddha's concluding remarks quoted immediately above which is very important for those Westerners who rush in to become ordained. As one who was ordained as a Buddhist monk for some years before returning to household life, and especially as one who studied for many years with the incomparable Chogyam Trungpa Rinpoche who insisted on the householder's life for his followers, I see that this sūtra gives a very direct message about the weakness of those who remain as celibate, ordained bodhisatvas compared to the great capability of householder bodhisatvas like Uncouth. This message is directly applicable to Westerners thinking of becoming ordained let alone those who have already been ordained.

### 2.b.2. *Learning to Read the Sutras and Honouring the Master who Teaches Them*

What has been said above highlights a key point about this sūtra, which is that it cannot be taken at face value. It is easy to miss the actual meanings embodied in the sūtra if it is read without paying attention to the details of the discourse and events surrounding it. For example, it could easily seem that the sūtra is a statement that the ordained life is the one which is better in every way for a bodhisatva who is intent on spiritual progress, though a more careful reading shows that the Buddha was speaking in a way that suited the ordained members of the audience, yet at the same time was skilfully addressing Uncouth's questions and actually coming out in favour of Uncouth's approach, at least for those householders who are capable of it.

Generally speaking the sūtras are not easy to read because they contain substantial amounts of the technical vocabulary of enlightenment and because the actual intent behind the questions, answers, and doings of the people involved is often less than obvious. To overcome these two difficulties, one first needs a good understanding of the vocabulary and style of expression of dharma, at least as it is used in any given sūtra. To help the reader with that, we have provided extensive notes and a glossary.

Then it is necessary to have experience with the sūtras and how to read and interpret them. Traditionally, and for good reason, a person has always gained an understanding of their vocabulary and the knowledge needed to read them by going to a Buddhist master and requesting that he impart his knowledge. The process of going to a Buddhist master and requesting that he impart his knowledge is one of the important sub-themes of this sūtra, to the extent that the Buddha gives one title for the sūtra as "The Chapter on Performing Service and Honour for the Guru Through the Special Intention".

In general, the Buddha emphasized the importance of learning the dharma through person-to-person oral transmission of the words and their meaning. It has become overlooked these days, with many people thinking that they can properly understand dharma simply by reading books or watching a video, but, in fact, there is a need for transmission of the teaching received in person from someone who belongs to an unbroken lineage of transmission all the way back to the Buddha. Moreover, there is an etiquette involved in obtaining that transmission, an etiquette which is rooted in faith and respect for the person who himself has received the transmission of the meaning of dharma from his own teacher. The Buddha spends considerable time teaching that etiquette to Uncouth and the rest of the retinue present at the discourse. It will be difficult for most readers to get a sufficient explanation of this sūtra in the person-to-person style of transmission just discussed. Therefore, we have written this introduction so that the reader could understand the main import of the sūtra and not fall into the gross misunderstandings that could occur if the sūtra were taken at face value.

## 2.c. The Non-Dual Wisdom Theme of the Sutra

As explained earlier, a hidden yet main theme of this sūtra consists of teaching on non-dual wisdom. This sūtra is one of a group of sūtras that show the most profound approach to becoming enlightened, the approach of entering the all-knowing mind of a buddha—which is given the name "wisdom"[6]—directly and without any further involvement with saṃsāric mind. The point here, and this is echoed again and again in this sūtra, is that wisdom is not realized by making a logical approach to it but by directly entering it. And the only way that that can be done is to be with someone who has

---

[6] For wisdom, see the glossary.

already done it and can, through the sheer force of his being present in it, cause it to manifest in your own mindstream and then introduce you to it. In other words, at the highest level, non-dual wisdom is known by direct transmission coupled with the appropriate instruction. In relation to that, remember that the householder Uncouth did not merely want teachings on how to be a householder bodhisatva but wanted them at the highest level of spiritual practice. The Buddha obliges him in this sūtra by explaining that the various trainings of a bodhisatva are always to be done within this wisdom and, we suppose, directly transmits that wisdom to Uncouth through his personal presence of being in that pure wisdom.

To get a feel for this, imagine what it would be like to be in the presence of Śhākyamuni Buddha, a being who is living in totally unobscured wisdom in every moment. If you had faith in him and were willing to respect everything about him, you would make a point of being in his presence, just as Uncouth had done, so that you could be in the field of that wisdom. Then, if you were open and if the Buddha emphasized being in wisdom in his teaching—which is what he does in this sūtra—and if he avoided mention of lesser, logical approaches to being in wisdom—which he also does in this sutra—then it is very likely that you would have that wisdom woken up in you. In that case, it is almost certain that you would have received the transmission of wisdom directly, and you would have received the essential instruction on that kind of approach to wisdom, which is simply to go there and stay in it. A key point here is that you do not merely hear the instruction, as so many people do today, "that you can simply go to wisdom and stay in it", but that you are in the presence of someone who wakes up that wisdom in you and then introduces you to it. In this sūtra, the words and events recounted tell us that there has been this sort of transmission of wisdom directly, person to person, and we can see that the Buddha then consistently tells Uncouth that that wisdom is the approach for a householder bodhisatva like him to take.

There are many aspects of this sūtra which indicate that the Buddha is teaching at that level. It is beyond the scope of this introduction to write about all of them, though anyone with a very good knowledge of the dharma could, once the above has been pointed out, find them in the sūtra. Nevertheless, consider for example the fact that the Buddha had emphasized for his lay followers living in households the practice of observing the member of the eightfold path of the noble ones called "right action"[7]. In this sūtra, we do see the Buddha instructing Uncouth that a householder bodhisatva practising at the highest level is to take all the vows of a layperson and is to avoid the ten non-virtuous actions. However, we also see that the Buddha again and again instructs him not to be concerned with performing good karmic actions for the sake of good future results because that will simply keep him in saṃsāra. Instead, Uncouth is instructed that he should make the all-knowing wisdom of a buddha his prime interest and to step into that as much as possible. This is a very high level of teaching—the same instruction is found in both Mahāmudrā and Mahasaṅdhi or Dzogchen teaching.

A second prominent feature of the profound style of teaching present in this sūtra is the Buddha's continual use of the term "equalness". "Equalness", which could also be called "sameness", is not the same as equanimity. For example, the Buddha states in this sūtra that the householder bodhisatva must gain "equalness in regard to the eight worldly dharmas" and some readers might think that this means that one must develop the kind of equanimity in which one is not affected by those eight situations of gain and loss, and so on, in other words, that one must develop a state within saṃsāric mind of neither attachment nor aversion when those situations arise. However, that is not the meaning at all. The teaching here is at a much higher level. The word "equalness" always refers

[7] In fact, the name is "correct extremes of action" meaning that one should ascertain the two possible extremes of karmic actions—good and bad—and then live by adopting good karmic actions and rejecting bad ones.

to being in a state of all-knowing wisdom. Thus, equalness in this sūtra always refers to directly experiencing all phenomena while at the same time directly knowing their equalness or sameness—which is that they are equal or the same in being empty—all of which is only possible while dwelling in all-knowing wisdom.

The use of "equalness" in this sūtra is particularly important. Its use shows that the Buddha was teaching Uncouth that householder bodhisatvas intent on their path must work at the level of stepping directly into the all-knowing wisdom of a buddha. The Buddha was not sending householder bodhisatvas along the lesser path recommended for the average layperson living in a household of primarily observing adoption and rejection of good and bad karmic action. Moreover, he was not teaching entrance into wisdom in the lesser way of engaging in logical approaches to seeing emptiness and then developing wisdom through that, but was teaching it at the highest level of entering it directly. The Buddha's use of "equalness" goes with following a path of realization in which one leaps directly from dualistic mind into the actual state of reality in which all phenomena are both present and empty as known by all-knowing wisdom, rather than analyzing them away into emptiness, with prajñā and from there going to wisdom, which is a lesser approach.

### 2.c.1. *Modern Parallels*

This theme of entering wisdom and staying in it also relates directly to the situation of most Westerner Buddhists today. They prefer to live a householder's life. The approach of monastic life, in which they might have large amounts of time to gain attainment by analysing reality logically is not available to them. What could work for them is that, rather than spending time on attempting to analyse the mistaken mind of saṃsāra to death, they might find someone who has already received the transmission of wisdom and knows how to transmit it to others, and who has the short but special instructions needed for them to train in remaining in that wisdom.

### 2.c.2. Other Emptiness and This Sutra

The Buddha taught his sūtra teachings—we are leaving tantra aside in this book—in three, successive stages. They were called "the three turnings of the wheel of dharma". The hidden yet main theme of this sūtra of the direct teaching of non-dual wisdom was entrusted to Maitreya by the Buddha, who then transmitted it to Indian masters, from whom it eventually entered Tibet where it eventually became known as the teaching of "Other Emptiness".

In Tibet, there was one group—Tsongkhapa and the tradition which arose following him called the Gelugpa school—which said that the three turnings of the wheel were not taught in a sequence that progressed from least to most profound. Tsongkhapa in particular claimed that the second turning contained the most profound teachings. Few others in Tibet agreed, with the majority of Tibetan masters saying that the third turning of the wheel contained the most profound teachings. The proof of which of those assessments is correct is not hard to come by—the Buddha himself says in one of the major sūtras of the third turning, the *Great Vehicle Unravelling the Intent Sūtra*, that he taught in a progressively profound sequence of stages for the sake of his disciples so that they could gradually be led from their state of confusion into full realization of the truth, then illustrated his approach with the analogy of spoon-feeding children. Moreover, he made that approach exceptionally clear in *The Sūtra Petitioned by King Dharaṇeśhvara* which says,

> Son of the family, it is like this. For example, there is a skilled jeweller who knows the craft of jewellery well. Of the various types of precious jewel, he has taken a precious jewel which is totally impure. He wets it with a penetrating, chemical salt solution then thoroughly cleans it with a hair cloth and in that way gives it a thorough cleaning. He does not stop his efforts at just that, either. Beyond that, to clean it he wets it with a penetrating decoction then thoroughly cleans it with a woollen

> flannel and in that way gives it a thorough cleaning. He does not stop his efforts at just that, either. Beyond that, to clean it he also wets it with a strong chemical liquid then thoroughly cleans it with a fine cotton cloth and in that way thoroughly cleans it. Thoroughly cleansed and free of encrustation, it is now called "an excellent type of Lapis Lazuli".
>
> Son of the family, in the same way, the tathāgata, knowing the element of totally impure sentient beings[8], uses the story of renunciation which is about impermanence, suffering, lack of self, and impurity to arouse disenchantment in those sentient beings who are attracted to cyclic existence and to get them into the taming that goes with the noble dharma. The tathāgata does not stop his efforts at just that much, either. Beyond that, he utilizes the story of emptiness, signlessness, and wishlessness to make them realize the mode of a tathāgata. The tathāgata does not stop his efforts at just that much, either. Beyond that, he utilizes the story of the non-regressing wheel and the story of the total purity of the three spheres to make those sentient beings whose causes vary in nature enter the tathāgata's place.

The disagreement over whether it is the second or third turning sūtras that are more profound comes because of the following. The Prajñāpāramitā sūtras of the second turning of the wheel show how, using logical analysis, to arrive at a direct perception of emptiness and thereby to exit saṃsāra—theirs is a presentation of how to arrive at reality which comes from using saṃsāric mind to overcome saṃsāric mind. A number of sūtras of the third turning, including

[8] Element is a name for the buddha nature. In the third turning of the wheel, beings are classed into three types: buddhas, who are totally pure; those on the path, who are mixed pure and impure; and ordinary beings who are totally impure.

the sūtra in this book, emphasize that the highest approach to exiting saṃsāra is not that of analysing it to death with logical mind but of simply stepping into buddha-mind and staying there. Anyone familiar with the approach of the tantras, and especially with the teachings of Mahāmudrā or Dzogchen, will see immediately that this latter approach is also the approach of those highest teachings.

One of the features of the approach of the second turning of the wheel—of entering reality by analysing non-reality to death with saṃsāric mind—is that it involves a great deal of instruction and all of it is very logical and detailed in nature: "Think this, think that, analyse this way, analyse that way, meditate like this and that", and so on. However, for entering reality by simply stepping into the wisdom which is a buddha's mind—which is the approach of a certain set of sūtras found in the third turning of the wheel sutras—there is little to say. In fact, there is no great method for this—the teacher has to mention to the disciple that the wisdom-mind of a buddha exists and then has to create a situation in which, based on his own direct realization of that wisdom, the disciple gains direct perception of that wisdom for himself. After that, there are some straightforward instructions on how the student should familiarize himself with that wisdom-mind, so that the student can remain in it more and more. After reading this sūtra while paying attention to this point, you should come to the conclusion that the sūtra is indeed teaching in that way.

The Buddha taught the teaching on how to enter wisdom-mind directly in the third turning sūtras and entrusted such teaching to his regent Maitreya. Maitreya then taught it to the Indian master Asaṅga, who wrote down Maitreya's teachings in five treatises called *The Five Dharmas of Maitreya*. Later, in Tibet, the majority of Tibetan Buddhist schools understood this meaning and named it the teaching of "Other Emptiness" and referred to the system of meditation which contained this approach as "the profound meditation system of Maitreya"[9]. Moreover, they identified ten third turning of the wheel sūtras that presented this approach[10]. The most common listing of those sūtras is:

1. *The Sūtra Definitively Teaching the Tathāgata's Great Compassion* contains many chapters, several of which were spoken because of the questions of King Dharaṇeśhvara so is also known as *The Sūtra Requested by King Dharaṇeśhvara*
2. *The Sūtra requested by the Girl, Jewel*
3. *The Sūtra Requested by the Householder Uncouth*
4. *The Sūtra of No Increase nor Decrease*
5. *The Sūtra for the Benefit of Aṅgulimālā*
6. *The Sūtra Encouraging the Special Intention*
7. *Wisdom Appearance's Ornament Sūtra*
8. *Point of Passage Wisdom Sūtra*
9. *The Great Drum Sūtra*
10. *The Meeting of Father and Son Sūtra*

Note that there are other lists like this but with slight variations in the sūtras mentioned and that there also are listings of fifteen and twenty sūtras that fall into this category.

---

[9] In the writings of the Tibetan masters who proclaimed what they called "the Other Empty system", these sūtras were called "the sūtras of the profound meditation system" because they were regarded as the sūtras which show the meaning of the most profound system of view and meditation of the Buddha. These sūtras were also referred to as "the profound definitive-meaning sūtras" and "the core definitive meaning sutras" because they show the definitive rather than provisional meaning of the Buddha's teaching and so show the most profound level of the Buddha's teaching within the sūtra teachings.

[10] ... rather than following the more detailed and very logical teachings of the second turning of the wheel in which the mistaken mind of saṃsāra uses itself to analyse itself to death so that the wisdom-mind could manifest.

We translated the sūtra in this book precisely because it is listed as one of the sūtras which expresses the profound approach to meditation which is a hallmark of the third turning sūtras. We had already translated *The Point of Passage Wisdom Sūtra*, which is also in the list[11] and wanted to make at least one more of this class of sūtra available to Westerners who are interested in sūtras that show "Other Emptiness".

The following statements from *The Point of Passage Wisdom Sūtra* will give further insight into the direct transmission of wisdom mentioned in this sūtra petitioned by the householder Uncouth. In *The Point of Passage Wisdom Sūtra* sūtra, the Buddha first makes a statement that teaches how to find the non-dualistic mind of wisdom and then stay in it:

> If mind is realized, it is wisdom, and that being so, he shall utterly cultivate the perception that buddha is not to be sought elsewhere.

The versified version of this statement adds something useful:

> Mind is the cause of wisdom's occurrence;
> Do not seek buddha elsewhere!

Wisdom is found in mind and nowhere else, a point which is mentioned in the sūtra for Uncouth. The Buddha taught in the second turning of the wheel that enlightenment is to be sought through logical dissections of the phenomena external to mind. He now teaches that the ultimate way to seek enlightenment is through examination of the mind itself. Realizing mind, meaning realizing the very nature of the dualistic saṃsāric mind by seeing its essential nature in direct perception, is the cause of, or the doorway to, finding wisdom. Once wisdom has been found, there is nothing to

---

[11] The sūtra is published under its own name *The Noble One Called "Point of Passage Wisdom", A Great Vehicle Sutra* by Padma Karpo Translation Committee, 2011, ISBN 978-9937-572-58-3, translated by Tony Duff and Sergey Dudko.

do other than to remain disengaged from the ignorant process of dualistic mind. Thus, the first statement sums up the ultimate view and the second sums up the ultimate meditation as taught by the Buddha.

## 3. Related Matters

### 3.a. Sources

We used the Derge edition of the Tibetan Kangyur to translate the sūtra. A copy of the Tibetan text is provided later in the book to assist those who are knowledgeable of Tibetan, and especially to give translators further insights into how to translate sūtras.

Note that there is a new edition of both the *Translated Word* and *Translated Treatises* which was published in Beijing, China, about two years ago. It is a comparative edition which uses the Derge edition as the basis but meticulously notes every difference with the seven other major editions of the *Translated Word* and *Translated Treatises*. It is a truly excellent reference. Theoretically, we should have compared all editions and tried to rectify the resulting translation into English. However, that would have been an enormous task and one which would ultimately have confused the reader, therefore we have not done it.

### 3.b. Sanskrit and diacriticals

Sanskrit terms are an important aspect of the technical explanations found in the commentary. They are properly rendered into English with diacritical marks, therefore, for the sake of precision, diacritical marks have been used with them throughout this book.

The IATS system of transliteration of Sanskrit, which is the one generally in use in academic circles is hard for non-scholars to read. Therefore, we have modified that system slightly to make the transliterated Sanskrit more readable even when the meaning of the diacritical marks is not understood. This same approach seems to be commonplace amongst translators of Tibetan Buddhism. In it:

ś is written the way it sounds, as śh ;
ṣ is written similarly as ṣh ; and
ṛ is written similarly as ṛi ;
ca is written as cha;
cha is written as chha.

The other letters for transliteration are used in the same way as they are used in the IATS scheme. In general, if you do not understand the system, simply read the letters as though they did not have the diacritical marks and, with our modified system, you will have a good approximation to the actual pronunciation.

## 3.c. Supports for Study

Padma Karpo Translation Committee has amassed a range of materials to help those who are studying this and related topics. In particular, several books on Other Emptiness have been published, all of which support each other and each of which clarifies another important aspect of the teaching. Please see the chapter containing information on supports for study at the end of the book for the details.

Lama Tony Duff, director
Agócs Tamás, translator
Christopher Duff, manager

Padma Karpo Translation Committee
Swayambunath,
Nepal,
February 2013

# The nineteenth chapter of *The Noble One, The Great Stack of Jewels'* dharma enumerations in a hundred thousand chapters: The One Petitioned by the Householder Uncouth[12]

First bundle[13].

In Sanskrit: ārya gṛihapati ugra paripṛhcchā nāma mahāyāna sūtra

In Tibetan: 'phags pa khyim bdag drag shul can gyis zhus pa zhes bya ba theg pa chen po'i mdo

---

[12] The householder's name in Sanskrit is Ugraḥ. This name conveys the sense of a man who was not educated and very rough in his ways, with a demeanour that tended to be very fierce or intense. The name fits well with the content of the sūtra, given that he represents those bodhisatva types who would find it hard to live as a monk within the very regimented and polite atmosphere of a monastic community. This very point is examined at length by the Buddha in the sūtra when he describes the various very polite styles of monastic conduct that are to be followed by all who enter a monastic environment.

[13] Indian Buddhist texts were written on palm leaves which were then stitched together into bundles. When they were translated, there was often an indication of the bundles involved put into the translation. That was done with this sūtra which came in three bundles.

In English: The Noble One, The Great Vehicle Sūtra Called "Petitioned by the Householder Uncouth"[14]

Homage to every buddha and bodhisatva.[15]

I heard these words at one time. The bhagavan[16] was residing in Śhrāvastī, in the enclosure of Anāthapiṇḍada within the grove of prince Jetṛi[17], together with a great monk community of one thousand, two hundred and fifty monks and with the bodhisatva

---

[14] The system for translating texts from other languages into Tibetan included adding this header before the actual translation, giving the name of the text as written in the source language followed by the name of the text as it had been translated into the Tibetan language. We think that this system should be extended by adding the translation of the original name in the target language as a third item, as done here for this translation into English.

[15] Note the spelling of bodhisatva, a spelling which is correct according to all Tibetan traditions of Buddhism. See the entra "satva and sattva" for more.

[16] "Bhagavan" is a term of respect used throughout Indian religions for a person who is regarded to be very advanced spiritually. The term literally means "one who has overcome the defilements" preventing enlightenment and is also explained to mean "one who has good qualities". Very extensive explanations of the meaning of "bhagavan" are given in *Unending Auspiciousness, the Sutra of the Recollection of the Noble Three Jewels* by Tony Duff, published by Padma Karpo Translation Committee, 2010, ISBN: 978-9937-8386-1-0.

[17] Skt. jetavana. This is often called "Jetavana Grove".

mahāsattvas[18] Maitreya, Mañjuśhrī, Apāyajaha, Avalokiteśhvara, Mahāsthāma-prāpta[19], and others, five thousand bodhisatvas in all.

At that point, the bhagavan was completely surrounded by a retinue of many hundreds of thousands and, looking straight ahead, was teaching dharma—he was teaching correctly and to the utmost the dharma which is pure conduct, virtuous at the beginning, virtuous in the middle, virtuous at the end, of excellent meaning, of excellent wording, un-adulterated, totally complete, total purity, and total purification[20].

Then, the householder Uncouth with five hundred underlings appeared from the great city of Śhrāvastī. They came there to the enclosure of Anāthapiṇḍada within the grove of prince Jetṛi where the bhagavan was and, having arrived there, prostrated by placing their heads at the feet of the bhagavan, then circled the bhagavan three times, and then arranged themselves to one side. Similarly, other householders too—householder Nandaruchi, householder Yaśhokāmaḥ, householder Samāptaḥ, householder Nandaka, householder Yaśhodatta, householder Sudhana, householder Śhilānanda, householder Anāthapiṇḍada, householder Nāgaśhrī, and householder Satyānanda—and, furthermore, very many householders

---

[18] For bodhisatva mahāsattva, see the glossary. Here it has the common meaning.

[19] One of the names of Vajrapāṇi.

[20] The list of features of the dharma starting with "pure conduct" and going down to "total purification" is the listing of the good qualities of dharma given by the Buddha himself in a teaching he named "recollection of the dharma". A complete presentation of the recollections of buddha, dharma, and saṅgha, together with extensive commentaries on the meanings of each of the items in the recollections is contained in the book *Unending Auspiciousness, the Sutra of the Recollection of the Noble Three Jewels* by Tony Duff, published by Padma Karpo Translation Committee, 2010, ISBN: 978-9937-8386-1-0.

each with five hundred underlings appeared from the great city of Śhrāvastī. They came there to the enclosure of Anāthapiṇḍada within the grove of prince Jetṛi where the bhagavan was and, having arrived there, prostrated by placing their heads at the feet of the bhagavan, then circled the bhagavan three times, and then arranged themselves to one side.

All of those householders and mostly their underlings as well had truly entered the Great Vehicle, produced roots of virtue, and definitely made for unsurpassed, truly complete enlightenment, and that alone[21].

Then householder Uncouth understanding that he was part of such a great retinue of householders[22] and by the power of the bhagavan rose from his seat, draped his outer robe over one shoulder, knelt down on his right knee, and bowing with joined palms in the direction of the bhagavan, supplicated the bhagavan in these words:

"Were the bhagavan to give me the opportunity to petition him for an authoritative statement[23], I would ask the bhagavan, tathāgata, arhat, truly complete buddha about some matters."

---

[21] "And that alone" means that they were not mixing up religious paths but were following the path of the bodhisatva and that alone. They were not attempting to go to a buddhist enlightenment and to one or more others such as the Hindu enlightenment—there were many possibilities in ancient India just as there are today—but were focussed solely on the unsurpassed truly complete enlightenment taught uniquely in this world age by Śhākyamuni Buddha.

[22] The sense here is that he had realized the extent of the assembly that he had joined and was in awe of it and therefore proceeded in the most respectful way possible.

[23] See the introduction and glossary for more on authentic statement.

He supplicated in those words and the bhagavan instructed the householder Uncouth in these words:

"Householder, the tathāgata has always given that opportunity to you! You the householder, ask the tathāgata which things you wish! In that way, through that question and its authoritative statement, I will make your mind happy."

He instructed in those words and Householder Uncouth supplicated the bhagavan in these words:

"Bhagavan, there are sons of the family and daughters of the family who have aroused the mind for unsurpassed, truly complete enlightenment, and have taken interest in the Great Vehicle, and are utterly abiding in the Great Vehicle, and seek right accomplishment in the Great Vehicle, and seek entrance into the Great Vehicle, and have committed to the Great Vehicle, and have taken all sentient beings into their care, and rescue all sentient beings, and seek armour so that they can be a refuge for all sentient beings, and take up the great burden for the sake of all sentient beings saying 'I will liberate those who have not crossed over, release those who have not been released, rescue those who have not been rescued, and take across to parinirvāṇa those who have not crossed over to parinirvāṇa', and are utterly abiding in the tremendously powerful entrance, and having heard of the unfathomable buddha wisdom seek armour so that they can have the right accomplishment of that wisdom, and who do not wish for the many faults of the sufferings of saṃsāra but have minds which do not become weary and even though cycling in saṃsāra for countless kalpas[24] will not be

---

[24] Skt. kalpa. "Kalpa" is the general term for a long period of time. Indian culture defined many degrees of kalpa, going from thousands of years up to cosmic ages.

daunted[25]. And bhagavan, among them are sons of the family or daughters of the family following the bodhisatva's vehicle who having come forth from staying in a household[26] are truly and correctly accomplishing the dharmas of the side of enlightenment[27] while not staying in a household. If everyone who is staying in a household truly and correctly accomplishing the dharmas of the side of enlightenment—the ones who are not coming forth from staying in a household—also are included, then, bhagavan, due to your mind of love for the world with gods, men, and asuras, and for the sake of your accepting them in the Great Vehicle, and of ensuring that they are not cut off from the Three Jewels' family, and of ensuring that they abide for a long time in all-knowing wisdom[28], bhagavan please give a good explanation of the ways in which the good qualities of the trainings of the bodhisatva householders should be presented.

"How should the bodhisatva householders staying in the place of a household be in accord with the command of the tathāgatas and not

---

[25] The bodhisatva undertakes the journey of remaining in saṃsāra for the sake of completing his own path and benefiting others despite the suffering nature of saṃsāra. To be able to do that, he develops a mind which never wearies of the task he has set himself.

[26] "To have come forth" or to have gone forth means to have left life in a household and gone into a life of full-time spiritual seeking. Having come forth, there is the further but separate possibility of becoming ordained as a monk or nun.

[27] "The dharmas of the side of enlightenment" refers to the thirty-seven dharmas which sum up the entire path of the Great Vehicle.

[28] For wisdom, see the glossary. The principal quality of wisdom is that it knows everything, knowing each of every one of all phenomena and knowing the actual nature of each of all of those phenomena all at once.

slip back, not slip back at all[29], from the dharmas of the side of enlightenment, so that they do not have unmentionable actions[30] in this life and will have the particulars[31] in others? And, bhagavan, there are the bodhisatvas who have come forth from staying in a household, the ones who, having left behind joy and sorrow[32], have

---

[29] "To not slip back" is part of the vocabulary of the Great Vehicle teaching. It is used when discussing the irreversibility of a bodhisatva's progress towards enlightenment. Here, irreversibility not only means not going backwards but also means not reverting into lesser approaches such as those of the śhrāvaka monks. Uncouth is saying that he is not convinced that the approach of being ordained is actually part of the higher spirituality of the bodhisatva, so he wants to know how he can remain as a bodhisatva who has not gone forth from his household yet fully follow the teachings of the tathāgata without falling back into lesser types of spirituality. His questions are breath-taking because he is, in the most polite way possible, and using the very wordings of the bodhisatva vehicle, suggesting that perhaps coming forth from a household and becoming ordained is not actually the highest form of spirituality.

[30] "Unmentionable actions" is one of several terms used by the Buddha to indicate "bad karmic actions" in general, "wrongdoings". Because such actions are impure, they are something that pious people would prefer not to mention.

[31] "Having the particulars" means being someone who has taken a set of the vows explained by the Buddha in the Vinaya, each of which has a full set of details on what the vows mean, what action is appropriate and which is inappropriate, and so on.

[32] "Joys and sorrows" refers to that aspect of family life to which many people are attached and which is a mark of the life of a householder. Householders see the joys and sorrows of household life as very desirable, and even a necessary part of life, whereas the spiritual seeker sees them as pure saṃsāric misery.

shaved the head and facial hair, donned saffron[33] clothing, and through true faith that took them from being in a household to not being in a household become ordained. Please correctly and utterly explain, using as much both advice and suitable teaching, their dharma practices and virtuous behaviours. How are the householder and ordained bodhisatvas to dwell? How are they to accomplish?"

He supplicated in those words and the bhagavan instructed the householder Uncouth in these words:

"Householder, this is good, this is good. Your thinking to ask me a question about this subject is in accord with your situation! Therefore, listen well with your fullest attention and retain it in mind! I will explain to you how the bodhisatva householders and ordained ones will correctly take up the good qualities of the training and will stay in the supreme conduct, and how they will go about accomplishment."

He said, "Bhagavan, as you say", then the householder Uncouth listened in accord with the bhagavan, and the bhagavan instructed him in these words:

"Householder, for this, the bodhisatva householder staying in a household is to go to the buddha for refuge, is to go to the dharma for refuge, and is to go to the saṅgha for refuge. The roots of virtue

---

[33] Although it has become standard to translate the original term as "saffron", what it actually means is the colour that comes from using the left over dregs of dyes, which were a yellowish-red colour. The buddha emphasized the use of cast off cloths to be dyed not with the best dye available but with the left over dregs of dye solution.

of having gone to the three for refuge are to be thoroughly dedicated[34] to unsurpassed, truly complete enlightenment.

"Householder, what is it like for a bodhisatva householder to have gone for refuge to the buddha? Householder, for this, a bodhisatva householder actually forms the mind that thinks, "I will entirely accomplish a buddha's body nicely adorned with the thirty-two marks of a great being". Then, he undertakes perseverance in order to truly accomplish the roots of virtue whatever they might be that will end up as the true accomplishment of the thirty-two marks of a great being. When it is like that, householder, a bodhisatva has gone for refuge to the buddha.

"Householder, what is it like for a bodhisatva householder to have gone for refuge to the dharma? Householder, for this, the bodhisatva householder having physical respect and mental veneration for the dharma[35], finding meaning in the dharma, desiring dharma, taking joy and interest in the totally joyous dharma, settling on dharma, alighting on dharma, having alighted on dharma, guarding dharma, hiding and living dharma, living in the fame of dharma and conduct of dharma, controlled by dharma, seeking dharma, having the strength of dharma, having the weapon of the gift of dharma, and doing the deeds of dharma fully achieves the reflection,

---

[34] In the Great Vehicle teachings, the Buddha does not speak of bodhisatvas "dedicating" their merits but of "thoroughly dedicating" them. This refers to making a dedication that is complete in every way. That in turn means that the dedication is done for all sentient beings and that it is done with all the aspects taught for a bodhisatva's way of dedication, which appear especially in the Prajñāpāramitā sūtras.

[35] Respect of body, speech, and mind each has its own term in the Buddhist vocabulary. That is absent from English so I have used "physical respect", "verbal respect", and "veneration" or "mental veneration" consistently throughout the book to indicate the three.

'Because of possessing dharma in this way, I will achieve unsurpassed truly complete enlightenment, becoming a manifest complete buddha, then through dharma will share dharma with the world with gods, men, and asuras'. Householder, when it is like that, a bodhisatva householder has gone for refuge to the dharma.

"Householder, what is it like for a bodhisatva householder to have gone for refuge to the saṅgha? Householder, for this, a bodhisatva householder who has gone for refuge to the saṅgha fully achieves the reflection, 'Suppose I see a monk stream-enterer or one-time returner or non-returner or arhat or individualized being[36] or Śhrāvaka Vehicle follower or Pratyekabuddha Vehicle follower or Great Vehicle follower, then I will show physical respect and verbal respect, and make the effort to rise, and will be happy with instructions given[37] and remain in harmony. By serving and honouring those who have gone into being authentic and are engaged in being authentic, I will attain unsurpassed truly complete enlightenment, becoming a manifest complete buddha, and then moreover will teach the dharma in order that the śhrāvaka good qualities will be entirely accomplished and the pratyekas' good qualities will be entirely accomplished'. He is physically and verbally respectful to

[36] For noble one, see the glossary. Noble beings are those who have made significant spiritual progress; they have exited saṃsāra by having seen the absence of self. Their counterpart is ordinary beings, the ones who have not reached that level of development, and who are still, spiritually speaking, commoners. Ordinary beings believe in the idea of self and so cut themselves out as individualized entities. Thus "noble beings" and "individualized or ordinary beings" are the terms used to indicate the two major types of beings when speaking of their spiritual development.

[37] To be "happy with instructions given" is one of many terms indicating a respectful approach to the community of Buddhist monks. When one is with them and they give an instruction to do something, one happily receives that instruction and does not complain or otherwise make a disturbance because of it.

them, rather than showing them dislike, which he does not do. When it is like that, householder, a bodhisatva householder has gone for refuge to the saṅgha.

"Householder, furthermore, if a bodhisatva householder has four dharmas[38], he has gone for refuge to the buddha. What are the four? They are: not rejecting the enlightenment mind; not breaking the commitments; not at all letting go of great compassion; and not referring to another vehicle. Householder, if a bodhisatva householder has those four dharmas he has gone for refuge to the buddha.

"Householder, furthermore, if a bodhisatva householder has four dharmas he has gone for refuge to the dharma. What are the four? They are: relying on and serving persons who speak the dharma—that is, giving them service and honour and showing them esteem—he listens to dharma; and he hears dharma and correctly discriminates it; and then he also teaches others and truly and utterly explains to them the dharmas as he has heard and as he has internally comprehended them; and he thoroughly dedicates to unsurpassed truly complete enlightenment the roots of virtue which have arisen from the gift of dharma. Householder, if a bodhisatva householder has those four dharmas he has gone for refuge to the dharma.

"Householder, furthermore, if a bodhisatva householder has four dharmas he has gone for refuge to the saṅgha. What are the four? They are: putting those who are truly and faultlessly engaged in the śhrāvaka vehicle into the all-knowing mind; bringing those who include themselves within material things into being included within dharma; relying on the saṅgha of the non-regressing bodhi-

---

[38] The word dharma is accepted in Buddhism as having ten distinct meanings. In this sūtra, it either refers, as it does here, to "feature" or "quality", or to dharma being the teaching of the Buddha, or to phenomena.

satvas, and not relying on the saṅgha of the śhrāvakas; and not seeking the good qualities of the śhrāvakas nor taking interest in their complete liberation. Householder, if a bodhisatva householder has those four dharmas he has gone for refuge to the sangha.

"Householder, furthermore, a bodhisatva householder who having seen the bodily form of a tathāgata utterly gains the recollection of the buddha, is one who has gone for refuge to the buddha; who having heard the dharma utterly gains the recollection of the dharma, is one has gone for refuge to the dharma; who having seen the saṅgha of śhrāvakas of the tathāgata recollects the enlightenment mind, is one who has gone for refuge to the saṅgha.

"Householder, furthermore, a bodhisatva householder staying in a household who prays to be in the company of the buddha and practices generosity is one who has gone for refuge to the buddha; who in order to truly protect the holy dharma practises generosity is one who has gone for refuge to the dharma; who thoroughly dedicates that generosity to unsurpassed truly complete enlightenment is one who has gone for refuge to the saṅgha.

"Householder, furthermore, a bodhisatva householder residing in a household does the actions of a holy being and does not do the actions of a bad being. Householder, what are the actions of a holy being, not the actions of a bad being? Householder, for this a bodhisatva householder seeks possessions through dharma not through non-dharma, which he does not do; seeks through harmony not disharmony, which he does not do. He has livelihood through right means not livelihood through wrong means, so when he obtains possessions through dharma, it does not involve harm for others; doing much meditation on impermanence, he makes his life valuable as follows: he serves and honours his parents; he uses in a right way his children, wife, male servants, female servants, workers, and those of independent livelihood[39]; he shows esteem for close acquaintances, ministers, relatives, and siblings of the same parents and not[40]; and by installing any of them into dharma, works at developing his giving.

"Householder, furthermore, a bodhisatva householder is like this: he undertakes perseverance for the honourable task of having taking up the burden, which is carrying the burden of the five aggregates of all sentient beings. He is like this: he undertakes perseverance for the honourable task of having taken up the burden, which is not rejecting śhrāvaka and pratyekabuddha vehicles. He will ripen all sentient beings but is entirely without weariness because of it. May there be no happiness for me; I work to make all sentient beings have happiness. Unmoved by gain and loss, fame and infamy, praise and blame, and happiness and suffering, he truly transcends the worldly dharmas. He does not become vain because of gain and a perfection of possessions; he is not dejected at absence of the sweet sounds that express gain and fame. He acts with the utmost consideration of what he is doing, totally guarding right accomplishment and taking no interest in wrong accomplishment. He sees the events that occur due to rational mind[41] which is not abiding and thinks that, without a mind like a sheet of finely-

---

[39] The people from children down to workers will all be people who stay within his household, receiving room and board. The independent workers are those who live elsewhere and who might or might not work for him full-time; they are responsible for their own livelihood and sustenance.

[40] "Siblings of the same parents and not" means all of a person's siblings, whether they are siblings where both parents are the same or where one of the parents is different.

[41] For rational mind, see the glossary. Here it means a dualistic mind which is producing all sorts of mental events.

combed cotton[42], how could I totally complete my commitments, do the deeds for others, entirely reject deeds for myself, not hope for benefit in return for what has been done for others, not hold a grudge against those who have done harm, remember deeds done, feel for deeds done, do actions that do good, distribute possessions to the poor[43], break the pride of those who are strong, rescue from fear those who are afraid, remove the pain of misery of those assailed by misery, be tolerant and accepting of those lesser in power, completely abandon being prouder than proud and physically respect the gurus[44], attend those who have much hearing[45], be

---

[42] Cotton here means raw cotton. The bodhisatva householder realizes that he needs to have a very highly pacified, and hence soft mind, a mind of well-developed śhamatha.

[43] Distributing one's own possessions to the poor, also called "distributions of generosity" was a standard practice amongst householders who had sufficient means to do so. In ancient times and even today in India and Nepal, a wealthy householder will distribute large amounts of food or goods to beggars who will gather in a certain location to receive the distribution.

[44] Prouder than proud is one of seven variations on pride that the Buddha enumerated in the Abhidharma teachings. It means not merely being proud but having the extra level of pride in which one thinks one is better than everyone else, including even people like very capable masters.

[45] "Much hearing" is a common phrase in the sūtras. It refers to the necessary quality of having heard a very large body of dharma teaching. Note that this can include knowledge gained through reading but that is not the main point. Buddha's realization is transmitted in two ways, he said. One is oral transmission of the authentic statements of the Buddha from person to person. When transmitted that way, there is an imparting of the energy of the original teaching that goes from mind to mind. Thus the emphasis here is on having heard a tremendous amount of dharma from people who also heard that dharma in

(continued...)

highly inquisitive with those who are expert[46], conduct myself with a straighter view and without guile, have loving kindness for all sentient beings without deceit or artifice, not be satiated when seeking out 'What is virtue?', be not satisfied in relation to having much hearing, be firm in my commitment to things undertaken, keep company with noble beings, have a greater level of compassion for beings who are not noble ones[47], be a steady friend, be even-minded towards both those who are and are not friends, in regard to all of the buddha's dharma not to keep the texts of the master for myself, utterly teach the dharmas as I have heard them, meditate afterwards on the meaning of what was heard, perceive all desirable things liked and loved as impermanent, perceive the body as unclean, perceive life as like a dew drop, perceive possessions as like an illusion and mirage, perceive children and wife as sentient beings of the hell of unending torment, perceive the extremes of action of field and household[48] and the ownership of various types of clothes as the joys of the impoverished, perceive that roots of virtue sought

---

[45](...continued)
person, in a transmission that goes all the way back to the Buddha.

[46] "Experts" are those who know the tradition and all of its ways extremely well. It is important to go to them and be very inquisitive, so that one can develop one's own expertise in the tradition.

[47] "Noble beings" and "noble ones" refers to those who are sufficiently developed spiritually that they see emptiness directly in their meditation and hence are not bound by clinging to a self. They can correctly explain what is right and wrong, not making the many mistakes that would come if they were grasping at a self. In Buddhism, one tries to spend as much time with such beings as possible.

[48] The extremes of action refers to good and bad karmic actions. Ordinary householders know no other type of action. The householders of the time of this sūtra were mainly farmers or carried out their livelihood at home.

after are completely transitory,[49] perceive that a household abode is like an executioner, perceive close associates, ministers, relatives, and siblings of the same parents and not as the guardians of sentient beings in hell, perceive that 'the particulars that I have for day and night' are to be entirely met, perceive that from a body which is without value a body with value can be obtained, perceive that from a life which is without value a life with value can be obtained, and perceive that from possessions which are without essence an essence can be taken.

"In that, what is perceiving that from a body which is without value value can be obtained? There is the one who takes delight in doing the works of others, speaks respectfully to the gurus, and does the acts of prostrating, rising, joining the palms, and bowing; this is referred to as 'perceiving that from a body without value value can be obtained'.

"In that, what is perceiving that from a life which is without value value can be obtained? There is the one who works at preventing the roots of merit made previously from declining in any way and increasing them even more; this is referred to as 'perceiving that from a life which is without value value can be obtained'.

"In that, what is perceiving that from possessions which are without value value can be obtained? There is the one who works at ending

---

[49] In this sūtra the Buddha frequently makes the point that the usual approach of Buddhist householders, that of pursuing good karmic actions and rejecting bad ones, is folly because such actions are still part of the sphere of saṃsāra. The implication here is that the dedicated Buddhist, whether he is a householder or ordained, is not to make the pursuit of adoption of good and rejection of bad karmic action his main priority. What should his main priority be? The answer lies in a key thread that runs throughout this sūtra, which is that the dedicated Buddhist aims for the all-knowing wisdom of unsurpassed truly complete enlightenment.

the mind of avarice and increasing the mind of great giving, and who truly makes distributions of generosity; this is referred to as 'perceiving that from possessions which are without value value can be obtained'.

"Householder, when it is like that, a bodhisatva householder who does these sorts of actions is doing the actions of a holy being, not the actions of a bad being. If he does such, the tathāgatas do not refer to it as faulty but say that it is family[50], it is dharma. It is like this: beforehand he commits to unsurpassed truly complete enlightenment and after that does not slip back, does not slip back from that at all.

"Householder, furthermore, a bodhisatva householder is one who has entirely taken up every one of the bases of training[51], which is as follows.

"Having entirely taken up five bases of training he is to abandon killing, because of which he will get rid of sticks, get rid of weapons, have embarrassment and compassion, have a nature of not harming any living being or elemental spirit[52], be even-minded towards all sentient beings, and perpetually abide in loving kindness.

---

[50] "Family" here means that it is the accepted behaviour of people within the family of those going to unsurpassed enlightenment.

[51] The bases of training for a Buddhist householder are the five vows of a layman: not to kill, not to take that which has not been offered (often incorrectly translated as "not to steal"), not to lie, not to engage in improper sexual conduct, and not to drink alcohol. A householder can take none, one, and so on up to all five of the vows. The Buddha here is saying that a householder intent on his training takes all five of them. The Buddha will now explain each of those vows and what it means for a bodhisatva householder like Uncouth.

[52] Elemental spirits are those spirits who are attached to earth, fire, water, and air.

"He is to abandon taking what is not given, because of which he is to be content with his own possessions, not to have strong liking for others' possessions, be without attached and covetous minds, be without desire for another's wealth, and not to take what has not been given, starting from something as minor even as a blade of grass or leaf.

"He is to abandon sexual misconduct with what is desirable, because of which he is to remain satisfied with his own wife, be without desire for another's wife, to look with eyes of detachment, to have a mind of renunciation, and to make the effort to produce detachment in the mind, thinking, 'Desirable things are extreme suffering'.

"When he has discursive thinking that desires his own wife, at that time also he has fallen under the influence of affliction, in which case he is to attend to the desire with a mind that views his own wife as unattractive and which is afraid. At that time, he is not to be gripped by clinging but, by perceiving the situation as impermanent, suffering, without self, and unclean, he must think, 'If I will not by any means act out desire even for mental gratification, then why mention something like engaging in the meeting of the two genitals or in what is not a branch[53]—I will not do that'.

"He is to abandon speaking falsely, because of which he is to speak truthfully, speak honestly, do just as he has said he would, not be misleading, have perfect intention, and have mindfulness and alert-

---

[53] "What is not a branch" refers to all the ways of sexual penetration proscribed by the Buddha, including homosexual activities of all kinds. (This was the Buddha's teaching, even if it hearing it is unpalatable for many people in the social climate of our world at present.) He explained that these modes of penetration create excessive amounts of bad karma and various other problems.

ness[54]. Doing that, saying what he has seen and heard will have fallen under the protection of dharma, so even at the cost of body and life, with alertness, he will not speak falsely.

"He is to abandon the intoxicating drinks of brewed and prepared liquors[55], because of which he is to see that they have no special taste, and that without them there is no intoxication, no confusion, no uncontrolled speech, no becoming high, no becoming wild, no being distracted, and that mindfulness remains close and he has alertness. In that case, he might have the idea to give without reservation all material goods and think, 'I will give food to those wanting food and drink to those wanting drink', in which case he will also be giving brewed liquor to others, so, together with his idea he is to think as follows, 'This is an occasion of the pāramitā of generosity and now the time has come to give someone what he wants, so I will do it as follows.' Then he is to generate this perception, 'While giving brewed liquor to such and such and so and so, it will be done in such a way that the act of giving is without confusion, and for this, I will engage in truly maintaining mindfulness and alertness in relation to the details, this and that, of the giving.' Why is it that way? To work at totally completing all the intentions is to fully conduct oneself in the bodhisatva's pāramitā of generosity. Householder, when it is like that, the bodhisatva householder could give liquor to others but the tathāgatas would not refer to it as wrongdoing.[56]

---

[54] Mindfulness and alertness are the two great causes of having a completely calm and heedful mind. They are the roots of the development of one-pointedness as well as many of the good-qualities of enlightenment. See mindfulness and alertness in the glossary.

[55] This means brewed alcohol such as beer and distilled alcohol such as whiskey.

[56] In other words, if as a bodhisatva he is going to give, he has to give what people ask for. Therefore, he first reminds himself that the

(continued...)

"Householder, that bodhisatva householder is to thoroughly dedicate the roots of virtue that come from having held the five bases of training to unsurpassed truly complete enlightenment. He is also to make an exceptional effort to keep those five bases of training[57].

"He never will speak divisively and always will reconcile those who are divided[58]. He also will not use rough speech and he will use gentle speech, speaking with pleasant words and speaking sincerely. He also will not gossip and will speak in a timely way[59], and will speak honestly, speak meaningfully, speak dharma, speak reasonably, speak in a tamed way, give nice replies, and do just as he has said he would.

---

[56](...continued)
giving is motivated by enlightenment mind. Then he takes the view that the act of giving must be unconfused and that the way to do that is to maintain mindfulness and alertness throughout the act. Given that the motivation is correct and the action is done without saṃsāric confusion, it becomes an action of a bodhisatva. Moreover, a bodhisatva is to fulfil all of his intentions of becoming enlightened, and that includes giving in all ways, so by approaching it this way, his act of giving becomes part of the bodhisatva's conduct and is part of his going to enlightenment.

[57] "Keep" here means to hold the vows while guarding against any breakage of them.

[58] The ten non-virtues are, together with the five vows, the most fundamental teachings on how a Buddhist householder is to behave. The actions of keeping the five vows of a layman already include avoidance of four of the ten non-virtues—killing, stealing, sexual misconduct, and lying. So, the Buddha now proceeds to explain how the remaining six non-virtues also must be followed. They are: for speech, not to speak divisively, roughly, or to gossip, and then for mind, not to have covetousness, ill-will, or wrong views.

[59] Speaking in a timely way means to speak when it is appropriate. It is the opposite of chattering, which is an aspect of gossiping.

"He is not to engage in covetous mind and is to think of benefit and ease[60] for all sentient beings. He is not to engage in ill-will and is to always wear the armour of the strength of patience. He is to engage in right view and to separate from all wrong views. He has taken up the thought that the buddha is the deity and is not to hold to another deity[61].

"Householder, furthermore, a bodhisatva householder wherever he stays be it a village, city, town, province, or district of a province is to tell the story of dharma to the sentient beings there: the ones who have no faith should be installed into faith; the sentient beings who are not respectful and do not hold to father, do not hold to mother, do not hold to trainees in virtue, do not hold to

---

[60] "Benefit and ease" is a standard phrase in Buddhist teaching. Benefit means to help sentient beings in a worldly way, assisting them as much as possible. Ease means to help sentient beings in a transcendent way, bring them into the ease of unsurpassed enlightenment.

[61] This last sentence applies to not holding wrong views. Taking refuge entails accepting a set of precepts; the prime one that goes with having taken refuge in the Buddha as the teacher is that one will not go to another teacher of another religious tradition. The Buddha explained the difficulties that come with trying to follow the instructions of more than one system of spiritual teaching, so he made a very strong point of the need, having taken refuge in buddha, not to go to another teacher representing another religion and attempt to follow his ways.

Personally, I had for long thought that this was not so important for our time. However, in recent years, I have seen how hopelessly confused many Westerners have become as they attempt to follow multiple religious traditions. Especially, I note that those who want to do the very highest practices, such as Mahāmudrā and Dzogchen, seem to believe that they can follow Buddhist and other traditions at the same time. Having spoken to many of them, I see their confusion. There is no doubt in my mind that this simple little sentence here has a tremendous meaning for everyone who claims to be a follower of the Buddha.

Brahmans[62], do not perform rituals of respect for the head of the family, who do not keep customs and have stepped away from them[63], should be installed into respect for the guru and doing the dharma activities[64]. Sentient beings who are of lesser hearing are to be connected with much hearing. The ones with avarice are to be installed into giving, the ones with lax discipline into discipline, the ones with ill-will into patience and good-naturedness, the ones with laziness into undertaking perseverance, the forgetful ones into mindfulness and alertness, and the ones with lax prajñā into prajñā. Poor sentient beings are to have his possessions truly shared with them. Sick sentient beings are to be given medicine. He is to be a guardian of sentient beings without a guardian. He is to be a refuge

---

[62] The Buddha referred to his own followers as "trainees in virtue", a name he coined to distinguish them from spiritual practitioners following other systems of teaching. The other big group of spiritual practitioners in his time were the Brahmans of the Hindu tradition.

[63] This is a long list of the customs of respect that were and still are part of the fabric of Indian life. Holding one's parents, children, and so on in high regard should not need further explanation. Note that, although the Buddha did not agree with the views of the Brahmans regarding ultimate reality, he did see many points of value in their customs and encouraged a general level of respect for them amongst his followers. One such custom was the performance of rituals of respect and longevity for the head of the family and this custom is still very much part of Indian culture.

[64] In Tibetan Buddhism, it is common to quote a statement by Maitreya, the Buddha's regent, in which he says that dharma activity in general is comprised of ten specific activities that Buddhists should take up:

> Copying letters, offering, giving,
> Hearing, reading, comprehending,
> Explaining, reciting,
> Contemplating it, and meditating …

for those without refuge and a supporting friend for those without a supporting friend. Staying in harmony with those provinces and districts within provinces according to their needs, he does not allow even a few sentient beings to fall into wrong and in that way he protects with the dharma.

"Householder, suppose a bodhisatva householder has taught those sentient beings according to their needs one time, two times, three times up to seven times, but instead of being set in good qualities they have not developed any good qualities whatsoever. Householder, at that point, that bodhisatva householder is to generate great compassion for those sentient beings—he is to don the subtle armour of all-knowingness and together with that is to express these words, 'For as long as these savages, these hard-to-tame sentient beings have not been entirely ripened, I will not go to unsurpassed truly complete enlightenment, manifest complete buddhahood.' Why is that? He thinks, 'I have donned armour for them, not for straight sentient beings, ones without guile, ones without cunning, nor for ones having discipline. My not donning armour for ones who have good qualities will certainly result in my efforts being meaningful, in sentient beings liking me immediately upon seeing me, and in their gaining faith. That is how it will be. That is how I will accomplish. That is how I will undertake perseverance.'

"Householder, suppose that bodhisatva staying in some village or city or town or province or district of a province has not encouraged or remembered the area; if sentient beings are born in any of the bad migrations[65] whatsoever, that bodhisatva will be denounced by the tathāgatas. Householder, it is as follows. For example, if a skilled doctor staying in some village or city or town or province or district of a province is not able at very least to alleviate the poison of some sentient beings, then when it comes time for him to die,

[65] Bad migrations are births in the hells, preta realms, or animal realms.

that doctor will be denounced by many beings. Householder, similarly, for that bodhisatva staying in some village or city or town or province or district of a province who has not encouraged or remembered even a few sentient beings in the area, if anyone is born in one of the bad migrations whichever it might be, that bodhisatva will be denounced by the tathāgatas. Householder, that being so, for this the bodhisatva householder who stays in some village or city or town or province or district of a province certainly is to don the sort of armour that thinks, 'I will not allow even a few sentient beings to fall down. That is how it will be. That is how I will accomplish. That is how I will undertake perseverance.'

"Householder, furthermore, a bodhisatva householder staying in a household is to be expert in the faults of staying in a household. He is to train in each of the following. This so-called 'household' destroys the roots of virtue, puts an end to the events[66], makes the tree of virtue fall down—that is why it is called 'a household'. This so-called 'staying in a household' is staying with all the afflictions, staying with discursive thoughts directed at the roots of non-virtue, staying with the childish individualized beings[67] who are untamed and unhidden[68], staying with the ones who act out non-virtue, and joining in with bad beings—that is why it is called 'staying in a

---

[66] "The events" are the two events of coming forth from a household and becoming ordained.

[67] "Individualized beings" was explained in an earlier note. Compared to the noble beings, the ones who have a superior level of spiritual development and who are expert in reality and meditations on it, the individualized beings are like children who have not yet developed themselves at all.

[68] "Unhidden" is one of several terms for beings who have not entered spiritual training and hence have not developed their being. A person who is not trained generally makes a show of himself, a person who is trained generally has a reserved demeanour, hiding his good qualities and not making a show of himself.

household'. This so-called 'staying in a household' is referred to as 'a place with all the dharmas of suffering'. It causes the degeneration of the roots of virtue made through familiarization in the past[69]—that is why it is called 'staying in a household'.

"This so-called 'household' is such that staying there causes unsuitable activities. Due to staying there, respect for parents, trainees in virtue, and Brahmans does not happen—that is why it is called 'a household'. This so-called 'household' is, because of finding great joy in the creeping vine of becoming[70], the source of misery, lamenting, suffering, mental unhappiness, and disturbance—that is why it is called 'a household'. This so-called 'household' collects the ways of murder, bondage, beating, menacing, harm, and unpleasant words, criticism, derision, and words designed to have a bad effect—that is why it is called 'a household'. This so-called 'household' does not establish one in having made roots of virtue; roots of virtue that have been made are completely transitory, and experts, buddhas, and all of the Buddha's śhrāvakas denounce them[71].

"Staying in this will lead to birth in the bad migrations. Staying in this leads to not progressing because of desire. It leads to not progressing because of anger, fear, and delusion[72]—that is why it is

---

[69] Familiarization is similar to meditation, but means to have habituated oneself to what is already one's nature where meditation means to develop good qualities afresh where they have not existed before.

[70] "Becoming" is another term for saṃsāra; see the glossary for more.

[71] As explained in the introduction, there is an emphasis in this sūtra on not following the expected behaviour of a layman in which there is a strong emphasis on adopting good karmic action and rejecting bad karmic action but instead on realizing the all-knowing wisdom of a buddha.

[72] "Delusion" is the term used for the ignorant states of mind that
(continued...)

called 'a household'. This is non-protection of all the aggregates of discipline[73]; it is the abandonment of the aggregate of concentration; it is non-entrance into the aggregate of prajñā; it is non-attainment of the aggregate of complete liberation; it is non-production of the aggregate of seeing complete liberation's wisdom—that is why it is called a 'household'[74].

"Staying in a household is to have the craving[75] involved in caring for father, mother, child, wife, male servants, female servants, workers, those of independent livelihood, close friends, ministers, relatives, siblings of same parents and not, and underlings. This staying in a household is as difficult to fill up as is filling an ocean with drops of water. Staying in a household one cannot be satisfied,

---

[72](...continued)
operate in the saṃsāric mind once it has formed through fundamental ignorance. It is one of the three root afflictions, with desire and anger being the other two.

[73] Discipline which has the following six aspects is called "the aggregate of discipline": keeping possession of the disciplines of personal emancipation; being bound by the vows one has; perfection of liturgy; perfection of behaviour; viewing with fear even the slightest unmentionable; and properly keeping and training in the bases of training.

[74] You will see "aggregate" used in this way in various places in the sūtra. It is the same word as in "the five aggregates or skandhas". It means that heap or aggregate of things which are discipline, and so on. In the case of discipline it is plural because there are seven major levels of discipline taught within the Vinaya and each of these is an aggregate of discipline.

[75] Craving here means craving for saṃsāric types of existence. Craving for any type of existence is a key factor in the cycle of interdependent origination that provides the impetus needed for another birth to be taken within saṃsāric existence. Laypeople are usually severely involved with this type of craving so the Buddha here lists the big points of craving for a layman.

like a fire cannot be satisfied with wood. Staying in a household consists of no end of discursive thinking, like a sandstorm has no end to it. Staying in a household is transitory like a city of sand is transitory. Staying in a household is adulterated like good food adulterated with poison. Staying in a household is perpetual suffering because of discord such as with those who are not friends. Staying in a household creates obstacles to accomplishing the dharma of the noble ones. Staying in a household is troublesome because of the conditions of mutual interaction[76]. Staying in a household is perpetually disagreeable because of ill-will between one another. Staying in a household involves more harms done because it entails the extremes of doing good and doing bad of karmic action. Staying in a household involves perpetually putting forth effort because there is no end to the extremes of karmic action. Staying in a household is impermanence because what has been accumulated over a long period has the feature of being completely transitory. Staying in a household is suffering because of being consumed with seeking things and protecting them. Staying in a household is perpetual anxiety because of those with whom one is not friendly, such as enemies. Staying in a household is to be heedless because of being in the grip of what is wrong. Staying in a household is the production of a world through one's own mental analysis, so it is empty of entity, similar to the colours of a dancer[77].

---

[76] Staying in a household, you are not alone, so the troubles that occur in situations of two or more people interacting happen. Conditions here also carries a sense of conditions produced by each person which then cause karmic seeds to ripen.

[77] The household world is a projection of one's own thoughts about it (mental analysis is a specific mental event which in this case means "one's own way of thinking about it"). Because it is a mere production of dualistic mind, there is actually no reality to it at all—it is without an entity. It is a colourful show to be sure, but nothing more than a charade of colours, like the colourful women dancers of India, wearing their many colourfully embroidered and dyed cloths, flashing and

(continued...)

Staying in a household ends in decay and change because of rapid mutual partings[78]. Staying in a household is analogous to viewing an illusion because the adventitious congregating of beings means that it never has an entity. Staying in a household is analogous to a dream because all circumstances no matter how perfect end in decay. Staying in a household is analogous to drops of dew because of the rapid separation involved. Staying in a household is analogous to drops of honey because it is entirely meeting with things of little taste. Staying in a household is analogous to a network of thorns because of being entirely needled by visual forms, sounds, smells, tastes, touches, and dharmas. Staying in a household is analogous to insects with a needle for a mouth because of not being wearied at all by discursive thought directed at non-virtue. Staying in a household is complete transitoriness of life because of the conmanship that goes on between one another. Staying in a household is perpetual disturbance because it is done in a context of polluted minds. Staying in a household is vulgar because of defeat at the hands of kings, robbers and thieves, fire, water, and the need to share. Staying in a household is of little taste because it has more disadvantages. Householder, in that way a bodhisatva householder staying in a household is to be expert in the faults of staying in a household.

"Householder, furthermore, a bodhisatva householder staying in a household is to do much generosity, taming, right following of vowed restraints, and ascertainment[79]. He also is to examine like this, 'What has been given, that is mine. What has been placed in

---

[77](...continued)
whirling about in a great pageant.

[78] People come and go from households, joining together and splitting apart again, so it is a great show of impermanence.

[79] He is to emphasise being generous to others, and is to tame himself, and is to keep his layman's vows properly, and is to study the dharma and contemplate it in order to ascertain it correctly.

the household, that is not mine. What has been given, that has value[80]. What has been placed in the household, that has no value[81]. What has been given, that is happiness for other. What has been placed in the household, that is happiness for the present. What has been given, that does not need to be protected. What has been placed in the household, that has to be protected. What has been given, that will exhaust craving. What has been placed in the household, that will thoroughly increase craving. What has been given, that is without mine. What has been placed in the household, that is with mine. What has been given, that is not owned[82]. What has been placed in the household, that is owned. What has been given, that is without fear. What has been placed in the household, that is with fear. What has been given, that very much teaches the enlightenment path. What has been placed in the household, that very much teaches the side of māra[83]. What has been given, that does not know exhaustion. What has been placed in the household, that will be exhausted. What has been given, that is happiness. What has been placed in the household, that is suffering because of needing always to be protected. What has been given, that is the abandonment of affliction. What exists in the household, that causes the increase of affliction. What has been given, that will become a great possession[84]. What has been placed

---

[80] It has value because, in having given properly, one has progressed further on the path to enlightenment.

[81] It is without value, that is, there is no meaning to it.

[82] The theme of ownership is also strongly present in this sūtra. Ownership brings with it firstly an increased sense of I and mine, and then the various other troublesome efforts required to maintain the ownership.

[83] For māra, see the glossary.

[84] As explained elsewhere in the sūtra, "great possession" refers to a good result of developing further on the path and also the good karmic (continued...)

in the household, that will not become a great possession. What has been given, that is the action of a holy being. What has been placed in the household, that is the action of a bad being. What has been given, that is commended by all buddhas. What has been placed in the household, that is commended by childish beings.' Householder, in that way a bodhisatva householder is to make his life valuable.

"Householder, furthermore, if a bodhisatva householder sees someone requesting something, he is to generate three perceptions. What are the three? They are: perceiving that person as a virtuous friend[85]; perceiving that person as becoming a great possession in a later life; and perceiving that person as someone very much teaching the enlightenment path. Householder, if a bodhisatva householder sees a requester, he is to generate those three perceptions.

"Householder, furthermore, if a bodhisatva householder sees a requester[86], he is to generate three perceptions. What are the three? They are: the perception of putting an end to avarice; the perception of giving all material goods without reservation; and the perception of viewing of all-knowing wisdom. Householder, if a bodhisatva householder sees a requester, he is to generate those three perceptions.

"Householder, furthermore, if a bodhisatva householder sees a requester, he is to generate three perceptions. What are the three? They are: the perception that he is to do in accordance with the tathāgata's command; the perception of putting an end to māra; and

---

[84](...continued)
results that come from it.

[85] Skt. kalyāṇamitra. A virtuous or spiritual friend is a spiritual teacher.

[86] A "requester" is anyone asking for something to be given to him.

the perception of having no hopes in regard to full-ripening[87]. Householder, if a bodhisatva householder sees a requester, he is to generate those three perceptions.

"Householder, furthermore, if a bodhisatva householder sees a requester, he is to generate three perceptions. What are the three? They are: perceiving that he is a servant to the requester; perceiving that the giving is not being done because of the four things of gathering; and perceiving that it is arising from the ownership of someone who is not holy[88]. Householder, if a bodhisatva householder sees a requester, he is to generate those three perceptions

"Householder, furthermore, if a bodhisatva householder sees a requester, he is to generate three perceptions. What are the three? They are: the perception of being free of desire; the perception of cultivating loving kindness; and the perception of not engaging in delusion[89]. Householder, if a bodhisatva householder sees a requester, he is to generate those three perceptions. Why is that? Householder, it is because if a bodhisatva householder sees a requester, he will come to have subtle desire, anger, and delusion. Householder, how is it that, if a bodhisatva householder sees a requester, he will come to have subtle desire, anger, and delusion? This having equanimity for the thing given and giving it without reservation is the subtle delusion involved in that. This practice of loving kindness for the requesters is the subtle anger involved in

---

[87] "No hopes in regard to full-ripening" means not to be thinking about the good results that will come in the future when the karma of giving comes to fruition. Full-ripening as it is used in this sūtra always refers to the maturation of a karmic latency into its result.

[88] In other words, oneself, as the giver, is not to think how good a person one is because of doing such giving.

[89] This comes down to not being involved in the three root poisons of desire, anger, and delusion because the generation of loving kindness mentioned here is the antidote to anger.

that. This thoroughly dedicating to unsurpassed truly complete enlightenment after the thing has been given is the subtle delusion involved in that. Householder, in that way then, if a bodhisatva householder sees a requester, he will come to have subtle desire, anger, and delusion.

"Householder, furthermore, if a bodhisatva householder sees a requester, he will totally complete his cultivation of the six pāramitās. Householder, for this, immediately a thing, whatever it might be, has been requested, a bodhisatva householder does not grasp at that thing with his mind and, in that way then, will totally complete his cultivation of the pāramitā of generosity. He is one who, having based himself in enlightenment mind, gives without reservation, and in that way then, will totally complete his cultivation of the pāramitā of discipline. He is one who practices loving kindness for those requesters, so does not produce anger or ill-will, and in that way then, will totally complete his cultivation of the pāramitā of patience. He is one who remains dauntless, not having a wavering mind that thinks, 'Suppose I were to give this, then what would I do?' and in that way then, will totally complete his cultivation on the pāramitā of perseverance. He is one who gives to the requester and as well as that has no distress and regret over it. Always joyful and utterly cheered by the prospect of giving, he generates bodily bliss and mental happiness for himself and then gives while abiding in enlightenment mind, and in that way then, will totally complete his cultivation of the pāramitā of absorption. Having given, he also is not referencing any dharmas at all and has no hopes for full-ripening, so, just as the experts[90] do not overtly cling to any dharmas, he, likewise, by being without overt clinging, thoroughly dedicates to unsurpassed truly complete enlightenment, and in that way then, will totally complete his cultivation of the

[90] "Experts" here means those practitioners who have attained the path of insight, the noble ones, and who are therefore expert in their approach to reality.

pāramitā of prajñā. Householder, in that way then, if a bodhisatva householder sees a requester, he will totally complete cultivation of the six pāramitās.

Second bundle.

"Householder, furthermore, a bodhisatva householder staying in a household is to achieve equalness[91] in regard to the eight worldly dharmas by being without attachment and aversion. He might acquire possessions, or a wife, or a child, or wealth, or grain, but he is not to be haughty or joyful because of it and he might not obtain any of them, but he is not to be daunted or gloomy because of it; instead, he is to examine as follows. 'All compounds having been produced as superficies which are illusory constructions have the character of being individually present. Thus, parents, children, wife, male servants, female servants, workers, those of independent livelihood, close friends, ministers, relatives, and siblings of the same parents and not have come to exist through the complete ripening of karma, so neither are they mine nor am I theirs. Why is that? Those parents, and so on, are not my guardian or refuge or supporter or dwelling or sanctuary or self or mine. After all, if even the aggregates, dhātus, and āyatanas[92] which I have taken are not self, not mine, then why would my parents, and so on, become self and mine, and why even mention the case of my self being theirs? What is this about? Self also comes to function as mine when it behaves as karmic allotment, that is, when virtuous karmas and evil actions and this and that whatever has been done behave as karmic allotments. They will be individually experienced as their fruitions. They will be behave as their full-ripenings. These also come to function as mine when they behave as karmic allotments, that is, when virtuous karmas and evil actions and this and that whatever

---

[91] See the introduction for a discussion of the importance of the teaching of equalness.

[92] For aggregates, dhātus, and āyatanas, see the glossary.

has been done behave as karmic allotments. They will be individually experienced as their full-ripenings. They will be individually experienced as their fruitions. The self which is the actual formation of non-virtuous karma in this life because of them[93] is not a part of mine. The following things will function as happiness of mine in this life, not function as happiness of mine in another life. That which is mine will have self enter into it, that is to say, the virtues included in and actually produced by generosity, taming, right vowed restraints, patience, ascertainment, perseverance, heedfulness, and the branches of enlightenment are mine, and on whichever path I go these also will go.' And then, even because of his life or because of his children and wife he does not engage in actually forming the evil karmic actions.[94]

---

[93] This is the exact wording of the sūtra. If you read very carefully, you will understand the reference "them".

[94] Paraphrase. There are the eight worldly dharmas and these should be eliminated through the knowledge of the equalness of all dharmas that comes with all-knowing wisdom. There are all the people with whom I relate and in relation to whom worldly dharmas happen. We and all of our doings are actually illusions even though they each one seems to exist. Therefore, the self that I see in them and the self that I see in myself are fabrications. Self or I or me or myself can be understood as the actual forming of karmic action as it occurs and mine can be understood as the results belonging to myself when those karmic actions ripen. If I follow the eight worldly dharmas and actually produce non-virtues, I might think that this is happiness of mine now, but that would be a mistake given that what is mine comes later as the fruition of the non-virtue. On the other hand, if I think of this life and not results in a future life, I will be the actual formation of the virtues included under the branches of enlightenment. However, that will produce happiness now and, of course, all the goodness that goes with it will always be with me as mine in future lives. The householder bodhisatva having thought that way becomes determined to never, even at the cost of life or family, do karmically bad actions
(continued...)

"Householder, that bodhisatva householder staying in a household is to generate three perceptions in regard to his wife. What are the three? They are: the perception of impermanence; the perception of unsteadiness, and the perception of change. Householder, a bodhisatva householder is to generate those three perceptions in regard to his wife.

"Householder, furthermore, a bodhisatva householder is to generate three perceptions in regard to his wife. What are the three? He thinks, 'This is a companion of liking and loving, this is not a companion of another world. This is a companion of eating and drinking, this is not a companion of experiencing the full-ripening of karma. This is a companion of happiness, this is not a companion of suffering.'[95] Householder, a bodhisatva householder is to generate those three perceptions in regard to his wife.

"Householder, furthermore, a bodhisatva householder is to generate three perceptions in regard to his wife. What are the three? They are: perceiving as unclean; perceiving as a temptress[96]; and perceiving as unharmonious.

"Householder, furthermore, a bodhisatva householder is to generate three perceptions in regard to his wife. What are the three? They are: perceiving as an enemy; perceiving as an executioner; perceiving as an assailant.

---

[94](...continued)
because he him*self* will have done them and then they will be his (*mine*) to experience in the future.

[95] Another world means a future existence. The meaning here is that he focusses on the realities of the present and does not engage in the romantic thinking and everything that goes with it of her as a future companion.

[96] The actual term means one who tempts, lures, baits, and so on in order to get what she wants.

"Householder, furthermore, a bodhisatva householder is to generate three perceptions in regard to his wife. What are the three? They are: perceiving as a she flesh-eater; perceiving as a rākṣhasī[97]; and perceiving as an unattractive form.

"Householder, furthermore, a bodhisatva householder is to generate three perceptions in regard to his wife. What are the three? They are: perceiving as difficult to fill; perceiving as deep; and perceiving as not being appreciative of what has been done.

"Householder, furthermore, a bodhisatva householder is to generate three perceptions in regard to his wife. What are the three? They are: perceiving as going to the hells; perceiving as going to an animal birth place; and perceiving as going to the world of the Lord of Death.

"Householder, furthermore, a bodhisatva householder is to generate three perceptions in regard to his wife. What are the three? They are: perceiving as a burden; perceiving as becoming; and perceiving as absorbed in caring for becoming.

"Householder, furthermore, a bodhisatva householder is to generate three perceptions in regard to his wife. What are the three? They are: perceiving as not mine; perceiving as nothing to care for; and perceiving as a female on loan.

"Householder, furthermore, a bodhisatva householder is to generate three perceptions in regard to his wife. What are the three? They are: perceiving as a place that does duties by body; perceiving as a place that does duties by speech; and perceiving as a place that does duties by mind.

---

[97] A very nasty female spirit powerful, willing to kill, and willing to eat the flesh. Like a she-troll of Norwegian legend.

"Householder, furthermore, a bodhisatva householder is to generate three perceptions in regard to his wife. What are the three? They are: perceiving as a place of the discursive thinking of desire; perceiving as a place of the discursive thinking of ill-will; and perceiving as a place of the discursive thinking of being harmful.

"Householder, furthermore, a bodhisatva householder is to generate three perceptions in regard to his wife. What are the three? They are: perceiving as a dungeon; perceiving as murder; and perceiving as fetters.

"Householder, furthermore, a bodhisatva householder is to generate three perceptions in regard to his wife. What are the three? They are: perceiving as creating obstacles to discipline; perceiving as creating obstacles to concentration; and perceiving as creating obstacles to prajñā.

"Householder, furthermore, a bodhisatva householder is to generate three perceptions in regard to his wife. What are the three? They are: perceiving as a snare; perceiving as a cage; and perceiving as a trap.

"Householder, furthermore, a bodhisatva householder is to generate three perceptions in regard to his wife. What are the three? They are: perceiving as infectious disease; perceiving as harm; and perceiving as the onset of disease.

"Householder, furthermore, a bodhisatva householder is to generate three perceptions in regard to his wife. What are the three? They are: perceiving as trouble-making; perceiving as a doorway to mishap; and perceiving as hail.

"Householder, furthermore, a bodhisatva householder is to generate three perceptions in regard to his wife. What are the three? They are: perceiving as sickness; perceiving as aging; and perceiving as death.

"Householder, furthermore, a bodhisatva householder is to generate three perceptions in regard to his wife. What are the three? They are: perceiving as a container for māra; perceiving as based on māra; and perceiving as fearsome.

"Householder, furthermore, a bodhisatva householder is to generate three perceptions in regard to his wife. What are the three? They are: perceiving as misery; perceiving as lamenting; and perceiving as suffering, unhappy mind, and disturbance.

"Householder, furthermore, a bodhisatva householder is to generate three perceptions in regard to his wife. What are the three? They are: perceiving as a great she-wolf, perceiving as a great she-crocodile; and perceiving as a great she-cat.

"Householder, furthermore, a bodhisatva householder is to generate three perceptions in regard to his wife. What are the three? They are: perceiving as a black she-snake; perceiving as a child-killing crocodile; and perceiving as a robber of vitality.

"Householder, furthermore, a bodhisatva householder is to generate three perceptions in regard to his wife. What are the three? They are: perceiving as having no guardian; perceiving as having no refuge; and perceiving as having no place.

"Householder, furthermore, a bodhisatva householder is to generate three perceptions in regard to his wife. What are the three? They are: perceiving as fullness; perceiving as waning; and perceiving as ill.

"Householder, furthermore, a bodhisatva householder is to generate three perceptions in regard to his wife. What are the three? They are: perceiving as a robber and thief; perceiving as a prison guard; and perceiving as a guard of the sentient beings in hell.

"Householder, furthermore, a bodhisatva householder is to generate three perceptions in regard to his wife. What are the three? They are: perceiving as a river; perceiving as an application; and perceiving as a knot.

"Householder, furthermore, a bodhisatva householder is to generate three perceptions in regard to his wife. What are the three? They are: perceiving as mud; perceiving as being caught; and perceiving as being contained inside.

"Householder, furthermore, a bodhisatva householder is to generate three perceptions in regard to his wife. What are the three? They are: perceiving as rope, perceiving as cuffs, and perceiving as a trap.

"Householder, furthermore, a bodhisatva householder is to generate three perceptions in regard to his wife. What are the three? They are: perceiving as a bed of coals; perceiving as like a torch of burning grass; and perceiving as like a dagger.

"Householder, furthermore, a bodhisatva householder is to generate three perceptions in regard to his wife. What are the three? They are: perceiving as meaningless; perceiving as a thorn; and perceiving as poison.

"Householder, furthermore, a bodhisatva householder is to generate three perceptions in regard to his wife. What are the three? They are: perceiving as exaggeration into extra; perceiving as totally coating everything with extra; and perceiving as being attached to extra.

"Householder, furthermore, a bodhisatva householder is to generate three perceptions in regard to his wife. What are the three? They are: perceiving as caring for the flesh; perceiving as severing by cutting; and perceiving as holding a weapon.

"Householder, furthermore, a bodhisatva householder is to generate three perceptions in regard to his wife. What are the three? They are: perceiving as divisive; perceiving as argumentative; and perceiving as a picker of faults.

"Householder, furthermore, a bodhisatva householder is to generate three perceptions in regard to his wife. What are the three? They are: perceiving as having met with the unattractive; perceiving as having separated from the attractive; and perceiving as intimidating.

"In sum, he is to generate perceiving her as the smell of a cook; perceiving her as all the grime of a cook; perceiving her as having become the cause of all harm; and perceiving her as the root of all non-virtue.

"Householder, a bodhisatva householder staying in a household examines his wife by bringing these sorts of perceptions into mind.

"Householder, furthermore, a bodhisatva householder is not to generate a mind that sees his child as specially attractive. Householder, if he were to generate a mind seeing his child as specially attractive and likewise seeing other sentient beings as not, he must censure his own mind using three types of censure. What are the three? They are: enlightenment is for the bodhisatva who has an even-mindedness towards others, not non-even-mindedness; enlightenment is for the bodhisatva who has right application, not wrong application; enlightenment is for the bodhisatva who conducts himself without creating polarization, not who conducts himself with creating polarization. He censures his own mind using those three censures, then he is to generate the perception of his child being unattractive.

"In regard to this being unattractive, he is to generate three perceptions, thinking, 'If it were not attractive to my heart, what purpose would be served in generating special attractiveness in relation to the child, and, if I do not view other sentient beings that way, it would be contradictory to the trainings advised by the Buddha. I would, because of doing that, have harmed the roots of virtue and been careless about and harmful to the life as well, so this would be harming myself. I would, because of that, be engaged in a path not in accord with the enlightenment path, so this would be attacking myself.'

"Making an example of the child, he is to generate the mind like so and like so: similar to having a mind which sees the child as attractive, he generates loving kindness for all sentient beings, and similar to having a mind of not caring for himself, he generates loving kindness for them.

"He also examines it in accord with how it actually is, like this, 'This child will indeed part from me and I too will part from him, and given that all sentient beings have been my child previously and I too have been a child of theirs, there is no such thing as a sentient being who is mine or another's or whoever's. What is that about? It is about discordance[98]. Other than being friendly to the five types of migrator[99] one will be unfriendly to them, so the way that I will approach this is that whoever it might be, I will not be friendly or unfriendly. Why? Because if I were to apprehend them with unfriendliness, then everyone, just everyone would become unwanted, whereas if I were to apprehend them with friendliness, then most would become wanted—the two minds of attachment and anger are not able to cause internal understanding of the equalness of dharmas. Why is that? Acting in non-equality will turn into non-equality; acting in equality will become equality. In relation to

[98] "Discordance" here is a term of logic; it refers to two things being dissimilar to the point of mutual exclusion. In other words, if it is one, it cannot be the other at the same time.

[99] For migrator, see the glossary. The five types of migrator are: hell-beings, pretas, humans, asuras, and gods.

that, if I were not to act in non-equality but instead were to act in equality, that would lead to the internal comprehension of all-knowingness.[100]

"Householder, in that way a bodhisatva householder is, for every thing whatever, not to apprehend it with the thought 'mine', not to get attached to it, and not to make the latencies of guile or craving for it. Householder, a beggar-woman comes before a bodhisatva householder and begs for some thing but suppose he does not give the thing? He is to contemplate like this to make certainty of mind, 'It will be all right whether I give the thing or not given that there is no doubt that I will part from this thing—it might be unwanted but I will die, and then this thing will discard me! So, I discard this thing not because of the happiness that comes of giving this thing, but because of making life valuable in connection with the time of death. If I have given this without reservation, then when it is time for me to die, because of my having thoroughly held the mind, the mind's situation will not change. Through this, when it is time for me to die, I will be happy and supremely happy and joyful, and without regret will change lives'.

"Suppose he has contemplated like that but is still unable to give that thing. In that case, he is to develop understanding for the beggar through the three things which bring total understanding, saying, 'I am still of little power and with roots of virtue not entirely ripened; I am a beginner at the Great Vehicle who has fallen under the influence of the mind not to give, who has the view of appropriation happening[101], and who remains in grasping at a self and

---

[100] Note again the emphasis on all-knowing wisdom and the equalness that goes with it.

[101] For appropriation, see the glossary. "A view of appropriation" means that he is still on the wheel of the twelve links of interdependent origination, a wheel which, driven by grasping at a self, results in the
(continued...)

grasping at mine. Therefore, you holy beings please be tolerant and do not be upset at all. Just as you go about totally completing the intentions of yourself and all sentient beings, that is how I will do it, that is how I will accomplish, that is how I will undertake perseverance.' Householder, in that way a bodhisatva householder is to develop understanding for the beggar through the three things which bring total understanding.

"Householder, furthermore, a bodhisatva householder staying in a household is to be expert at always and continuously making thorough dedications. Suppose it has happened that, although the excellent speech of a teacher[102] who has passed exists, no buddha has arisen, nor is there a dharma teacher, nor is there a saṅgha of noble ones who could be met. In that case, he is, having prostrated to all the buddhas of the ten directions, to recall their behaviour of the past and to rejoice in behaviour consistent with that, and similarly for the virtuous conduct, intentions, and perfect special intentions[103], and the entire accomplishment of all the buddha dharmas of those who have attained enlightenment.

"He also is to do the following: during three days and three nights he is to engage in entirely pure actions of body, entirely pure actions of speech, entirely pure actions of mind, cleanliness, pure intention, and skill at loving kindness meditation, and to nicely adorn himself with clean clothes and the minds of embarrassment

---

[101](...continued)
appropriation of a new birth in saṃsāra.

[102] "The excellent speech" is the name for the recorded teachings of a buddha. "Teacher" here means a founding teacher, which in this case is a buddha, one who has set in motion the teaching of dharma.

[103] "Perfect special intentions" here means special intentions in general which are as pure and perfect as they could be. See also special intentions in the glossary.

and shame[104], and to accumulate and complete the accumulation of merit—the roots of virtue, and to take utter joy in beauty[105] and enlightenment mind, and to be glad of the company of those who have certainty in it, and to do the actions which are good doings[106], and to have physical respect, and be happy with instructions given, and by having truly cut pride, arrogance, and haughtiness to lay aside all the faults of non-virtuous actions and then henceforth restrain himself from them, and to rejoice in all merit, and to act to utterly complete the accumulation of marks[107], and to supplicate all the buddhas to utterly turn the wheel of dharma, and to retain all dharma, and in order to completely guard a life in the fathomless buddha fields to recite the dharma enumeration of the three heaps.[108]

---

[104] The two minds of embarrassment and shame are necessary foundations for being able to keep pure behaviour and pure vows in accordance with the Buddha's teaching. Embarrassment is the mind which is sensitive to and prevents wrong behaviour because of what one thinks about it oneself and shame is the mind which is sensitive to and prevents wrong behaviour because of what others will say about it.

[105] Beauty here is one of the several names for enlightenment. It is explained in the Recollection of the Buddha that the "gata" in "tathāgata" has several meanings, one of which is that he has gone beautifully to beauty, where beauty is enlightenment. Again, the complete explanation can be read in *Unending Auspicious, The Sūtra of the Recollection of the Noble Three Jewels* by Tony Duff.

[106] As explained earlier, there are two extremes of karmic actions.

[107] "Marks" are the thirty-two marks of a great being which appear on a buddha's physical body.

[108] *The Sūtra of the Three Heaps* is a sūtra in which various matters are taught, and which focusses especially on how to lay aside evil deeds using the thirty-five buddhas of laying aside.

"Householder, furthermore, a bodhisatva householder staying in a household is to take up the fasting rite of eight limbs.[109]

"He is to serve, attend, and serve and honour those who have disciplines, that is, those among the trainees in virtue and the Brahmans who have good qualities and who have virtuous dharma. He is to serve and attend them, meaning to give them service and honour, and is, without observing their confused conduct, to see his own faults. Though he sees a fully ordained monk who has slipped from the conduct of a trainee in virtue, he is not to harbour even the slightest mind of disrespect. He is to generate the mind that thinks as follows, 'The bhagavan tathāgata arhat truly complete buddha is without pollution, free of all polluting afflictions. His saffron garments indicate his being wholly clothed in discipline, wholly clothed in concentration, prajñā, complete liberation, and sight of the place of complete liberation—it is the victory banner of the ṛiṣhis who are noble ones.' Having generated the utmost respect for them, he is to generate great compassion for that monk as follows, 'This conduct of evil deeds is not good. This conduct of total affliction[110] is not good. Thus, although he wears the victory

[109] "The fasting right of the eight limbs" consists of taking of a set of eight vows at daybreak followed by either completely fasting or eating only one meal during the twenty-four hours after the vows have been taken. The practice was very common in Buddhist cultures where it was used as the container which laypeople would set up for a day of intensive Buddhist practice.

[110] In the Lesser Vehicle teachings, the Buddha made a distinction between "total affliction" which he used to summarize the saṃsāric situation and its opposite, "complete purification" which he used to summarize the nirvanic situation which results from the complete purification of the saṃsāric situation by the practices of the path to enlightenment. Note that "complete purification" refers to the result of having followed the path and is only used in relation to "total affliction"; it is not the same as complete purity, which is also men-

(continued...)

banner of the ṛiṣhis of the bhagavan tathāgata arhat truly complete buddha who is tamed, peaceful, hidden, and who knows everything, this one's conduct is the conduct of one who is not purified, not pacified, not hidden, and not tamed—it is the conduct of one who does not know everything[111]. The bhagavan has said, 'Do not speak badly of those who have not completed the training!' so he is not bad. It is the afflictions themselves, the afflictions which have made these non-virtues show, that are bad. If through the buddha bhagavans' teaching which includes the mental events these afflicted things are fully comprehended then known for what they are, then the primary fruition will be obtained, which exists as the topic of definitely becoming unsurpassedly truly completely enlightened. Why is that? It is because the afflicted states will be made known by wisdom, so the bhagavan also said, 'One person is not to assess another person—if one person assesses another person, he will slip back.'[112] The tathāgata is utterly knowing whereas I am not utterly knowing.' Having thought that, he is also to generate an attitude to that monk which is without ill-will, aversion, anger, or aggression.

---

[110](...continued)
tioned in this sutra.

[111] In this case, the words "one who does not know everything" refer to the fact that overcoming of all obscuration and gaining the attainment of all-knowing wisdom is the essence of Buddhism. Later in the sūtra "knowing everything" is used in the more conventional sense of simply having complete knowledge of a particular situation.

[112] In other words, you cannot criticize another person based on your own dualistic consciousness because only wisdom can correctly assess what is at fault, what comes from affliction, and so on. Thus, one person—where person is defined as anyone who is not a buddha—does not have the capacity to determine whether another person is at fault, only a buddha has the capacity to do that—and, on top of that, if a person does make that attempt, it will result, the Buddha said, in the person dragging himself down.

"Householder, furthermore, if that bodhisatva householder wants to enter a vihāra, he will, with a mind knowing everything, a mind become workable, possessing physical respect, possessing verbal respect, possessing faith, and possessing veneration, stay at the door to the vihāra where he will prostrate with all five limbs to the vihāra, and then first enter the vihāra. He also is to examine like this, 'This is a place of residing in emptiness. It is a place of residing in signlessness, of residing in wishlessness, of residing in loving kindness, compassion, joy, and equanimity. This is a place of the absorptions; it is a place of having truly cut all abodes. This is a place of those who have gone into being authentic and are engaged in being authentic. I too will come forth from a place of dust, the place of a household, and one day will have this sort of conduct. I too one day will stay in a place where there are the actions of the saṅgha, the action of poṣhada[113], action of lifting restrictions[114], and action of bowing.' Having thought that, he is to take joy in a mind set on being ordained.

"There are no bodhisatvas staying in a household who are achieving unsurpassed true complete enlightenment, manifest complete buddhahood! Every one of them has come forth from the place of a household then had a mind to go to a remote monastery, settled on the idea of a remote monastery, and gone to a remote monastery where they achieved unsurpassed truly complete enlightenment, manifest complete buddhahood. That assembly, moreover, is engaged in true accomplishment whereas staying in a household is totally harmful to that—progress is halted. Ordination has been

---

[113] "Poṣhada" is the name for the practice done by monks and nuns on full moons and new moons of declaring, repairing, and healing their downfalls and other faults in regard to their vows. It is one of the big features of monastic life.

[114] Tib. dgag dbye. "Lifting restrictions" is another feature of monastic life. It is a ceremony done at the end of the rains retreat to end the restrictions that have been in effect during the retreat.

commended by the buddhas and their śhrāvakas. Staying in a household entails more faults of wrongdoing happening. Ordination entails more perfect good qualities happening. Staying in a household is intimidating. Ordination is carefree. Staying in a household has the stain of ownership. Ordination is complete liberation from ownership. Staying in a household is a basis for engaging in wrong doings. Ordination is a basis for engaging in good doings. Staying in a household is staying within dirt[115]. Ordination is not staying within dirt. Staying in a household is to be drowning in the mud of desire. Ordination is to be extracted from the mud of desire. Staying in a household is to be engaged in a childish level of being. Ordination is to be engaged in expert level of being. Staying in a household it is difficult to train in livelihood. Ordination makes it easy to train in livelihood. Staying in a household there are more competitors. Ordination is without competitors. Staying in a household there is much poverty. Ordination is without poverty. Staying in a household is staying in misery. Ordination is joy. Staying in a household is a stairway to the bad migrations. Ordination is a stairway to the higher ones. Staying in a household is to be bound. Ordination is emancipation. Staying in a household is to be with fear. Ordination is without fear. Staying in a household is living cut off. Ordination is living not cut off. Staying in a household is to be with the use of weapons. Ordination

---

[115] The view within Buddhism was that householders lived in the dust of ordinary houses where the ordained community did not. A dusty environment was and still is a feature of India and surrounding countries, though the use of the words has the added connotation of "dirty and impure compared to the monastic environment". There is a very interesting interchange between Ānanda and Uncouth at the end of the sūtra regarding this point, one which is essential to understanding one of the several main threads of meaning in the sūtra. In it, Ānanda accuses Uncouth of being weak and so staying in the dirty situation of a householder rather than becoming ordained. Uncouth points out that there is, for him as he goes about his bodhisatva householder path, essentially no impurity in staying in a household.

does not have the use of weapons. Staying in a household is to be with complete distress. Ordination is to be without complete distress. Staying in a household is suffering because of always seeking something. Ordination is happiness because of being without always seeking something. Staying in a household entails wildness. Ordination is very peaceful. Staying in a household involves clinging and being attached. Ordination does not involve clinging and being attached. Staying in a household is to be in the underprivileged class. Ordination is not underprivileged[116]. Staying in a household is low class. Ordination is high class[117]. Staying in a household is to be totally ablaze. Ordination is the blaze pacified. Staying in a household is about others' aims. Ordination is about both aims[118]. Staying in a household is of lesser meaning. Ordination is of greater meaning. Staying in a household is less brilliant. Ordination is more brilliant. Staying in a household is suffering due to total affliction. Ordination is happiness due to having come forth. Staying in a household is production of thorns. Ordination is removal of thorns. Staying in a household is to possess small dharma. Ordination is to possess great dharma. Staying in a household is doing what is not taming. Ordination is doing what

---

[116] "Underprivileged class" refers to the lowest situation within any culture in which the common people have no great power or say within the society; they are its underdogs. The average householder is still in that situation. Living a monastic life bypasses that altogether.

[117] "Low and high class" in this couplet, do not refer to position within the larger society but to the kind of person one is. Monastics are generally regarded as high class and honoured whereas the ordinary householders are generally regarded as inferior to them.

[118] Staying in a household would usually be said to be only about one's own aims, with the emphasis on selfishness. Here it is said to be about others' aims with the emphasis on always being at the mercy of others' demands. In the ordained situation, one is working on the aims of both oneself and others: the aims of enlightening oneself and enlightening all other sentient beings.

is taming. Staying in a household is regretful. Ordination is not regretful. Staying in a household is to develop oceans of tears, breast-milk, and blood. Ordination is to dry up oceans of tears, breast-milk, and blood. Staying in a household is to denigrate the buddhas, pratyekas, and śhrāvakas. Ordination is to commend the buddhas, pratyekas, and śhrāvakas. Staying in a household is to be discontent. Ordination is to be content. Staying in a household is to like the māras. Ordination makes misery for the māras. Staying in a household becomes the ultimate great pollution. Ordination is the ultimate pacification of all pollution. Staying in a household is to remain totally untamed. Ordination is to be totally tamed. Staying in a household is to do the work of a servant. Ordination is to act as a lord. Staying in a household becomes the saṃsāra extreme. Ordination becomes the nirvāṇa extreme. Staying in a household is to be at a precipice. Ordination is to be gone from the precipice. Staying in a household is deep darkness. Ordination is illumination. Staying in a household is not controlling the faculties. Ordination is controlling the faculties. Staying in a household is to create haughtiness. Ordination is to tame haughtiness. Staying in a household is to create what is not holy. Ordination is to create what is holy. Staying in a household is to create the bad migrations. Ordination is to create the good migrations. Staying in a household is to have an unsuitable view. Ordination is to have a suitable view. Staying in a household involves great work. Ordination involves small work. Staying in a household is a smaller fruition. Ordination is a greater fruition. Staying in a household is being crooked. Ordination is being straight. Staying in a household there is more mental unhappiness. Ordination has mental happiness. Staying in a household has acute pain. Ordination has the acute pain removed. Staying in a household is to be sick. Ordination makes the absence of sickness. Staying in a household causes dharma to diminish. Ordination causes dharma to flourish. Staying in a household causes heedlessness. Ordination causes heedfulness. Staying in a household is the source of prajñā becoming lax. Ordination is the increase of prajñā. Staying in a household causes obstacles to prajñā. Ordination causes prajñā to come alive.

Staying in a household is to be on standby watching for any attempt at deception. Ordination is not to be on standby watching for any attempt at deception. Staying in a household involves more doings. Ordination involves less doings. Staying in a household is like drink with poison. Ordination is like drink with nectar. Staying in a household is harmful. Ordination is without harm. Staying in a household involves mixing with adulterating influences. Ordination is not mixing with them. Staying in a household is like the Kimpāka fruit[119]. Ordination is like a nectar fruit. Staying in a household causes meeting with what is unattractive. Ordination causes separation from what is unattractive. Staying in a household causes separation from what is attractive. Ordination causes meeting with what is attractive. Staying in a household is made heavy by delusion. Ordination is made light by wisdom. Staying in a household application completely falls apart. Ordination is complete training in application. Staying in a household intentions completely fall apart. Ordination is complete training in intention. Staying in a household the special intention[120] completely falls apart. Ordination is complete training in the special intention. Staying in a household makes for being without supporters. Ordination causes supporters. Staying in a household makes for being without a guardian. Ordination causes having a guardian. Staying in a household makes for having no place. Ordination causes having a place. Staying in a household makes for being without a refuge. Ordination causes having a refuge. Staying in a household there is more ill-will. Ordination has more loving kindness. Staying in a household is to carry a burden. Ordination is to lay down the burden. Staying in a household is to behave without limit. Ordination is to bring all conduct to its limit[121].

---

[119] The Kimpāka fruit is a gourd with a particularly foul taste.

[120] See special intentions in the glossary. Here it refers to enlightenment mind.

[121] In a household, you can do anything you want. An ordained person (continued...)

Staying in a household has the unmentionable actions. Ordination is without the unmentionable actions. Staying in a household there will be distress. Ordination will not involve distress. Staying in a household involves affliction. Ordination is without affliction. Staying in a household involves material things. Ordination is without material things. Staying in a household involves overt pride. Ordination is without overt pride. Staying in a household is to make wealth the essence. Ordination is to make good qualities the essence. Staying in a household there is infectious disease. Ordination is a pacifier of infectious disease. Staying in a household there is decrease. Ordination is increase. Staying in a household acquisition is easy. Ordination is that even for one hundred thousand kalpas acquisition is difficult. Staying in a household it is easy to do things. Ordination is that it is difficult to do things. Staying in a household goes towards continuous involvement. Ordination turns away from and leaves continuous involvement. Staying in a household is a river. Ordination is a boat. Staying in a household is a river of afflictions. Ordination is a bridge. Staying in a household is the approach to this shore. Ordination is the approach to the other shore[122]. Staying in a household is easy to do. Ordination is not easy to do. Staying in a household one cares for the flesh. Ordination pacifies caring for the flesh. Staying in a household one does according to the king's edicts. Ordination means that one does according to the Buddha's teaching. Staying in a household is to be in a feeble situation. Ordination is without feebleness. Staying in a household suffering occurs. Ordination has happiness occur. Staying in a household is shallow. Ordination is deep. Staying in a household there are indeed companions. Ordination is a situation where companions are rare. Staying in a household one associates with a wife. Ordination is to associate

---

[121](...continued)
strives to bring all conduct into the final form of enlightened conduct.

[122] "This shore" is our side, the side of saṃsāra, and "the other shore" is the side of the noble beings, the side of nirvāṇa.

with one's intent. Staying in a household is similar to a trap. Ordination is to break the trap. Staying in a household is to attach great importance to harming others. Ordination is to attach great importance to benefiting others. Staying in a household is to see a need for material gifts. Ordination is to see a need for the gift of dharma. Staying in a household is to bear the victory banner of māra. Ordination is to bear the victory banner of the Buddha. Staying in a household is the basis for suffering. Ordination is true defeat of the basis of suffering. Staying in a household is the complete increase of the aggregates. Ordination is the certain casting away of all the aggregates[123]. Staying in a household involves gathering denseness[124]. Ordination is emancipation from the gathering denseness. Householder, in that way a bodhisatva householder is to settle on the idea of ordination.

"He, moreover, is to generate the mind that thinks as follows. 'Suppose during many days I have made offerings of worship equal to the amount of sand in the Ganges River; all that giving without reservation of material goods is outshone by the mind which has been ordained in the Vinaya dharma which has been well-explained[125]. Why is that? Householder, those of no faith, those

---

[123] Staying in a household only results in the increase of saṃsāric being, which is summed up under the heading of the five aggregates or skandhas. Being in the ordained situation means that those five saṃsāric aggregates are completely cast off but also means that the five aggregates of the nirvāṇa side—which are mentioned on a few occasions in this sūtra—are developed to perfection.

[124] "Denseness" here means the gathering of thick, difficult complexity, like storm clouds gathering.

[125] "The Vinaya dharma which has been well-explained" refers to the Vinaya in which all the levels of Buddhist ordination and all the rules and customs that go with them are explained. Well-explained here does not mean "well-explained" *per se* but means that the Buddha's

(continued...)

with no appreciation for what has been done, robbers and thieves, outcastes[126], king's appointees, and ministers also engage in performing acts of generosity but theirs is the generosity of material things, which is inferior.

"Householder, a bodhisatva householder is to generate the mind that thinks like this, 'I will not be content with making generosity essential, rather, I also will make discipline and hearing and celibacy essential.'

"If he comes into a vihāra, he is to prostrate to the representations of the tathāgata. Having made prostrations to those he is to generate three perceptions. What are the three? They are the thoughts, 'I too am to become worthy of this sort of offering, and for the sake of heartfelt love for sentient beings also will bless my body. And I too as soon as I have achieved unsurpassed truly complete enlightenment and become a truly complete buddha, will do the activities of a buddha. And, having done them, I will, by the tathāgata having gone to parinirvāṇa, do the activity of going to parinirvāṇa. I will train like that and be assiduous like that.'

"Having entered the vihāra, he is to completely examine all conducts of the saṅgha of monks, asking, "Who is: the monk of much

---

[125](...continued)
explanations of a system for taming oneself (the Vinaya) were good explanations because they were taught correctly and in accord with reality, whereas the explanations given by other spiritual teachers of the time were not good. This "the Vinaya dharma which has been well-explained" is one of the epithets of the dharma and is thoroughly explained in the book *Unending Auspiciousness, the Sutra of the Recollection of the Noble Three Jewels* cited in note 20.

[126] "Outcastes" are those in the lowest of the four castes of Hindu culture and literally were not allowed to live with the other casts of Hindu culture. For this reason, they were often found living in remote places.

hearing; the monk who explains dharma; the monk who upholds the Vinaya; the monk who cares for the older women; the monk who upholds the bodhisatva's piṭaka; the monk who stays in a remote monastery; the one who goes begging for alms; the one who wears cast-off clothing, the one of little desire, the one of contented mind, and the one who stays in utmost isolation; the monk who practices yoga; the monk who stays in meditative absorption; the monk who follows the bodhisatva vehicle; the monk who is the top hand[127]; the monk who acts as a servant[128]; and the monk who is the leader of the monks.'

"Having completely examined their conducts, he is, in order to enter in a way that is in harmony with all, to stay in harmony as required.

"He is not to show another form of conduct in front of them. Why is that? What happens inside the vihāra is secret from the village. What happens in the village is secret from the vihāra. Keeping his actions of speech extremely restrained, he is not to tell the secrets of the vihāra in the village and not to tell the secrets of the village in the vihāra.

"In regard to monks who have faults of the dharma robes, faults of the begging bowl, faults of medicines for curing illness or of articles[129], he is to be generous by having the approach of not criticising or become angry towards them. Why is that? The

---

[127] "Top hand" is the position within the monastic order of the one in charge of work. It is like saying "leading hand" or "foreman".

[128] "Who acts as a servant" is a specific position within the Buddhist monastic order. It is a position where one does specific tasks that are assigned, so that one is a servant to the community. The job entails the approach "Yes venerable sir, I will do it!"

[129] These are faults that a monk can have because of not following the rules of his vowed conduct. They make the monk less than pure.

enmeshments[130] of gods and men are jealousy and avarice, and that being so, what is to guarded to the utmost by individualized beings is not so for the arhats. Why is that? From individual beings wrongdoings are produced, from arhats it is not so. Thus, attending the one of much hearing, he is to be diligent at seeking hearing. Attending the one who expresses dharma, he is to be diligent at the stories of thorough ascertainment. Attending the one who upholds the Vinaya, he is to be diligent at taming wrongdoing and taming affliction. Attending the one who cares for the older women, he is to be diligent at vowed restraints of body, speech, and mind. Attending the one who upholds the bodhisatva collection of sūtras, he is to be diligent at the six pāramitās and skilful means. Attending the one who stays in a remote monastery, he is to be diligent at utter isolation. Attending the one who goes begging for alms, he is to be diligent at not being shaken by gain and loss, fame and infamy, praise and blame, happiness and suffering. Attending the one who wears cast-off clothing, he is to be diligent at being warmed by dharma robes and not taking joy in ornamentation. Attending the one of little desire, he is to be diligent at having little desire. Attending the one who is content, he is to be diligent at being content. Attending the one who stays in utter isolation, he is to be diligent at utter isolation. Attending the one who practices yoga, he is to be diligent at correctly setting himself internally, with an internal mind of śhamatha and vipaśhyanā that is operating in accord with what is. Attending the one who stays in meditative absorption, he is to be diligent at removing affliction. Attending the one who follows the bodhisatva's vehicle, he is to be diligent at generosity, speaking nicely, meaningful conduct, and consistency of aim—the four things of gathering[131]. Attending the top hand, he

---

[130] "Enmeshments" is a technical term for the afflictions that keep sentient beings totally joined to saṃsāric existence.

[131] "The four things of gathering" is a set of four things taught for bodhisatvas in the Prajñāpāramitāsūtra as the means to attract and

(continued...)

is to be diligent at taking delight in how things are totally given. Attending the monk who acts as a servant, he is to be diligent at doing every 'do it'. Attending to the leader of the monks, he is to be indefatigable. Householder, in that way a bodhisatva householder staying in a household is to be diligent at a style of entering that follows in exact accordance with their conduct.

"If a monk who is engaged in true faultlessness does what is included with dharma robes or what is included with the begging bowl, that monk is one who will be engaged in truly holding unsurpassed truly complete enlightenment. Why is that? Because there is the issue of what is included under material things creating inclusion under dharma. Householder, in that way a bodhisatva householder is to become expert in the conduct of trainees in virtue.

"He is also to reconcile monks who are not in a state of reconciliation.

"In that the holy dharma is utterly transitory, he is to give without reservation even his life and to totally uphold the holy dharma.

"Householder, if any bodhisatva householder sees a sick monk, he is to cure that monk of that disease even if it takes his own flesh and blood to do so.

"Householder, furthermore, a bodhisatva householder is to care for others as guests by giving and being generous and also, having

---

[131](...continued)
retain disciples. As mentioned here: first one gives things to attract people; then one speaks very nicely to them to get them interested; then one gradually introduces them to the disciplines of the Buddhist path; and, in order for them not to feel cheated and so to stay, one shows a way of behaving which is entirely consistent with the teachings on discipline that one has taught them.

given, is not to generate a mind of regret. As well, he is to turn to the enlightenment mind prior to producing every root of virtue.

"Householder, when it is like that, the bodhisatva householder staying in the place of a household is acting in accordance with the command of the tathāgatas, and is not slipping back from the dharmas of the side of enlightenment, not slipping back from them at all. Also, there are no unmentionable actions in this life and there will be the particulars in another."

Then, householder Uncouth, and those other householders unanimously highly praised what the bhagavan had said, then supplicated the bhagavan in these words:

"The extent to which the bhagavan has spoken well of these matters of the faults of staying in a household and the benefits of the good qualities of vows, conduct, and ordination is wondrous! Bhagavan, we too at this point have directly seen how many faults of wrongdoing happen in relation to staying in a household and the infinite good qualities and benefits of being ordained. Thus, bhagavan, we would be ordained; please perform the approach completion[132] in the Vinaya dharma which the sugata has well explained."

They supplicated in those words and the bhagavan instructed those householders in these words:

---

[132] "Approach completion" is the technical term found in the Vinaya teachings for full ordination of Buddhist monk or nun. There are different levels of ordination for monastics. The lesser levels only go part of the way to training in enlightenment. In comparison to them, the highest level of ordination, the level of being a full monk or nun, completes the approach to enlightenment, being a complete training in enlightenment. Thus, the householders are asking for ordination at the level of a full monk. The meaning of "well explained" is given in note 125.

"Householders, it is difficult for ordination to happen; it is difficult for the conduct which is extremely completely pure to be accomplished."

He instructed in those words and those householders supplicated the bhagavan in these words:

"Bhagavan, ordination is indeed difficult to have happen, nevertheless, please would the bhagavan create an opportunity on account of our becoming ordained? We seek to practise assiduously the bhagavan's teaching."

The bhagavan created an opportunity for ordination for those householders, then the bhagavan instructed the bodhisatva Maitreya and the bodhisatva Sarvacharyavimala in these words:

"You two holy beings do the approach completion for these householders' ordination!"

The bhagavan having granted it, the bodhisatva Maitreya ordained nine thousand householders. Seven thousand householders were ordained through all bodhisatva conducts being completely pure[133]. In explaining this enumeration of dharma in which the flow of the trainings of the bodhisatva householders has been taught, the mind for unsurpassed truly complete enlightenment was born in a full one thousand living beings.

The third and last bundle.

Then householder Uncouth supplicated the bhagavan in these words:

---

[133] This means that seven thousand of them additionally took the bodhisatva vows.

"The bhagavan having explained the mistakes made by bodhisatva householders and the mistakes of staying in a household, would the bhagavan please explain well the perfections of the accomplishing[134], discipline, hearing, ascetic training's good qualities[135], diminished articles[136], conduct, and liturgies connected with being ordained of the bodhisatvas who are included among the ordained. And, how is it for the bodhisatvas who have been ordained in the Vinaya dharma which has been well explained; it does not mean, does it, that they do not have the tasks of speaking respectfully, prostrating, rising, joining palms, and bowing?"

He supplicated in those words and the bhagavan instructed the householder Uncouth in these words.

"Householder, all of what you have asked the tathāgata concerning the perfections of the accomplishing, discipline, hearing, ascetic

---

[134] "Accomplishing" here refers to what the ordained bodhisatvas are to practise and accomplish. The details are explained a little further on and then summed up as the practise and accomplishment of dharma.

[135] There were twelve ascetic trainings that, generally speaking, monks could choose to follow or not, though some of them, such as begging for food and being allowed the use of only a few articles are an integral part of being a monk. The twelve fall into three groups: 1) begging for alms, one seat, and not taking food later; 2) three robes, felt robes, and cast offs; and 3) staying in a remote place, sitting at the foot of a tree, and being without a canopy. The following are major topics in this sūtra: begging for alms, three robes, cast offs, and staying in a remote place. Each of these trainings produces one or more beneficial qualities of body, speech, and mind, and these also are sometimes dealt with at length in the sūtra.

[136] "Diminished articles" is the ascetic practice of having very few possessions, both clothing and utensils. There are extensive rules on how many articles in total a monk can have, what they can be, and so on.

training's good qualities, diminished articles, conduct, and liturgies connected with being ordained is good, is good!

"Householder, therefore, listen well with your fullest attention and retain it in mind! And I will explain to you how bodhisatvas included among the ordained are to stay and how they are to accomplish."

He said "Very well bhagavan", then the householder Uncouth listened according to the bhagavan and the bhagavan instructed him with these words.

"Householder, for this, an ordained bodhisatva is to evaluate, thinking like this, 'On whose account have I, in going from householder to not householder, been ordained?' And then he is, as though his head and clothes were on fire, to undertake perseverance because of seeking wisdom.

"He, by thoroughly evaluating in that way, to begin with is to utterly remain within the four families of noble ones and to take great joy in ascetic training's good qualities and in diminished articles. Householder, how is it for an ordained bodhisatva to utterly remain within the four families of noble ones? Householder, for this, the ordained bodhisatva has the attitude of being content with the worst kind of dharma robes. He also expresses approval for the attitude of being content with the worst kind of dharma robes, because he does not have to go seeking in various ways for the sake of dharma robes. Even if he does not acquire dharma robes, he does not become dejected and remains totally without distress. Even if he does acquire dharma robes, he is without attachment, without stupidity, without joy, and without clinging and will not start to cling. Seeing the disadvantages and having utterly known the events[137], he conducts himself without attachment; the attitude of being content with the worst kind of dharma robes entails no praise for oneself and no blame for other.

Householder, furthermore, the ordained bodhisatva has the attitude of being content with the worst kind of alms. He also expresses approval for the attitude of being content with the worst kind of alms, because he does not have to go seeking in various ways for the sake of alms. Even if he does not acquire alms, he does not become dejected and remains totally without distress. Even if he does acquire alms, he is without attachment, without stupidity, without joy, and without clinging and will not start to cling. Seeing the disadvantages and having utterly known the events, he conducts himself without attachment; the attitude of being content with the worst kind of alms entails no praise for oneself and no blame for other.

Householder, furthermore, the ordained bodhisatva has the attitude of being content with the worst kind of bedding. He also expresses approval for the attitude of being content with the worst kind of bedding, because he does not have to go seeking in various ways for the sake of bedding. Even if he does not acquire bedding, he does not become dejected and remains totally without distress. Even if he does acquire bedding, he is without attachment, without stupidity, without joy, and without clinging and will not start to cling. Seeing the disadvantages and having utterly known the events, he conducts himself without attachment; the attitude of being content with the worst kind of bedding entails no praise for oneself and no blame for other.

---

[137] "Events" here and in the subsequent paragraphs means "the mental events involved, virtuous and unvirtuous, and which ones should be followed and not".

Householder, furthermore, the ordained bodhisatva has the attitude of being content with the worst kind of medicines for curing sickness and articles. He also expresses approval for the attitude of being content with the worst kind of medicines for curing sickness and articles, because he does not have to go seeking in various ways for the sake of medicines for curing sickness and articles. Even if he does not acquire medicines for curing sickness and articles, he does not become dejected and remains totally without distress. Even if he does acquire medicines for curing sickness and articles, he is without attachment, without stupidity, without joy, and without clinging and will not start to cling. Seeing the disadvantages and having utterly known the events, he conducts himself without attachment; the attitude of being content with the worst kind of medicines for curing sickness and articles entails no praise for oneself and no blame for other.

"He also finds joy in abandoning, which is that he intends to abandon and is diligent at applying himself to being joyful at abandoning. He becomes joyful because of having abandoned evil deeds, non-virtuous dharmas, and does not because of not having abandoned them. He finds joy in cultivating, which is that he is diligent at applying himself to being joyful at cultivating. He becomes joyful because of having cultivated virtuous dharmas, and does not because of not having cultivated them. Joy at abandoning, intending to abandon, diligence at applying himself to being joyful at abandoning, joy at cultivating, intending to cultivate, diligence at applying himself to being joyful at cultivating, all of which entails no praise for oneself and no blame to others.

"Householder, when it is that way, the ordained bodhisatva is abiding in the four families of the noble ones. Why are they called 'families of the noble ones'? All the dharmas of the side of enlightenment are present in this, because of which they are called 'families of the noble ones'.

"Householder, furthermore, an ordained bodhisatva is, through ten joys at the benefits involved, to decide on dharma robes for the body. What are the ten? They are as follows. He thinks, 'Being bound by embarrassment and avoidance, and being covered against contact with meat flies, small insects, wind, sun, and evil snakes, and having the colours of a trainee in virtue, showing the sign of a trainee in virtue, and saffron, these are a stūpa of the world which has gods, men, and asuras.' Because of being a stūpa it is to be properly owned. So, those robes signify a change of colour because of renunciation and separation from desire, not a change of colour due to desire. And they are consistent with being highly pacified, they are not consistent with the blazing up of afflictions. And, having been bound and covered by these saffrons I am to turn away from evil actions, do the actions which are good acts, not make efforts at showing myself to being underway because of the dharma robes[138], and having understood that these saffrons are consistent with the aggregates of the path of the noble ones[139] not by any means to contaminate them even for an instant, and not provide the saffron garments to companions but to keep them for myself. Householder, an ordained bodhisatva is through those ten joys at the benefits to have decided on dharma robes for the body.

"Householder, furthermore, an ordained bodhisatva is, through seeing the ten benefits involved, not to let go of the conduct of begging for alms for as long as he is alive. What are the ten? They are: one will survive by independent means, not in dependence on others; the sentient beings from whom I desired alms and who gave alms also will, having been arranged in the Three Jewels, later take

---

[138] In other words, not to use the wearing of the dharma robes as a way of showing that he has progressed significantly on the dharma path.

[139] "The aggregates of the path of the noble ones" in general means the various things that comprise it, though it could also be seen as the five aggregates of the nirvāṇa side, which are mentioned a couple of times in this sutra.

up begging for alms; having generated compassion for the sentient beings from whom I desired alms but who did not give alms, those sentient beings will undertake perseverance for the sake of taking up giving; having done the activity, the alms are eaten; I become one who has done in accordance with the tathāgata's command; now, I will have created the causes for doing what is easy and obtaining easy sustenance; I will have shown the breakage of pride; I will have accumulated the roots of virtue of my unseen crown protuberance; having seen me, they will train in that same way, and will not attend a man or woman or boy or girl; and as well as the conduct of truly taking up alms, I will, because of having an even mind in regard to all sentient beings, come into the aggregate of all-knowing wisdom. Householder, an ordained bodhisatva having seen those ten benefits is not to let go of the conduct of begging for alms for as long as he is alive.

"Suppose one group calls him to be a guest; he is to go for the sake of generating the special intention[140], faith, and admiration, not because of luring them or manipulation. If he is capable of making acceptance of the group's alms into completion of the aims of oneself and others, then I grant permission for the bodhisatva to go as a guest.

"Householder, furthermore, an ordained bodhisatva is, through seeing the ten benefits involved, to be content with massage medicinals for as long as he is alive. What are the ten? They are: one will have engaged in the teaching of the tathāgata; one will not look at another's side[141]; I will attend to the perception of what is unattractive; I will standby, perceiving each and every case of what

---

[140] See special intentions in the glossary. Here it refers to enlightenment mind.

[141] This means that, having taken refuge formally in the Buddha, one will not go to another teacher and his ways, as explained in an earlier note.

is not in harmony with me; even though something is tasty, I will abandon it with little hardship; all childish individualized beings will take me as a reliance; I will become one who has actually lessened his consumption of food; I will become one without the poverty of having to search for medicine; I will become one who has made himself to be without the harm to the mind of the illness of afflictions and, having entered into such, will quickly obtain separation from the illness of afflictions. Householder, an ordained bodhisatva through seeing those ten benefits is to be content with massage medicinals for as long as he is alive.

"Householder, furthermore, an ordained bodhisatva is, through seeing the ten benefits involved, to not give up at all on staying in a remote monastery up until the end of his staying alive. What are the ten? They are: being happy in myself and going under my own control; having no mine and no owning; being loose about bedding; not being separated from the joy of being in a remote monastery; attaching little to holy places and doing little; casting aside the requirements of a servant and not looking out for body and life; taking joy in solitude and completely abandoning frivolous entertainments; completely giving up the benefits of the good qualities of having done work; having a one-pointed mind consistent with concentration; and having no canopy-like mentations, no obscuring mentations. Householder, an ordained bodhisatva through seeing those ten benefits is to not give up at all on staying in a remote monastery up until the end of his staying alive.

"Householder, suppose an ordained bodhisatva staying in a remote monastery has come to the place of a village because of desiring to listen to dharma, desiring to see a master or preceptor, or having questions about an illness. He is to generate the mind to go based on intending to return again. Suppose he is thinking to take authoritative statement or do recitation[142], something that happens in dependence on others; he is staying in a vihāra, nevertheless, because his mind is settled on a remote monastery, everything is perceived in terms of the remote monastery and he will contemplate, 'The dissatisfaction that comes with seeking dharma is what causes staying in a remote monastery.'

"Householder, furthermore the ordained bodhisatva staying in a remote monastery is to examine in this way, thinking, 'Why am I staying in a remote monastery? Staying in a remote monastery of itself is not training in virtue. In here there are ones who are not purified, hidden, tamed, industrious, utterly diligent—it is gentle creatures, monkeys, many birds, robbers and thieves, and outcastes

---

[142] Taking authoritative statement and doing recitation will be mentioned several times in the coming part of the discourse, where they are being used as prime examples of the sorts of things one might do in relation to or with others. "Taking authoritative statement" means to go before a master, preceptor, or other person expert in the Buddhist teaching and to ask him to impart words that have been passed down through the tradition, originating either with the Buddha himself or with someone else in the tradition who was highly accomplished and could provide authoritative statements himself (for example, these days a group of six and another group of two masters of ancient India are regarded as the ones who were best and most capable at giving authoritative explanations.) Taking authoritative statement is something that can only happen in dependence on others, so the issue of how those others who are in a position to impart authoritative statement should be respected. "Doing recitation" means to join with a group of monks and recite the sūtras, something that was usually done at the request of householders who would invite the monks in a group to come to the house and do the recitation. The householders would then serve the monks in whichever way was needed—for example, giving them food and refreshment—and would honour them as needed, which would usually include making offerings of material things to them in thanks for their efforts. All the points mentioned in this note are germane to understanding what follows.

that mostly stay here. Moreover, they do not possess the good qualities of training in virtue, so why do I stay in a remote monastery? The answer is: to totally complete the purpose of training in virtue'.

"Householder, what is an ordained bodhisatva's purpose of training in virtue? It is: utterly gaining mindfulness, alertness, undistractedness, and retention, and attending to loving kindness, attending to compassion, mastering the extra-perceptions, totally completing cultivation of the six pāramitās, not letting go at all of the mind of all-knowing, cultivating the wisdom of skilful means, gathering sentient beings, entirely ripening sentient beings, not letting go at all of the four things of gathering, recollecting the six recollections, not casting aside hearing and perseverance, utterly distinguishing dharmas according to their actual mode, being diligent for the sake of true complete liberation, knowing the gaining of fruitions, remaining in entering without fault, guarding the holy dharma, right view through trust in full-ripening of karma, right thought through having utterly cut all thought and discursive thought, right speech through teaching dharma in exact accord with intentions[143], right extremes of action through having totally completed the exhaustion of action, right livelihood through truly having defeated the junctures of latencies[144], right effort through having internally comprehended complete enlightenment, right mindfulness through the situation of being without forgetfulness, right concentration through having completely attained all-knowing wisdom itself, not being scared by emptiness, not being daunted by signlessness, not being intimidated by wishlessness, caring to the utmost for

---

[143] "Intentions" here means the intentions of the listeners, their thoughts about what they want to do and how they will do it. For example, some will think to follow the Lesser Vehicle path and some will think to follow the Greater Vehicle path.

[144] "Junctures of latencies" refers to the process of one karmic latency or another ripening into its effect.

becoming as a whole through wisdom in accordance with the intentions[145], relying on meaning not relying on letters, relying on wisdom not relying on consciousness, relying on dharma not relying on persons, relying on the sūtra section of definitive meaning not relying on the sūtra section of provisional meaning, and not conceiving of an entitiness of dharmas through their mode of not having arisen to begin with and not disintegrating. That, householder, is called 'the ordained bodhisatva's purpose of training in virtue'.

"Householder, also the ordained bodhisatva will mostly be without companion. He is also to examine in this way, thinking, 'I am not to mix in with sentient beings; I am not to generate the roots of virtue of a single sentient being, instead, I am to generate the roots of virtue of all sentient beings.'

"It is indeed like that householder, nevertheless, the following four companions of an ordained bodhisatva are granted by the tathāgata. What are the four? They are: a companion because of hearing the dharma; a companion because one will entirely ripen sentient beings; a companion because of making offerings of worship to and doing practices of respect for the tathāgata; and the companion of the mind of all knowingness being without adulteration. Householder, those four companions of an ordained bodhisatva are granted by the tathāgata. Householder, in that way then, an ordained bodhisatva is to have complete liberation from companions.

---

[145] "Intentions here has the same meaning as explained in a note just above. Here though, it mentions "becoming" which means that it is in reference to the intentions of all beings in saṃsāra (see becoming in the glossary". In other words, this item means that the bodhisatva is to care to the utmost for the beings in saṃsāra by having all-knowing wisdom which, in knowing exactly their thoughts and aims, knows exactly the right way and right time to do whatever needs to be done to care for them.

"Householder, furthermore, an ordained bodhisatva due to staying in a remote monastery is to examine with the thought, 'Why did I come to a remote monastery?' He is also to fully analyse like this, thinking, 'I came to a remote monastery because of being frightened and scared. What is frightening and scaring me? Frivolous entertainments frighten and scares me. Companions frighten and scare me. Desire, anger, and delusion frighten and scare me. Pride, infatuation, and concealment frighten and scare me. Attachment, jealousy, and avarice frighten and scare me. Visual form, sound, smell, taste, and touch frighten and scare me. The aggregates' māra frightens and scares me. The afflictions' māra frightens and scares me. The death māra frightens and scare me. The son of god māra frightens and scares me. Wrongly seeing impermanent as permanent frightens and scares me. Wrongly seeing suffering as happiness frightens and scares me. Wrongly seeing lack of self as self frightens and scares me. Wrongly seeing impure as pure frightens and scares me. Mind, mentality, and consciousness[146] frighten and scare me. Craving frightens and scares me. Samsara frightens and scares me. Obscuration, obstacles, and total obstruction frighten and scare me. The view of the transitory collection frightens and scares me. Grasping at self and grasping at mine frighten and scare me. Agitation frightens and scares me[147]. Regret and doubt frighten and scare me. Companions who do evil actions frighten and scare me. Gain and honour frighten and scare me. Non-spiritual friends[148] frighten and scare me. Grasping with the thought 'I see'

---

[146] Tib. sems yid rnam shes. "Mind, mentality, and consciousness" is a group of three things which sums up all the possibilities of dualistic saṃsāric mind. One should be afraid of them because they are the mind of saṃsāra, with all the unsatisfactoriness which that entails.

[147] "Agitation" here refers to one of the two enemies of being able to develop a calmly abiding mind, the other being sinking and sleeping.

[148] "Non-spiritual friends who are those who, proclaiming themselves as a spiritual teacher, teach non-virtuous ways or ways which are

(continued...)

when I do not see frightens and scares me. Grasping with the thought 'I hear' when I do not hear frightens and scares me. Grasping with the thought 'I remember' when I do not remember frightens and scares me. Grasping with the thought 'I have distinguished the details' when I have not distinguished the details frightens and scares me. Grasping with the thought 'I know' when I do not know frightens and scares me. Stains on training in virtue frighten and scare me. The mind that thinks to harm one another frightens and scares me. The desire realm, the form realm, and the formless realm frighten and scare me. Death and transference followed by birth in all the migrations in becoming frightens and scares me. Going to the hellish sentient beings, animal birthplaces, and place of the pretas frightens and scares me. Non-freedom[149] frightens and scares me. In sum, mental involvement with all the non-virtuous dharmas frightens and scares me. Being frightened and scared like that, I was afraid of those things so came to a remote monastery. Staying in a household and staying with frivolous entertainments, not being industrious and putting effort into yoga[150], and staying in mental involvements that are not how it is, I am unable to be completely freed from those sorts of frightening, scary things. All of the bodhisatva mahāsattvas who arose in past times were, due to staying in a remote monastery, completely liberated from all fears in that they attained unsurpassed truly complete enlightenment which is fearless. Moreover, all of the bodhisatva

---

[148](...continued)
counter to true spirituality.

[149] "Non-freedom" here refers to the non-freedom taught in relation to precious human rebirth, which is the eight non-freedoms discussed under that heading. It is tantamount to saying that I am afraid of being born in one of the many places in saṃsāra in which the conditions there give me no freedom to be able to pursue dharma.

[150] "Yoga" here means doing the meditations of combined śhamatha and vipaśhyanā in which one attempts to re-unite (the meaning of yoga) oneself with reality.

mahāsattvas who will arise in the future times will, due to staying in a remote monastery, be completely liberated from all fears, in that they will attain unsurpassed truly complete enlightenment which is fearless. The bodhisatva mahāsattvas who have arisen in the present time will attain unsurpassed truly complete enlightenment; moreover, all of them will, due to staying in a remote monastery, be completely liberated from all fears in that they will attain unsurpassed truly complete enlightenment which is fearless. So it is that I too being frightened and scared of this want to utterly transcend all fears. No fear is what I desire to subsequently obtain, so I will stay within a remote monastery.'

"Householder, furthermore, an ordained bodhisatva who, due to having become frightened and scared, has gone to stay in the place of a remote monastery, has slight fears of it, all of which are produced from grasping at a self. They are produced from strong attachment to a self, entirely grasping at a self, basis of a self, craving self, perceiving self, appropriation that speaks of a self, viewing a self, abode of a self, entirely conceiving a self, and protecting a self. He is to train in the thought, 'Suppose I, in staying in a remote monastery, were not to have entirely abandoned grasping at a self, not to have entirely abandoned strong attachment to a self, entirely grasping at a self, basis of a self, craving self, perceiving self, appropriation that speaks to a self, viewing a self, abode of a self, totally conceiving of a self, and protecting a self. In that case, my staying in a remote monastery would have been meaningless.'

"For the perceiving of a self there is no need to stay in a remote monastery. For the perceiving of other there also is no need of it. For strong clinging to grasping at I and grasping at mine there is no need to stay in a remote monastery. For viewing references[151] there is no need to stay in a remote monastery. For viewing the wrong way around there is no need to stay in a remote monastery.

---

[151] For references, see the glossary.

"Householder, if even for perceiving of nirvāṇa there is no need to stay in a remote monastery, what need is there to mention it in respect for someone who has perception of all the afflictions? Householder, what is called 'staying in a remote monastery' is staying in not being based in any dharmas. It is staying in not grasping at all dharmas. It is staying in detachment from all concept tokens[152]. It is staying in not being based in all visual forms. It is staying in not being based in all sounds, smells, tastes, and touches. It is staying in not being contrary to the equalness of all dharmas[153]. It is staying in being thoroughly processed[154] through thorough pacification of mind[155]. It is staying in being unafraid through having abandoned all fears. It is staying in having crossed over the river through complete liberation from all afflictions. It is staying in steadiness. It is staying in having utter joy in the families of the noble ones through the attitude of being content with the

---

152 For concept tokens, see the glossary. The meaning here is consistent with the meaning of the next sentence. This sentence explains not to stay in dualistic consciousness—anything with concept tokens is a dualistic consciousness. This could be approached either by coming to emptiness through prajñā in the style of the second turning of the wheel or by simply entering the non-dualistic wisdom of a buddha, which is the highest teaching of the sūtras and the overall thrust of this particular sūtra.

153 Again, the use of equalness here means taking the highest-level approach to actualizing the dharma of simply entering and remaining in non-dualistic wisdom. In that approach, all phenomena are directly known and at the same time the point of their equalness or sameness, which is that they are empty of a nature, is also directly known.

154 "Thorough processing" is the final outcome of the perfect development of calm-abiding or śhamatha. It includes bliss of body and mind, lightness of body and mind, utter workability of mind, the ability to fly, and many other features.

155 "Pacification of mind" means to develop calm-abiding, that is, śhamatha.

worst kinds of things and having little desire. It is staying in the attitude of being content with easy things and easy livelihood. It is staying in hearing through application to the actual mode for the sake of prajñā. It is staying in emancipation through individual discrimination in respect to the doors of complete emancipation—emptiness, signlessness, and wishlessness. It is staying in complete liberation through having cut the fetters. It is staying in pacification of those who are untamed through being in accord with interdependent origination. It is staying in having done the deeds through extreme complete purity.

"Householder, it is like this: for example, in a remote monastery one will not become frightened and scared despite staying in grass, spreading trees, and forests. Householder, accordingly, an ordained bodhisatva despite staying in a remote monastery is to generate the perception that his body is like grass, a spreading tree, a medicinal substance, a wall, wood, a visual distortion, and analogous to an illusion, and is to generate the mind that thinks, 'Who would be frightened of this? Who would be scared of this?' If he views it with fear and is scared, then he is to examine the body in accordance with its actual mode like this, 'In this body the self, sentient being, life, living being, sustainable being, small being, person, being of force, or being without force which I call 'frightened' is unreal, nothing but conceptual labelling[156], so I am not to conceive of such being in it.'

---

[156] "Nothing but conceptual labelling" is one aspect of the fundamental ignorance that creates and keeps one in saṃsāra. The first type of that ignorance is called "co-emergent ignorance". It means that every occurrence experienced automatically comes together with the wrong idea of a self. The second type, which builds on that layer of ignorance and which functions to solidify the ignorant state of being even further, is the one mentioned here. At this level, everything is a product of conceptual labelling, so everything is simply imagined and has little relation to the actual truth of the matter.

"He is to stay there and practise strongly through understanding that, 'In the same way as the grass, spreading trees, medicinal substances, and forests present in a remote monastery have no mine, no ownership, a bodhisatva also has no mine, no grasping at ownership because of which all dharmas are the remoteness of a monastery.' Why is that? To stay in a monastery is to sever afflictions—it is to be without mine, without grasping at ownership.

"Householder, furthermore, an ordained bodhisatva staying in a remote monastery is for this to train in thinking, 'Staying in a remote monastery is to be in harmony with the aggregate of discipline. Staying in a remote monastery is to be settled on the idea of the aggregate of concentration. Staying in a remote monastery is to assemble the aggregate of prajñā. Staying in a remote monastery is to accomplish the aggregate of complete liberation. Staying in a remote monastery is to give birth to the aggregate of seeing the wisdom of complete liberation. Staying in a remote monastery is to utterly attend to the dharmas of the side of enlightenment. Staying in a remote monastery is to gather the twelve good qualities of ascetic training[157]. Staying in a remote monastery is to realize the truths. Staying in a remote monastery is to wholly know the aggregates[158]. Staying in a remote monastery is for the dhātus to meet equally with the dharmadhātu[159]. Staying in a

---

[157] See note 135.

[158] This can mean both to wholly know the saṃsāric five aggregates so as to eliminate them and to wholly know all the aggregates of the path of the noble ones so as to actualize them.

[159] For the dhātus to meet equally with dharmadhātu means that the saṃsāric form of dhātus—as in aggregates, dhātus, and āyatanas—eventually will become enlightened forms of the same, in which case they will no longer be the individual elements of saṃsāric being but will become that fundamental expanse in which every phenomenon—the dharmadhātu—is produced. This is similar to the talk of being in

(continued...)

remote monastery is to dispel the āyatanas. Staying in a remote monastery is to not forget enlightenment mind. Staying in a remote monastery is not to be afraid because of discriminating emptiness. Staying in a remote monastery is to totally hold dharma. Staying in a remote monastery is to not squander all the roots of virtue. Staying in a remote monastery is commended by the buddhas. Staying in a remote monastery is praised by the bodhisatvas. Staying in a remote monastery is esteemed by the noble ones. Staying in a remote monastery is to be attended by those desiring emancipation[160]. Staying in a remote monastery is to serve[161] for the sake of internally comprehending all-knowing wisdom'.

"Householder, furthermore, an ordained bodhisatva staying in a remote monastery will, with little hardship, wholly complete the cultivation of the six pāramitās. Why is that? The bodhisatva who stays in a remote monastery does not look out even for body or life; in that way, the one who stays in a remote monastery will wholly complete his cultivation of the pāramitā of generosity. Householder, how is it that an ordained bodhisatva staying in a remote

---

[159](...continued)
equality which pervades this sūtra, in that the only way for the dhātus to meet with the dharmadhātu is to enter and remain in the state of equalness that comes with being in the non-dualistic wisdom of a buddha.

[160] This means that, just as much as one attends and apprentices oneself to the masters, preceptors, and experts who have progressed on the path to enlightenment, so, by staying in the remote monastery, others will eventually come to attend and apprentice themselves to oneself.

[161] One stays in a remote monastery serving and honouring those masters, preceptors, and experts who have themselves internally comprehended—meaning fully taken in and understood in direct perception—non-dual all-knowing wisdom so that one can do the same.

monastery's cultivation of the pāramitā of discipline will be wholly completed? Householder, the ordained bodhisatva who stays in a remote monastery utterly remains in ascetic training's good qualities and the diminished articles then undertakes true accomplishment through the three vowed restraints; staying in remote monastery in that way his cultivation of the pāramitā of discipline will be wholly completed. Householder, how is it that an ordained bodhisatva staying in a remote monastery's cultivation of the pāramitā of patience will be wholly completed? Householder, the ordained bodhisatva who stays in a remote monastery is without ill-will in mind and works at loving kindness for all sentient beings, which also is patience for all-knowingness; staying in a remote monastery in that way, his cultivation of the pāramitā of patience will be wholly completed. Householder, how is it that an ordained bodhisatva staying in a remote monastery's cultivation of the pāramitā of perseverance will be wholly completed? Householder, for this the ordained bodhisatva trains in thinking, 'For the sake of utterly attaining forbearance with respect to the unborn[162], I will not turn away from this remote monastery'; staying in a remote monastery in that way, his cultivation of the pāramitā of perseverance is wholly completed. Householder, how is it that an ordained bodhisatva staying in a remote monastery's cultivation of the pāramitā of absorption will be wholly completed? Householder, the bodhisatva who stays in a remote monastery devotes himself utterly to achieving the pāramitā of absorption yet this does not mean that he is forsaking the work of entirely ripening sentient beings, it is that he also wants to accumulate roots of virtue in that way; staying in a remote monastery in that way, his cultivation of the pāramitā of absorption will be wholly completed. Householder, how is it that an ordained bodhisatva staying in a remote monastery's cultivation of the pāramitā of prajñā will be wholly completed? Householder,

---

[162] "Attained forbearance with respect to the unborn" means that he gained acceptance of the fact that all phenomena are unborn, that is empty of a nature.

for this an ordained bodhisatva trains in thinking, 'In the same way as the body can be viewed, the remote monastery also is such, and in the way as the body can be viewed, enlightenment also is such', and then through that suchness does not think, does not think discursively; staying in a remote monastery in that way, his cultivation of the pāramitā of prajñā will be wholly completed. Householder, in that way then, an ordained bodhisatva staying in a remote monastery will, with little hardship, wholly complete cultivation of the six pāramitās.

"Householder, if an ordained bodhisatva possesses four dharmas he is granted permission to stay in a remote monastery. What are the four? Householder, for this, the ordained bodhisatva is one who has much hearing; one who holds to hearing, is expert at the complete ascertainment of dharma, is diligent at mentation in accord with the actual mode, and who accomplishes dharma and what follows in agreement with dharma, is granted permission to stay in a remote monastery. Householder, furthermore, if an ordained bodhisatva has a greater level of affliction, he is granted permission to stay in the remote monastery without companions for the sake of pacifying the afflictions; he is to eliminate the afflictions. Householder, furthermore, an ordained bodhisatva must gain the five extra-perceptions; he is to stay in a remote monastery for the sake of entirely ripening gods, nāgas, yakṣhas, and gandharvas[163]. Householder,

---

[163] This is a standard listing of non-human types. One has to develop the extra-perceptions for various reasons, including having the ability to know others' minds, an ability which is essential for teaching others. We often think that "teaching others" means other humans, but a person of some capacity has a much bigger responsibility of teaching humans and non-humans. Here, the most common non-humans that one would teach are listed. Gods who would be taught are those living in the levels above humans in the desire realm and also in the form realm; nāgas are snake-like beings who usually live near water and who often are interested in the dharma; yakṣhas are a very harmful and

(continued...)

furthermore, an ordained bodhisatva knowing that the Buddha has granted permission to stay in a remote monastery is to stay in a remote monastery; there, all the virtuous dharmas will be totally completed. When, by means of those roots of virtue, he has become very stable, he is to enter villages, cities, towns, provinces, regions with their beings, and palaces with their retinues, and teach dharma. Householder, an ordained bodhisatva possessing those four dharmas is granted permission to stay in a remote monastery.

"Householder, suppose an ordained bodhisatva, for the sake of taking authoritative statement or recital, enters the assembly. Even then, he must do so with respect for it; he is to do so with verbal respect for the masters and preceptors, the elders, the middling ones, and the new monks. He is to be knowledgeable of their ways. He is to do his own activities without being haughty and without causing distress to others. He is not to stew the system of serving and honouring[164]. He is to examine in this way, thinking, 'There is

---

[163](...continued)
powerful type of spirit who sometimes take an interest in dharma; and gandharvas are the equivalent of European fairies, and they too historically took an interest in dharma. You will often see this group of non-humans mentioned at the end of a sūtra as members of the audience.

[164] "To stew" means to cook up water and ingredients into a thick soup in which all the ingredients are mixed in together. The verb here refers to making a style of food that was and still is common in Asia, where a meal is often a thick soup made from watery start with ingredients put into the water and boiled together till there is a very thick broth.

This meaning is found here, where Buddha instructs his followers not to stew up the practice of serving and honouring others into something that is a mixture of all sorts of things and is nice for oneself. His meaning is that one should not take the purity of that practice and mix it up with all sorts of self-centred ideas, such as thinking that

(continued...)

the tathāgata arhat truly complete buddha who has become a place for generosity, a place of offerings of worship by the world with gods, with māras, with Braḥma, with trainees in virtue and nine-birth brahmans, and gods, men, and asuras, and as well as that, there are all sentient beings who, no matter who they are, are to be paid respect in every way. It is not that they are to do that for me. It goes without saying that I am to serve and honour our people who are untrained but desire to train[165] but in addition I am to serve and honour all sentient beings—it is not that they are in every way to give service and honour to me.' Why is that so? Householder, stewing the service and honour of monks wastes the dharmas of good qualities already held, so if he and the others who have gathered are thinking, 'We are gathered on account of service and honour, not because of dharma', then their faith in the great soul[166] will have become wasted and lost. In that case, the service and honour together with material things of the world[167] given to them will not become something of great meaning, will not have a great fruition. If he then goes to the place of the master and preceptor, the master and preceptor will, due to seeing that he has some kind of mind of no faith, say, 'It will be of no benefit to you for me to impart authoritative statement to you, make recitals with you, or teach you.' Those things can only happen when mind and body

---

[164](...continued)
service and honour is something that should be done for oneself, given that one is a monk, etcetera.

[165] "Untrained but desire to train" is another way of referring to all those followers of the buddha who might not be buddhas yet but have formally entered the Buddhist path by becoming a monk or nun so that they can train themselves up to being buddhas.

[166] As for example in Mahātma Gandhi and here meaning the Buddha.

[167] Offerings of food and other material goods that the lay people who had invited them to their houses or who were serving them in the monastery would have given in appreciation.

have been made workable and mind knows everything[168]. In order to be able to take authoritative statement or do recital, he has to have no consideration for even his body or life. To fulfil his desire for dharma, the master's and preceptor's wishes have to be fulfilled. And, he is not to find any meaning at all in gain, esteem, and verses that might come from his finding meaning in good qualities.

"Householder, if a bodhisatva who finds meaning in taking authoritative statement and doing recitation hears from others simply four lines of verse or hears from someone four lines of verse having the word generosity, discipline, patience, perseverance, absorption, or prajñā or words of the requirements of the bodhisatva path and the like, or takes authoritative statement or retains such, then definitely there has to be, for the sake of receiving dharma, respect for that master. Suppose that the bodhisatva offers worship without guile to the master who imparted the verse through performing service and honour, being a servant, fetching wood, and offering all honour and esteem for as many kalpas as there are names, grammatical phrases, and letters[169] comprising the verse, even then householder,

---

[168] It is usually said that body and mind are made workable through practices such as śhamatha which pacify the wildness and roughness of body and mind. However, the meaning here is more encompassing than that. It means to pacify that wildness and roughness by whichever forms of training are needed, which could be by putting oneself into a position of serving and honouring deliberately to develop humility and the appropriate manners. Here, mind knowing everything is not referring to all-knowing wisdom but to developing full knowledge of the situation that one has entered so as to be in complete harmony with that situation and not cause disturbances within it.

[169] Where letters and words are the two components from which English language is composed, "names, grammatical phrases, and letters" are the three components from which Sanskrit and Tibetan languages are composed. A full explanation would take up too much space so is not given, for that, see the book *Standard Grammar Volume I, The*

(continued...)

he still will not have completed the veneration of the master as a master. He might offer service and honour to the master for as many kalpas as the minds and mental events possessing virtue, or possessing buddha, or possessing dharma, or possessing saṅgha, or possessing separation from weariness and desire, or possessing purification, tameness, and peace that are involved in his engagement through faith—leaving aside through respect for what is not dharma—in listening and meditating, and in recitation, yet even then, householder, he will not have completed the veneration of the master as a master. Householder, what one is to understand by this enumeration is that the dharmas of full-ripening are measureless and that internally comprehended wisdom is measureless. Householder, if he takes that view and queries the matter in relation to the dharmas of full-ripening being measureless and internally comprehended wisdom being measureless, it will bring him to the thought, 'My master also is measureless', and then the bodhisatva will have measureless veneration for the dharma.

"Householder, furthermore, an ordained bodhisatva is to stay in the accomplishing that belongs to ordination. Householder, how is it that an ordained bodhisatva is to stay in the accomplishing that belongs to ordination? Householder, for this, if an ordained bodhisatva hears of totally pure discipline, he trains in that; the following four are the totally pure discipline. What are they? They are: staying in the families of the noble ones; taking great joy in ascetic training's good qualities and in diminished articles; the ordained not mingling with those who stay in a household; and staying in a remote monastery in an uncontrived manner. Those four are the totally pure discipline.

---

[169](...continued)
*Thirty Verses of Minister Thumi*, by Tony Duff, published by Padma Karpo Translation Committee, 2005, ISBN: 978-9937-572-35-4.

"Householder, furthermore, what are the four totally pure disciplines? They are: that by restrained[170] body one does not reference body; that by restrained speech one does not reference speech; that by restrained mind one does not reference mind; and that by separating from views the mind for all-knowing is generated. Those four are the totally pure discipline.

"Householder, furthermore, what are the four totally pure disciplines? They are: abandoning grasping at I; casting off grasping at mine; separating from nihilism and permanence; and entering into the dharma which is a basis. Those four are the totally pure discipline.

"Householder, furthermore, what are the four totally pure disciplines? They are: conceiving of the aggregates as having origination and disintegration; entirely meeting the dharmadhātu in the dhātus; perceiving the āyatanas as an empty village; and not overtly clinging to the designated conventions. Those four are the totally pure discipline.

"Householder, furthermore, what are the four totally pure disciplines? They are: not praising self through perceiving that in self there is absence of self; not disparaging other through not referencing other; being without conceit through a mind which has been thoroughly processed; and being without guile through the equalness of all dharmas. Those four are the totally pure discipline.

"Householder, furthermore, what are the four totally pure disciplines? They are: being intent on emptiness; not being scared of signlessness; compassion at a greater level for all sentient beings; and forbearance with respect to lack of self. Those four are the totally pure discipline.

---

[170] Restrained here means that one has taken vows in relation to it.

"Householder, furthermore, if an ordained bodhisatva hears of totally pure concentration, he trains in that. What is totally pure concentration? It is: being without conceived effort[171] for all dharmas; being without separation into two through the equalness of all dharmas; workable mind, one-pointed mind, renounced mind, mind not elaborating, mind not totally running[172], mind not abiding, certainty of mind, blessed mind, control over mind, no attachment to the qualities of a desirous mind, mind discriminating dharmas as illusions, the way that dharmadhātu is not to be actually formed, and the way that there is non-production, non-origination, and equalness. Householder, in that way an ordained bodhisatva discriminates totally pure concentration.

"Householder, furthermore, if an ordained bodhisatva hears of totally pure Prajñāparamita, he trains in it. What is totally pure prajñā? It is discriminated like this: knowing all dharmas in direct perception; knowing how to utterly distinguish words; knowing how to enter the individual correct knowledges[173]; and knowing how to make other sentient beings understand dharma. Householder, in that way an ordained bodhisatva discriminates totally pure prajñā.

"Householder, furthermore, an ordained bodhisatva for this is to utterly train in thinking, 'This prajñā being bodyless has the characteristic of being without impedance; being causeless has the characteristic of not being graspable; being without birth has the characteristic of being without dwelling; being space-like without entitiness has the characteristic of not being actually formed.'

---

[171] For conceived effort, see the glossary.

[172] This means literally for the mind not to be running and running and running without stop.

[173] The "individual correct knowledges" is a set of four insights which allow a bodhisatva to teach sentient beings in the best possible way.

Householder, that sort of discrimination of dharmas is what is an ordained bodhisatva's accomplishing."

"The bhagavan having explained this enumeration of dharma, one hundred thousand living beings have generated the mind for unsurpassed truly complete enlightenment. Householder, of all of them, the majority have utterly gained forbearance with respect to unborn dharmas. Thirty-two thousand living beings have had the dust on the dharma eye for dharmas removed and it has been completely purified into stainlessness."

Then the householder Uncouth was joyful and rejoiced, and being utterly joyful, was gratified and happy in mind. He supplicated the body of the bhagavan with a pair of manufactured cloths worth one hundred thousand times normal then supplicated in these words:

"Bhagavan, I bestow this root of virtue of mind on sentient beings. By this root of virtue of mine, may the dharmas of the bodhisatva householders whoever they are, the trainings of the bodhisatva householders however they have them, be totally completed! May the dharmas of the ordained bodhisatvas whoever they are, the trainings of the ordained bodhisatvas however the bhagavan has given them, be totally completed!

"I also make a petition to the bhagavan; if a bodhisatva householder staying in a household had how many dharmas would he be training in the trainings of the ordained?"

He supplicated in those words and the bhagavan instructed householder Uncouth in these words:

"Householder, for this, if a bodhisatva householder staying in a household has five dharmas he will be training in the trainings of the ordained. What are the five? Householder, for this, a bodhisatva householder staying in a household completely gives all things without consideration—because of possessing all-knowing wisdom he is without hope for full-ripening. And householder, furthermore, a bodhisatva householder staying in a household does not engage in celibacy and cleanliness—if he does not generate desire even for mental gratification, why mention something like engaging in the meeting of the two genitals or in what is not a branch? And householder, furthermore, a bodhisatva householder staying in a household who has disconnected from being truly without fault and is remaining in an empty household, having established the right conditions, enters the equilibria of the four absorptions. And householder, furthermore, a bodhisatva householder staying in a household who is being diligent at making all sentient beings happy undertakes perseverance at definite deliverance by prajñā pāramitā. And householder, furthermore, a bodhisatva householder staying in a household takes up the pure and holy dharma and furthermore applies himself to the genuine dharma. Householder, if a bodhisatva householder staying in a household has those five dharmas he is training in the trainings of the ordained."

Then the householder Uncouth supplicated the bhagavan in these words:

"Bhagavan, I desire to act in accordance with the command of the tathāgatas, will train in the trainings of the ordained, and also will in such way enter the equalness of dharmas."

Then, at that point, the bhagavan gave a smile. This was one of those circumstances when the buddha bhagavans give a smile, and at that point radiant light in many colours, in various colours such as blue, yellow, red, white, green, crystal, and silver came from the doorway of the bhagavan's mouth. They pervaded the infinite, boundless world realms, illuminating them with light, then, having gone very high, up as far as Braḥmā's world, came back again, circled the bhagavan three times, then sank into the crown protuberance atop the bhagavan's head.

Then, the Vitality-filled[174] Ānanda by the power of the bhagavan rose from his seat, draped his outer robe over one shoulder, knelt down on his right knee, and bowing with joined palms in the direction of the bhagavan, supplicated the bhagavan in these words:

"Bhagavan, given that the tathāgata does not give a smile without cause, without condition, what would be the cause, what would be the condition, of his giving a smile?"

He supplicated in those words and the bhagavan instructed the Vitality-filled Ānanda in these words:

"Ānanda, you, by means of this householder Uncouth, have made an offering of worship to the tathāgata[175]; have you seen a lion giving his roar because of his accomplishing the dharma?"

He supplicated:

"Bhagavan, yes indeed I have seen it! Sugata, yes indeed I have seen it!"

The bhagavan instructed:

"Ānanda, this householder Uncouth will offer respect to all those tathāgatas who will arise in this good kalpa. He will esteem them and will make offerings of worship to them using all the offerings of worship. He also will uphold the holy dharma. As well, always becoming a householder, he will stay in the trainings of the

---

[174] Skt. āyuṣhmat. This is a standard honorific term used in the monastic community when addressing other monks. It means that the person is full of life, full of vitality, because of having abandoned worldly pursuits and training in virtue.

[175] This is because Ānanda was the one who generally made the arrangements for people to have an audience with the Buddha.

ordained. Moreover, he will make the tathāgata's enlightenment become more widespread."

Then the vitality-filled Ānanda said these words to householder Uncouth:

"Householder, which cause and which condition are the reason for your staying in a household and taking joy in staying in dust?"

Uncouth said:

"Bhadanta[176] Ānanda, there is no dust, except for a slight amount! With the possession of great compassion, I do not hope for my own happiness. Bhadanta Ānanda, a bodhisatva even tolerates being tormented by all sufferings; he does not let go at all of sentient beings."

He said those words and the bhagavan instructed the Vitality-filled Ānanda in these words:

"Ānanda, this householder Uncouth in this good kalpa will, due to staying in the place of a household, engage in the entire ripening of utterly many sentient beings; an ordained bodhisatva would not be capable of such in even a thousand kalpas or many hundreds of thousands of kalpas. Why is that? Ānanda, it is that the good qualities had by this bodhisatva do not exist in even one thousand of the ordained bodhisatvas."

Then the Vitality-filled Ānanda supplicated the bhagavan in these words:

---

[176] Bhadanta is the common term used in the Buddhist tradition when a layman addresses a monk. It comes to mean "virtuous one".

"Bhagavan, what should be the name of this enumeration of dharma? How should it be retained?"

The bhagavan instructed:

"Ānanda, for that, retain this enumeration of dharma as 'Petitioned by Uncouth'! Also, retain it as 'Accomplishing the Householders' and Ordained Ones' Trainings'! Also retain it as 'The Chapter on Performing Service and Honour for the Guru Through the Special Intention'.

"Ānanda, immediately on hearing this dharma enumeration, the good qualities, perseverance, and many dharmas of the bodhisatva will utterly be gained; this is not the inferior class of perseverance that causes one to remain in the conduct of celibacy for one hundred kalpas.

"Ānanda, that being so, there should be the thought, 'I too desire to arouse perseverance for this, and, furthermore, want to install myself in perseverance for it. And I also want to stay in all the equalness dharmas of good qualities[177]. And, furthermore, because of wanting to arrange myself in all the equalness dharmas of good qualities, I am to listen to this enumeration of dharma, to totally absorb its meaning, to read it, and also to teach it vastly, correctly, and utterly to others.'

"Ānanda, for the sake of this enumeration of dharma being taught again and again vastly, correctly, and utterly, I fully entrust it to

---

[177] The "equalness dharmas of good qualities" means staying within the good qualities that belong to the state of equalness, in other words, staying within non-dual wisdom. This is yet another pointer to the fact that the Buddha is teaching at the highest level. It is one of the reasons that this is marked out as a sūtra that teaches Other Emptiness, as described in the introduction.

you. Why is that? This enumeration of dharma contains within it all good qualities because it has been explained by the tathāgata.

"Ānanda, a bodhisatva who remains unseparated from this enumeration of dharma will not be separated from the occurrence of a buddha. Ānanda, a bodhisatva who remains unseparated from listening to or retaining or reading this dharma enumeration will not be separated from the occurrence of a buddha or from seeing all buddhas. Why is that? Ānanda, because the tathāgata has correctly, utterly explained it, this enumeration of dharma contains within it all good qualities and this enumeration of dharma contains within it all good qualities of the path on which the trainings will be accomplished.

"Ānanda, sons of the family or daughters of the family who find meaning in truly complete enlightenment should, even if the third order great thousandfold world system catches and utterly fills with fire, listen to this enumeration of dharma, should totally absorb its meaning. Ānanda, having venerated the master with and then offered him the third order great thousandfold world system utterly filled with the seven types of precious things[178], this enumeration of dharma is to be listened to, is to have its meaning totally absorbed.

"Ānanda, a bodhisatva who offers worship with all the offerings of worship to each one of the precious stūpas of the past buddha bhagavans, and likewise who performs service and honour with all useful articles for as long as he lives to the buddha bhagavans who have arisen in the present together with their śhrāvaka saṅghas, and who will have done service and honour for the buddhas who will arise in the future and their servant bodhisatvas and those who have proclaimed themselves as their disciples, but who does not stay within doing and accomplishing the retention of, bearing of,

---

[178] The "seven types of precious things" are the seven attributes of a wheel-wielding or chakravartin king.

reading of, total absorption of the meaning of, and entrance into this, Ānanda, that bodhisatva would not have made offerings of worship to the tathāgatas arising in the past, future, and present.

"Ānanda, if a bodhisatva who listens to and totally absorbs the meaning of this enumeration of dharma also, for the sake of the holy dharma staying for a long time and the buddha family being uninterrupted, stays in this, teaching and accomplishing it vastly, correctly, and utterly to others too, then Ānanda, that bodhisatva will have made offerings of worship to the buddha bhagavans arising in the past, future, and present. He would also have, through having respect, done service and honour for them."

The bhagavan instructed in those words then the Vitality-filled Ānanda, the householder Uncouth, those monks, those bodhisatvas, and the world with gods, men, asuras, and gandharvas[179] rejoiced and highly praised what the bhagavan had said.

Of the hundred thousand chapters of dharma enumerations of the *Noble One, The Great Stack of Jewels*, this is the end of the nineteenth chapter called "The Noble One Petitioned by Uncouth".

Translated and edited by the Indian preceptor Surendrabodhi and by the chief editor translator Bande Yeshe De, this has been finalized.

[179] This is a standard listing of the beings who were in the audience, listening to the Buddha. Gods who could be taught dharma directly were the ones living in the levels above humans in the desire realm and also in the form realm; asuras are gods of the lowest god level of the desire realm who constantly war with the gods of the upper levels in an attempt to be like them; and gandharvas are the equivalent of European fairies, and they too historically took an interest in dharma.

# GLOSSARY OF TERMS

**Adventitious**, Tib. glo bur: This term has the connotations of popping up on the surface of something and of not being part of that thing. Therefore, even though it is often translated as "sudden", that only conveys half of the meaning. In Buddhist literature, something adventitious comes up as a surface event and disappears again precisely because it is not actually part of the thing on whose surface it appeared. It is frequently used in relation to the afflictions because they pop up on the surface of the mind of buddha-nature but are not part of the buddha-nature itself.

**Affliction**, Skt. kleśha, Tib. nyon mongs: This term is usually translated as emotion or disturbing emotion, etcetera, but the Buddha was very specific about the meaning of this word. When the Buddha referred to the emotions, meaning a movement of mind, he did not refer to them as such but called them "kleśha" in Sanskrit, meaning exactly "affliction". It is a basic part of the Buddhist teaching that emotions afflict beings, giving them problems at the time and causing more problems in the future.

**Aggregates, dhatus, and ayatanas**, Skt. skandha dhātu āyatana, Tib. phung po khams skyed mched: The Buddha taught this set of three in the Lesser Vehicle teachings where they were an essential part of the teaching on how saṃsāra is constructed and how it perpetuates itself. Skandhas are the "aggregates" that make up a samsaric being. Dhātus are the items within a samsaric being's makeup that are the "bases" of all samsaric minds; they are a detailed listing of the things that allow dualistic mind to occur with all of its attendant problems. Āyatanas are those specific members of the dhātus which cause saṃsāric consciousness to ignite. A very complete presentation of the skandhas, dhātus, and āyatanas can be found in the book *The Six Topics that All Buddhists Learn* by Tony Duff, published by Padma Karpo Translation Committee, 2012, ISBN: 978-9937-572-13-2.

**Alertness**, Tib. shes bzhin: Alertness is a specific mental event that occurs in dualistic mind. It and another mental event, mindfulness, are the two functions of mind that must be developed in order to develop śhamatha or one-pointedness of mind. In that context, mindfulness is what remembers the object of the concentration and holds the mind to it while alertness is the mind watching the situation to ensure that the mindfulness is not lost. If distraction does occur, alertness will know it and will inform the mind to re-establish mindfulness again.

**Appropriation**, Skt. upādāna, Tib. nye bar len pa: This is the name of the ninth of the twelve links of interdependent origination. Tsongkhapa gives a good treatment of all twelve links in his interdependent origination section of the *Great Stages of the Path to Enlightenment*, a translation of which is available for free download from the PKTC web-site. It is the crucial point in the process at which a karma that has been previously planted is selected and activated as the karma that will propel the being into its next existence. In other words, it is the key point in a being's existence when the next type of existence is selected. There is the further point that, at the time of death, the particular place that the wind-mind settles in the subtle body, a place related to the seed syllables mentioned in the tantras, also determines the next birth. The two points are not different. The selection of the karma that will propel the next life then affects how the wind-mind will operate at the time of death.

**Authoritative statement**, Skt. āgama, Tib lung. Although often translated as "scripture", authentic statement means statement made by someone who has the true knowledge needed to make fully reliable statements about a subject. It is often used to indicate dharma taught by the Buddha or his disciples which is authoritative because of its source. It is also used in the pair "authoritative statement and realization" which, the Buddha explained, summed up the ways of transmitting his realization.

**Becoming**, Skt. bhāvanā, Tib. srid pa: This is another name for samsaric existence. Beings in saṃsāra have a samsaric existence but, more than that, they are constantly in a state of becoming—becoming this type of being or that type of being in this abode or that, as they are driven along without choice by the karmic process that drives samsaric existence.

**Bodhichitta**, Tib. byang chub sems: See under enlightenment mind.

**Bodhisatva**, Tib. byang chub sems dpa': A bodhisatva is a person who has engendered the bodhichitta, enlightenment mind, and, with that as a basis, has undertaken the path to the enlightenment of a truly complete buddha specifically for the welfare of other beings. Note that, despite the common appearance of "bodhisattva" in Western books on Buddhism, the Tibetan tradition has steadfastly maintained since the time of the earliest translations that the correct spelling is bodhisatva; see under satva and sattva.

**Bodhisatva mahasattva**, Tib. byang chub sems dpa' sems dpa' chen po: In general, *bodhisatva* refers to a *satva* or heroic being who is on the path to *bodhi* truly complete enlightenment and *mahāsattva* refers to a *sattva* or sentient being who is at a greater level of being, a higher kind of person. Thus, the usual explanation of *bodhisatva mahāsattva* is that it means "a being on the path to truly complete enlightenment, one who is a great type of being because of his intention to reach truly complete enlightenment for the sake of all sentient beings. However, there is also a second, less common explanation, in which *mahāsattva* does not mean a great being in general but has the specific meaning of those bodhisatvas who, amongst all bodhisatvas, have attained a very great level of being. In this case, it particularly refers to bodhisatvas who have achieved and are dwelling on the highest bodhisatva levels, the eighth to tenth bodhisatva levels. Unlike bodhisatvas at all levels below that, these bodhisatvas have attained such a high level of purity that they cannot regress to a lower level. Their level of attainment is enormous and with it, they have many qualities which are very similar to those of a buddha. It is important to know of this second understanding of *bodhisatva mahāsattva*, because when it is used with that meaning, it says that the bodhisatvas being mentioned are the bodhisatvas above all other bodhisatvas, ones who are close to truly complete enlightenment.

**Clinging**, Tib. zhen pa: In Buddhism, this term refers specifically to the twofold process of dualistic mind mis-taking things that are not true, not pure, as true, pure, etcetera and then, because of seeing them as highly desirable even though they are not, attaching itself to or clinging to those things. This type of clinging acts as a kind of glue that keeps a person joined to the unsatisfactory things of cyclic existence because of mistakenly seeing them as desirable.

**Complete purity**, rnam dag: This term refers to the quality of a buddha's mind, which is completely pure compared to a sentient being's mind. The mind of a being in saṃsāra has its primordially pure nature covered over by the muck of dualistic mind. If the being practises correctly, the impurity can be removed and mind can be returned to its original state of complete purity.

**Conceived effort**, Tib. rtsol ba: In Buddhism, this term usually does not merely mean effort but has the specific connotation of effort of dualistic mind. In that case, it is effort that is produced by and functions specifically within the context of dualistic concept. For example, the term "mindfulness with effort" specifically means "a type of mindfulness that is occurring within the context of dualistic mind and its various operations".

**Concept tokens**, Tib. mtshan ma: This is the technical name for the structures or concepts which function as the words of conceptual mind's language. They are the very basis of operation of the third skandha and hence of the way that dualistic mind communicates with its world. For example, a table seen in direct visual perception will have no concept tokens involved with knowing it. However, when thought becomes involved and there is the thought "table" in an inferential or conceptual perception of the table, the name-tag "table" will be used to reference the table and that name tag is the concept token.

Although we usually reference phenomena via these concepts, the phenomena are not the dualistically referenced things we think of them as being. The actual fact of the phenomena is quite different from the concept tokens used to discursively think about them and is known by wisdom rather than concept-based mind. Therefore, this term is often used in Buddhist literature to signify that dualistic saṃsāric mind is involved rather than non-dualistic wisdom.

**Confusion**, Tib. 'khrul pa: In Buddhism, this term mostly refers to the fundamental confusion of taking things the wrong way that happens because of fundamental ignorance, although it can also have the more general meaning of having lots of thoughts and being confused about it. In the first case, it is defined like this "Confusion is the appearance to rational mind of something being present when it is not" and refers, for example, to seeing an object, such as a table, as being truly present, when in fact it is present only as mere, interdependent appearance.

**Consciousness**, Skt. vijñāna, Tib. rnam shes: The term means "awareness of superficies". A consciousness is a dualistic (jñā) awareness which simply registers a certain type of (vi) superfice, for example, an eye consciousness by definition registers only the superficies of visual form. A very important point is that the addition of the "vi" to the basic term (jñā) for awareness conveys the sense of a less than perfect way of being aware. This is not a wisdom awareness which knows every superfice in an utterly uncomplicated way but a limited type of awareness which is restricted to knowing one kind of superfice or another and which is part of the complicated—and highly unsatisfactory process—called (dualistic) mind. Note that this definition, which is a crucial part of understanding the role of consciousness in samsaric being, is fully conveyed by the Sanskrit and Tibetan terms but not at all by the English term.

**Cyclic existence**: See under saṃsāra.

**Dharmadhatu**, Skt. dharmadhātu, Tib. chos kyi dbyings: This is the name for the *dhātu* meaning range or basic space in which all *dharmas*, meaning all phenomena, come into being. If a flower bed is the place where flowers grow and are found, the dharmadhātu is the dharma or phenomena bed in which all phenomena come into being and are found. The term is used in all levels of Buddhist teaching with that base meaning but the explanation of it becomes more profound as the teaching becomes more profound. In Great Completion and Mahāmudrā, it is the all-pervading sphere of luminosity-wisdom, given that luminosity is where phenomena arise and that the luminosity is none other than wisdom. In this sūtra, it is always used with that sense, which is yet another pointer to this sūtra being a teaching given at the highest or Other Emptiness level as explained in the introduction.

***Dhyana***, Skt. dhyāna, Tib. bsam gtan: A Sanskrit term technically meaning all types of mental absorption. Mental absorptions cultivated in the human realm generally result in births in the form realms which are deep forms of concentration in themselves. The practices of mental absorption done in the human realm and the godly existences of the form realm that result from them both are named "dhyāna". The Buddha repeatedly pointed out that the dhyānas were a side-track to emancipation from cyclic existence.

The term also means meditation in general where one is concentrating on something as a way of developing oneself spiritually.

***Discursive thought***, Skt. vikalpa, Tib. rnam rtog: This means more than just the superficial thought that is heard as a voice in the head. It includes the entirety of conceptual process that arises due to mind contacting any object of any of the senses. The Sanskrit and Tibetan literally mean "(dualistic) thought (that arises from the mind wandering among the) various (superficies *q.v.* perceived in the doors of the senses)".

***Enlightenment mind***, Skt. bodhichitta, Tib. byang chub sems: This is a key term of the Great Vehicle. It is the type of mind that is connected not with the lesser enlightenment of an arhat but the enlightenment of a truly complete buddha. As such, it is a mind which is connected with the aim of bringing all sentient beings to that same level of buddhahood. A person who has this mind has entered the Great Vehicle and is either a bodhisatva or a buddha.

It is important to understand that "enlightenment mind" is used to refer equally to the minds of all levels of bodhisatva on the path to buddhahood and to the mind of a buddha who has completed the path. Therefore, it is not "mind striving for enlightenment" as is so often translated, but "enlightenment mind", meaning that kind of mind which is connected with the full enlightenment of a truly complete buddha and which is present in all those who belong to the Great Vehicle.

**Entity**, Tib. ngo bo: The entity of something is just exactly what that thing is. In English we would often simply say "thing" rather than entity. However, in Buddhism, "thing" has a very specific meaning rather than the general meaning that it has in English. It has become common to translate this term as "essence" *q.v.* However, in most cases "entity", meaning what a thing is rather than an essence of that thing, is the correct translation for this term.

**Five paths**, Tib. lam lnga: In the Prajñāpāramitā teachings of the Great Vehicle, the Buddha explained the entire Buddhist journey as a set of five paths called the paths of accumulation, connection, seeing, cultivation, and no more training. The first four paths are part of journeying to enlightenment; the fifth path is that one has actually arrived and has no more training to undergo. There are a set of five paths that describe the journey of the Lesser Vehicle and a set of five paths that describe the journey of the Greater Vehicle. The names are the same in each case but the details of what is accomplished at each stage are different.

**Great Vehicle**, Skt. mahāyāna, Tib. theg pa chen po: The Buddha's teachings as a whole can be summed up into three vehicles where a vehicle is defined as that which can carry a person to a certain destination. The first vehicle, called the Lesser Vehicle, contains the teachings designed to get an individual moving on the spiritual path through showing the unsatisfactory state of cyclic existence and an emancipation from that. However, that path is only concerned with personal emancipation and fails to take account of all of the beings that there are in existence. There used to be eighteen schools of Lesser Vehicle in India but the only one surviving nowadays is the Theravāda of south-east Asia. The Greater Vehicle is a step up from that. The Buddha explained that it was great in comparison to the Lesser Vehicle for seven reasons. The first of those is that it is concerned with attaining the truly complete enlightenment of a truly complete buddha for the sake of every sentient being where the Lesser Vehicle is concerned only with a personal liberation that is not truly complete enlightenment and which is achieved only for the sake of that practitioner. The Great Vehicle has two divisions: a conventional form in which the path is taught in a logical, conventional way, and an unconventional form in which the path is taught in a very direct way. This latter vehicle is called the Vajra Vehicle because it takes the innermost, indestructible (vajra) fact of reality of one's own mind as the vehicle to enlightenment.

***Habituation***, Tib. gom pa: Habituation is similar to but not the same as meditation (Tib. sgom pa). Where meditation is the process of creating then cultivating a certain quality which was not there before, habituation is the process of re-familiarizing yourself with a quality that is already present, even if it has become temporarily unavailable due to being covered over.

***Latency***, Skt. vāsanā, Tib. bag chags: The original Sanskrit has the meaning exactly of "latency". The Tibetan term translates that inexactly with "something sitting there (Tib. chags) within the environment of mind (Tib. bag)". Although it has become popular to translate this term into English with "habitual pattern", that is not its meaning. The term refers to a karmic seed that has been imprinted on the mindstream and is present there as a latency, ready and waiting to come into manifestation.

***Lay aside***, Tib. bshags pa: This term is usually translated as "confession" but that is not the meaning. The term literally means to cut something away and remove it from oneself. In Buddhism, it is used in the context of ridding oneself of the karmic seeds sown by bad karmic actions.

Buddhism is a totally non-theistic religion, so it is very important to understand that one is not confessing wrongdoings to anyone, including oneself. There is no granting of absolution in this system. As the Buddha himself said, he has no ability to purify the karmic stains of sentient beings, he can only teach them how to do so. The practice that he taught for ridding oneself of karmic wrongdoings is the practice of realizing for oneself that they hold the seed of future suffering, rousing regret, and distancing oneself from them. In doing so, one lays them aside.

There is a longer phrase that indicates the full practice of laying aside. The Tibetan phrase "mthol zhing shags pa" literally means "admitting and laying aside". Note that "admitting" also does not entail confession; it refers to that fact that one first has to admit or acknowledge to oneself that one has done something wrong, karmically speaking, and that it will have undesirable consequences. Without this, one cannot effectively take the second step of distancing oneself from the actions. Therefore, it is explained that the process of "laying aside" has to be understood to include the practice of "admission" because, without that acknowledgement, the laying aside cannot be done.

**Lesser Vehicle**, Skt. hīnayāna, Tib. theg pa dman pa: See under Great Vehicle.

**Mara**, Skt. māra, Tib. bdud: The Sanskrit term is closely related to the word "death". Buddha spoke of four classes of extremely negative influences that have the capacity to drag a sentient being deep into saṃsāra. They are the "maras" or "kiss of death": of having a samsaric set of five skandhas; of having afflictions; of death itself; and of the son of gods, which means being seduced and taken in totally by sensuality.

**Mentation**, Skt. manaskāra, Tib. yid la byed pa: Mentation is the act of using the mental mind in general and is also one of the omnipresent mental events *q.v.* Its use implies the presence of dualistic mind. Non-mentating could be simply not using the dualistic mind but is usually used to imply the absence of dualistic mind, that is, the presence of wisdom.

**Migrator**, Tib. 'gro ba: Migrator is one of several terms that were commonly used by the Buddha to mean "sentient being". It shows sentient beings from the perspective of their constantly being forced to go here and there from one rebirth to another by the power of karma. They are like flies caught in a jar, constantly buzzing back and forth. The term is often translated using "beings" which is another general term for sentient beings but doing so loses the meaning entirely: Buddhist authors who know the tradition do not use the word loosely but use it specifically to give the sense of beings who are constantly and helplessly going from one birth to another, and that is how the term should be read. The term "six migrators" refers to the six types of migrators within samsaric existence—hell-beings, pretas, animals, humans, demi-gods, and gods.

***Mind***, Skt. chitta, Tib. sems: There are several terms for mind in the Buddhist tradition, each with its own, specific meaning. This term is the most general term for the samsaric type of mind. It refers to the type of mind that is produced because of fundamental ignorance of enlightened mind. Whereas the wisdom of enlightened mind lacks all complexity and knows in a non-dualistic way, this mind of un-enlightenment is a very complicated apparatus that only ever knows in a dualistic way.

***Mindfulness***, Skt. smṛiti, Tib. dran pa: A particular mental event, one that has the ability to keep mind on its object. Together with alertness, it is one of the two causes of developing śhamatha. See under alertness for an explanation.

***Noble one***, Skt. ārya, Tib. 'phags pa: In Buddhism, a noble one is a being who has become spiritually advanced to the point that he has passed beyond cyclic existence. According to the Buddha, the beings in cyclic existence were ordinary beings, spiritual commoners, and the beings who had passed beyond it were special, the nobility.

***Prajna***, Skt. prajñā, Tib. shes rab: The Sanskrit term, literally meaning "best type of mind" is defined as that which makes correct distinctions between this and that and hence which arrives at correct understanding. It has been translated as "wisdom" but that is not correct because it is, generally speaking, a mental event belonging to dualistic mind where "wisdom" is used to refer to the non-dualistic knower of a buddha. Moreover, the main feature of prajñā is its ability to distinguish correctly between one thing and another and hence to arrive at a correct understanding.

***Provisional and definitive meaning***, Skt. neyartha and nītārtha, Tib. drangs don and nges don: This is a pair of terms used to distinguish which is an ultimate or final teaching and which is not. A teaching which guides a student along to a certain understanding where the understanding led to is not an ultimate understanding is called "provisional meaning". The teaching is not false even though it does not show the final meaning; it is a technique of skilful means used to lead a student in steps to the final meaning. A teaching which shows a student the final meaning directly is called "definitive meaning". The understanding presented cannot be refined or shown in a more precise way; it is the final and actual understanding to be understood. These terms are most often used in Buddhism when discussing the status of the three turnings of the wheel of dharma.

***Rational mind***, Tib. blo: Rational mind is one of several terms for mind in Buddhist terminology. It specifically refers to a mind that judges this against that. With rare exception it is used to refer to samsaric mind, given that samsaric mind only works in the dualistic mode of comparing this versus that. Because of this, the term is mostly used in a pejorative sense to point out samsaric mind as opposed to an enlightened type of mind.

This term has been commonly translated simply as "mind" but that fails to identify this term properly and leaves it confused with the many other words that are also translated simply as "mind". It is not just another mind but is specifically the sort of mind that creates the situation of this and that (*ratio* in Latin) and hence upholds the duality of saṃsāra. In that case, it is the very opposite of the essence of mind. Thus, this is a key term which should be noted and not just glossed over as "mind".

***Realization***, Tib. rtogs pa: Realization has a very specific meaning: it refers to correct knowledge that has been gained in such a way that the knowledge does not abate.

***Reference and Referencing***, Tib. dmigs pa: Referencing is the name for the process in which dualistic mind references an actual object by using a conceptual token instead of the actual object. Whatever is referenced is then called a reference. Note that these terms imply the presence of dualistic mind and their opposites, non-referencing and being without reference imply the presence of non-dualistic wisdom.

***Refuge***, Skt. śharaṇaṃ, Tib. bskyab pa: The Sanskrit term means "shelter", "protection from harm". Everyone seeks a refuge from the unsatisfactoriness of life, even if it is a simple act like brushing the teeth to prevent the body from decaying un-necessarily. Buddhists, after having thought carefully about their situation and who could provide a refuge from it which would be thoroughly reliable, find that three things—buddha, dharma, and saṅgha—are the only things that could provide that kind of refuge. Therefore, Buddhists take refuge in those Three Jewels of Refuge as they are called. Taking refuge in the Three Jewels is clearly laid out as the one doorway to all Buddhist practice and realization.

***Samsara***, Skt. saṃsāra, Tib. 'khor ba: This is the most general name for the type of existence in which sentient beings live. It refers to the fact that they continue on from one existence to another, always within the enclosure of births that are produced by ignorance and experienced as unsatisfactory. The original Sanskrit means to be constantly going about, here and there. The Tibetan term literally means "cycling", because of which it is frequently translated into English with "cyclic existence" though that is not quite the meaning of the term.

***Satva and sattva***: According to the Tibetan tradition established at the time of the great translation work done at Samye under the watch of Padmasambhava not to mention one hundred and sixty-three of the greatest Buddhist scholars of Sanskrit-speaking India, there is a difference of meaning between the Sanskrit terms "satva" and "sattva", with satva meaning "an heroic kind of being" and "sattva" meaning simply "a being". According to the Tibetan tradition established under the advice of the Indian scholars mentioned above, satva is correct for the words Vajrasatva and bodhisatva, whereas sattva is correct for the words mahāsattva, samayasattva, samādhisattva, and jñānasattva, and is also used alone to refer to any or all of these sattvas.

All Tibetan texts produced since the time of the great translations conform to this system and all Tibetan experts agree that this is correct, but Western translators of Tibetan texts have for last few hundreds of years claimed that they know better and have "satva" to "sattva" in every case, causing confusion amongst Westerners confronted by the correct spellings. Recently, publications by Western Sanskrit scholars have been appearing in which these great experts finally admit that they were wrong and that the Tibetan system is and always has been correct!

**Shamatha**, Skt. śhamatha, Tib. gzhi gnas: This is the name of one of the two main practices of meditation used in the Buddhist system to gain insight into reality. This practice creates a one-pointedness of mind which can then be used as a foundation for development of the insight of the other practice, vipaśhyanā. If the development of śhamatha is taken through to completion, the result is a mind that sits stably on its object without any effort and a body which is filled with ease. Altogether, this result of the practice is called "the creation of workability of body and mind".

***Skandhas, dhatus, and ayatanas***: See under Aggregates, dhātus, and āyatanas.

**Special intention**, Tib. lhag bsam: This term is used in general to refer to all specially pure intentions. In Great Vehicle literature it will more often refer specifically to enlightenment mind but even then, it can be used to mean enlightenment mind in general or an especially pure instance of enlightenment mind.

**Sugata**, Tib. bde bar gshegs pa: This term is one of many names for a buddha. It has the twofold meaning of someone who has gone on a good, pleasant, easy journey and who has arrived at a place which is good, pleasant, and full of ease. The meaning in relation to buddhahood is explained at length in *Unending Auspiciousness, the Sutra of the Recollection of the Noble Three Jewels* by Tony Duff, published by Padma Karpo Translation Committee, 2010, ISBN: 978-9937-8386-1-0.

**Superfice, superficies**, Tib. rnam pa: In discussions of mind, a distinction is made between the entity of mind which is a mere knower and the superficial things that appear on its surface and which are known by it. In other words, the superficies are the various things which pass over the surface of mind but which are not mind. Superficies are all the specifics that constitute appearance—for example, the colour white within a moment of visual consciousness, the sound heard within an ear consciousness, and so on.

**Third order thousandfold world system**, Tib. stong gsum 'jig rten: Indian cosmology has for its smallest cosmic unit a single Mt. Meru with four continents type of world system; an analogy might be a single planetary system like our solar system. One thousand of those makes a first order thousandfold world system; an analogy might be a galaxy. One thousand of those makes a second order thousandfold world system; an analogy might be a region of space with many galaxies. One thousand of those makes a third order thousandfold world system (1000 raised to the power 3); an analogy would be one whole universe like ours. The Buddha said that there were countless numbers of third order thousandfold world systems, each of which would be roughly equivalent to a universe like ours.

***Vipashyana***, Skt. vipaśhyanā, Tib. lhag mthong: This is the Sanskrit name for one of the two main practices of meditation needed in the Buddhist system for gaining insight into reality. The other one, śhamatha, keeps the mind focussed while this one looks piercingly into the nature of things.

***Wisdom***, Skt. jñāna, Tib. ye shes: This is a fruition term that refers to the kind of mind—the kind of knower—possessed by a buddha. Sentient beings do have this kind of knower but it is covered over by a very complex apparatus for knowing, that is, dualistic mind. If they practise the path to buddhahood, they will leave behind their obscuration and return to having this kind of knower.

The Sanskrit term has the sense of knowing in the most simple and immediate way. This sort of knowing is present at the core of every being's mind. Therefore, the Tibetans called it "the particular type of awareness which is there primordially". Because of the Tibetan wording it has often been called "primordial wisdom" in English translations, but that goes too far; it is just "wisdom" in the sense of the most fundamental knowing possible.

Wisdom does not operate in the same way as samsaric mind; it comes about in and of itself without depending on cause and effect. Therefore it is frequently referred to as "self-arising wisdom" *q.v.*

# ABOUT THE AUTHOR, PADMA KARPO TRANSLATION COMMITTEE, AND THEIR SUPPORTS FOR STUDY

I have been encouraged over the years by all of my teachers to pass on the knowledge I have accumulated in a lifetime dedicated to study and practice, primarily in the Tibetan tradition of Buddhism. On the one hand, they have encouraged me to teach. On the other, they are concerned that, while many general books on Buddhism have been and are being published, there are few books that present the actual texts of the tradition. Therefore they, together with a number of major figures in the Buddhist book publishing world, have also encouraged me to translate and publish high quality translations of individual texts of the tradition.

My teachers always remark with great appreciation on the extraordinary amount of teaching that I have heard in this life. It allows for highly informed, accurate translations of a sort not usually seen. Briefly, I spent the 1970's studying, practising, then teaching the Gelugpa system at Chenrezig Institute, Australia, where I was a founding member and also the first Australian to be ordained as a monk in the Tibetan Buddhist tradition. In 1980, I moved to the United States to study at the feet of the Vidyadhara Chogyam Trungpa Rinpoche. I stayed in his Vajradhatu community, now called Shambhala, where I studied and practised all the Karma Kagyu, Nyingma, and Shambhala teachings being presented there and was a senior member of the Nalanda Translation Committee. After the vidyadhara's nirvana, I moved in 1992 to Nepal, where I have been continuously involved with the study, practise, translation, and teaching of the Kagyu system and especially of the Nyingma system of Great Completion. In recent years, I have spent extended times in Tibet with the greatest living Tibetan masters of Great Completion, receiving very pure transmissions of the ultimate levels of this teaching directly in Tibetan and practising them there in retreat. In that way, I have studied and practised extensively not in one Tibetan tradition as is usually done, but in three of the four Tibetan traditions—Gelug, Kagyu, and Nyingma—and also in the Theravada tradition, too.

With that as a basis, I have taken a comprehensive and long term approach to the work of translation. For any language, one first must have the lettering needed to write the language. Therefore, as a member of the Nalanda Translation Committee, I spent some years in the 1980's making Tibetan word-processing software and high-quality Tibetan fonts. After that, reliable lexical works are needed. Therefore, during the 1990's I spent some years writing the *Illuminator Tibetan-English Dictionary* and a set of treatises on Tibetan grammar, preparing a variety of key Tibetan reference works needed for the study and translation of Tibetan Buddhist texts, and giving our Tibetan software the tools needed to translate and research Tibetan texts. During this time, I also translated full-time for various Tibetan gurus and ran the Drukpa Kagyu Heritage Project—at the time the largest project in Asia for the preservation of Tibetan Buddhist texts. With the dictionaries, grammar texts, and specialized software in place, and a wealth of knowledge, I turned my attention in the year 2000 to the translation and publication of important texts of Tibetan Buddhist literature.

Padma Karpo Translation Committee (PKTC) was set up to provide a home for the translation and publication work. The committee focusses on producing books containing the best of Tibetan literature, and, especially, books that meet the needs of practitioners. At the time of writing, PKTC has published a wide range of books that, collectively, make a complete program of study for those practising Tibetan Buddhism, and especially for those interested in the higher tantras. All in all, you will find many books both free and for sale on the PKTC web-site. Most are available both as paper editions and e-books.

It would take up too much space here to present an extensive guide to our books and how they can be used as the basis for a study program. However, a guide of that sort is available on the PKTC web-site, whose address is on the copyright page of this book and we recommend that you read it to see how this book fits into the overall scheme of PKTC publications.

This book presents an important sūtra of the third turning of the wheel of dharma, one which presents Other Emptiness. For other sūtras of the third turning which also presents Other Emptiness, see:

- *The Noble One Called "Point of Passage Wisdom", A Great Vehicle Sutra*;
- *Maitreya's Sūtras and Prayer, with Commentary by Padma Karpo*, which presents two sūtras petitioned by Maitreya and his famous prayer, and a commentary to the prayer by Padma Karpo.

And for publications of sūtras also from the *Great Stack of Jewels* collection of Great Vehicle sūtras, see:

- *Maitreya's Sūtras and Prayer, with Commentary by Padma Karpo*, which presents two sūtras petitioned by Maitreya and his famous prayer, and a commentary to the prayer by Padma Karpo;
- *Samantabhadra's Prayer with Commentaries by Noble Nāgārjuna and Tenpa'i Wangchuk and Tony Duff*, a large volume which presents a fresh translation of the prayer, both Indian and Tibetan commentaries, and an extensive commentary by Tony Duff which dispels many mistakes

in existing translations and shows very clearly the meaning contained in the original prayer.

Other books about Other Emptiness are:

- *The Noble One Called "Point of Passage Wisdom", A Great Vehicle Sutra*, the root sūtra of the twenty sūtras of Other Emptiness of the third turning of the wheel;
- *Other Emptiness, Entering the Wisdom Beyond Emptiness of Self*, a major and exceptionally complete exposition of Other Emptiness with many Tibetan texts and teachings included;
- *Instructions for Practising the View of Other Emptiness*, a text by the first Jamgon Kongtrul showing the practice of Other Emptiness according to the Jonang tradition;
- *The Lion's Roar that Proclaims Zhantong*, a text by Ju Mipham which shows the view of Other Emptiness then goes through arguments raised by Tsongkhapa's followers against the Other Emptiness system;
- *Maitripa's Writings on the View*, a selection of important texts written by the Indian master Maitrīpa showing his understanding of the Other Emptiness approach;
- *A Juggernaut of the Non-Dual View, Ultimate Teachings of the Second Drukchen, Gyalwang Je*, a set of sixty-six teachings on the non-dual view of the tantras which shows clearly the Other Emptiness view of the Kagyus.
- *The Theory and Practice Of Other Emptiness Taught Through Milarepa's Songs*, explanations of Other Emptiness based on two songs of Milarepa—*Authentic Expression of the View of the Middle Way* and *Ultimate View, Meditation, Conduct, and Fruition* showing both the view and meditation of Other Emptiness.

We make a point of including, where possible, the relevant Tibetan texts in Tibetan script in our books. We also make them available in electronic editions that can be downloaded free from our web-site, as discussed below. The Tibetan text for this book is included at the back of the book and is available for download from the PKTC web-site.

## Electronic Resources

PKTC has developed a complete range of electronic tools to facilitate the study and translation of Tibetan texts. For many years now, this software has been a prime resource for Tibetan Buddhist centres throughout the world, including in Tibet itself. It is available through the PKTC web-site.

The wordprocessor TibetDoc has the only complete set of tools for creating, correcting, and formatting Tibetan text according to the norms of the Tibetan language. It can also be used to make texts with mixed Tibetan and English or other languages. Extremely high quality Tibetan fonts, based on the forms of Tibetan calligraphy learned from old masters from pre-Communist Chinese Tibet, are also available. Because of their excellence, these typefaces have achieved a legendary status amongst Tibetans.

TibetDoc is used to prepare electronic editions of Tibetan texts in the PKTC text input office in Asia. Tibetan texts are often corrupt so the input texts are carefully corrected prior to distribution. After that, they are made available through the PKTC web-site. These electronic texts are not careless productions like so many of the Tibetan texts found on the web, but are highly reliable editions useful to non-scholars and scholars alike. Some of the larger collections of these texts are for purchase, but most are available for free download.

The electronic texts can be read, searched, and even made into an electronic library using either TibetDoc or our other software, TibetD Reader. Like TibetDoc, TibetD Reader is advanced software with many capabilities made specifically to meet the needs of reading and researching Tibetan texts. PKTC software is for purchase but we make a free version of TibetD Reader available for free download on the PKTC web-site.

A key feature of TibetDoc and Tibet Reader is that Tibetan terms in texts can be looked up on the spot using PKTC's electronic dictionaries. PKTC also has several electronic dictionaries—some Tibetan-Tibetan and some Tibetan-English—and a number of other reference works. The *Illuminator Tibetan-English Dictionary* is renowned for its completeness and accuracy.

This combination of software, texts, reference works, and dictionaries that work together seamlessly has become famous over the years. It has been the basis of many, large publishing projects within the Tibetan Buddhist community around the world for over thirty years and is popular amongst all those needing to work with Tibetan language or deepen their understanding of Buddhism through Tibetan texts.

# TIBETAN TEXT

༄༅། །འཕགས་པ་དཀོན་མཆོག་བརྩེགས་པ་ཆེན་པོའི་ཆོས་ཀྱི་རྣམ་གྲངས་ལེའུ་སྟོང་ཕྲག་བརྒྱ་པ་ལས་ལེའུ་བཅུ་དགུ་པ་སྟེ་ཁྱིམ་བདག་དྲག་ཤུལ་ཅན་གྱིས་ཞུས་པ། བམ་པོ་དང་པོ། །རྒྱ་གར་སྐད་དུ། ཨཱརྱ་གྲྀ་ཧ་པ་ཏི་ཨུ་གྲ་པ་རི་པྲྀ་ཙྪཱ་ནཱ་མ་མ་ཧཱ་ཡཱ་ན་སཱུ་ཏྲ། བོད་སྐད་དུ། འཕགས་པ་ཁྱིམ་བདག་དྲག་ཤུལ་ཅན་གྱིས་ཞུས་པ་ཞེས་བྱ་བ་ཐེག་པ་ཆེན་པོའི་མདོ། །སངས་རྒྱས་དང་། བྱང་ཆུབ་སེམས་དཔའ་ཐམས་ཅད་ལ་ཕྱག་འཚལ་ལོ། །འདི་སྐད་བདག་གིས་ཐོས་པ་དུས་གཅིག་ན། བཅོམ་ལྡན་འདས་མཉན་ཡོད་ན་རྒྱལ་བུ་རྒྱལ་བྱེད་ཀྱི་ཚལ་མགོན་མེད་ཟས་སྦྱིན་གྱི་ཀུན་དགའ་ར་བ་ན་དགེ་སློང་སྟོང་ཉིས་བརྒྱ་ལྔ་བཅུའི་དགེ་སློང་གི་དགེ་འདུན་ཆེན་པོ་དང་། བྱང་ཆུབ་སེམས་དཔའ་སེམས་དཔའ་ཆེན་པོ་བྱམས་པ་དང་། འཇམ་དཔལ་དང་། ངན་སོང་སྦྱོང་དང་། སྤྱན་རས་གཟིགས་དབང་ཕྱུག་དང་། མཐུ་ཆེན་ཐོབ་ལ་སོགས་པ་བྱང་ཆུབ་སེམས་དཔའ་ལྔ་སྟོང་དང་ཐབས་ཅིག་ཏུ་བཞུགས་ཏེ། །དེའི་ཚེ་བཅོམ་ལྡན་འདས་འཁོར་བརྒྱ་སྟོང་དུ་མས་ཡོངས་སུ་བསྐོར་ཅིང་མདུན་གྱིས་བལྟས་ནས་ཆོས་སྟོན་ཏེ། ཚངས་པར་སྤྱོད་པ། ཐོག་མར་དགེ་བ། བར་དུ་དགེ་བ། ཐ་མར་དགེ་བ། དོན་བཟང་པོ། ཚིག་འབྲུ་བཟང་པོ། མ་འདྲེས་པ། ཡོངས་སུ་རྫོགས་པ། ཡོངས་སུ་དག་པ་ཡོངས་སུ་བྱང་བ་ཡང་དག་པར་རབ་ཏུ་སྟོན་ཏོ། །དེ་ནས་ཁྱིམ་བདག་དྲག་ཤུལ་ཅན་གཡོག་ལྔ་བརྒྱ་དང་མཉན་ཡོད་ཀྱི་གྲོང་ཁྱེར་

ཆེན་པོ་ནས་བྱུང་སྟེ། རྒྱལ་བུ་རྒྱལ་བྱེད་ཀྱི་ཚལ་མགོན་མེད་ཟས་སྦྱིན་གྱི་ཀུན་དགའ་
ར་བ་ག་ལ་བ་དང་། བཅོམ་ལྡན་འདས་ག་ལ་བ་དེར་སོང་སྟེ་ཕྱིན་ནས་བཅོམ་ལྡན་
འདས་ཀྱི་ཞབས་ལ་མགོ་བོས་ཕྱག་འཚལ་ཏེ། བཅོམ་ལྡན་འདས་ལ་ལན་གསུམ་
བསྐོར་བ་བྱས་ནས་ཕྱོགས་གཅིག་ཏུ་འཁོད་དོ། །དེ་བཞིན་དུ་ཁྱིམ་བདག་གཞན་
རྣམས་ཀྱང་འདི་ལྟ་སྟེ། ཁྱིམ་བདག་དགའ་འདོད་དང་། ཁྱིམ་བདག་གྲགས་
འདོད་དང་། ཁྱིམ་བདག་ལེགས་བྱིན་དང་། ཁྱིམ་བདག་དགའ་བྱེད་དང་།
ཁྱིམ་བདག་གྲགས་བྱིན་དང་། ཁྱིམ་བདག་ནོར་བཟངས་དང་། ཁྱིམ་བདག་ཚུལ་
དགའ་དང་། ཁྱིམ་བདག་མགོན་མེད་ཟས་སྦྱིན་དང་། ཁྱིམ་བདག་ཀླུ་དཔལ་
དང་། ཁྱིམ་བདག་བདེན་དགའ་དང་། དེ་དག་དང་གཞན་ཡང་ཁྱིམ་བདག་རབ་
ཏུ་མང་པོ་རྣམས་གཡོག་ལྔ་བརྒྱ་ལྔ་བརྒྱ་དང་། མཉན་ཡོད་ཀྱི་གྲོང་ཁྱེར་ཆེན་པོ་ནས་
བྱུང་སྟེ། རྒྱལ་བུ་རྒྱལ་བྱེད་ཀྱི་ཚལ་མགོན་མེད་ཟས་སྦྱིན་གྱི་ཀུན་དགའ་ར་བ་ག་ལ་
བ་དང་། བཅོམ་ལྡན་འདས་ག་ལ་བ་དེར་སོང་སྟེ་ལྷགས་ནས་བཅོམ་ལྡན་འདས་ཀྱི་
ཞབས་ལ་མགོ་བོས་ཕྱག་འཚལ་ཏེ། བཅོམ་ལྡན་འདས་ལ་ལན་གསུམ་བསྐོར་བ་
བྱས་ནས་ཕྱོགས་གཅིག་ཏུ་འཁོད་དོ། །ཁྱིམ་བདག་དེ་དག་ཐམས་ཅད་ཕལ་ཆེར་ནི་
གཡོག་དང་བཅས་ཏེ་ཐེག་པ་ཆེན་པོ་ལ་ཡང་དག་པར་ཞུགས་པ་དང་། དགེ་བའི་རྩ་
བ་བསྐྱེད་པ་དང་། བླ་ན་མེད་པ་ཡང་དག་པར་རྫོགས་པའི་བྱང་ཆུབ་ཏུ་ངེས་པར་
བྱས་པ་ཤ་སྟག་གོ །དེ་ནས་ཁྱིམ་བདག་དྲག་ཤུལ་ཅན་གྱིས་ཁྱིམ་བདག་གི་འཁོར་
ཆེན་པོ་དེ་འདུས་པར་ཤེས་ནས་བཅོམ་ལྡན་འདས་ཀྱི་མཐུས་སྟན་ལས་ལངས་ཏེ་བླ་གོས་
ཕྲག་པ་གཅིག་ཏུ་གཟར་ནས་པུས་མོ་གཡས་པའི་ལྷ་ང་ས་ལ་བཙུགས་ཏེ། བཅོམ་
ལྡན་འདས་ག་ལ་བ་དེ་ལོགས་སུ་ཐལ་མོ་སྦྱར་བ་བཏུད་ནས་བཅོམ་ལྡན་འདས་ལ་འདི་
སྐད་ཅེས་གསོལ་ཏོ། །གལ་ཏེ་ཞུས་ནས་ཞུ་བ་ལུང་བསྟན་པའི་སླད་དུ་བཅོམ་ལྡན་
འདས་ཀྱིས་བདག་ལ་སྐབས་ཕྱེ་ན། བཅོམ་ལྡན་འདས་དེ་བཞིན་གཤེགས་པ་དགྲ་
བཅོམ་པ་ཡང་དག་པར་རྫོགས་པའི་སངས་རྒྱས་ལ་བདག་ཕྱོགས་འགའ་ཞིག་
ཞུའོ། །དེ་སྐད་ཅེས་གསོལ་པ་དང་། བཅོམ་ལྡན་འདས་ཀྱིས་ཁྱིམ་བདག་དྲག་

ཤུལ་ཅན་ལ་འདི་སྐད་ཅེས་བཀའ་སྩལ་ཏོ། །ཁྱིམ་བདག་ཁྱོད་ལ་དེ་བཞིན་གཤེགས་པས་རྟག་ཏུ་སྐབས་ཕྱེས། ཁྱིམ་བདག་ཁྱོད་ཅི་དང་ཅི་འདོད་པ་དེ་བཞིན་གཤེགས་པ་ལ་དྲིས་ཤིག་དང་། དེ་ལྟར་དྲིས་པ་དེ་དང་དེའི་ལུང་བསྟན་པས་ངས་ཁྱོད་ཀྱི་སེམས་རངས་པར་བྱའོ། །དེ་སྐད་ཅེས་བཀའ་སྩལ་པ་དང་། བཅོམ་ལྡན་འདས་ལ་ཁྱིམ་བདག་དྲག་ཤུལ་ཅན་གྱིས་འདི་སྐད་ཅེས་གསོལ་ཏོ། །བཅོམ་ལྡན་འདས་རིགས་ཀྱི་བུ་འམ། །རིགས་ཀྱི་བུ་མོ་གང་དག་བླ་ན་མེད་པ་ཡང་དག་པར་རྫོགས་པའི་བྱང་ཆུབ་ཏུ་སེམས་བསྐྱེད་པ་དང་། ཐེག་པ་ཆེན་པོ་ལ་མོས་པ་དང་། ཐེག་པ་ཆེན་པོ་ལ་རབ་ཏུ་གནས་པ་དང་། ཐེག་པ་ཆེན་པོ་ལ་ཡང་དག་པར་སྒྲུབ་པར་འཚལ་བ་དང་། ཐེག་པ་ཆེན་པོ་ལ་འཇུག་པར་འཚལ་བ་དང་། ཐེག་པ་ཆེན་པོ་ལ་དམ་བཅའ་བ་དང་། སེམས་ཅན་ཐམས་ཅད་གཉེར་བ་དང་། སེམས་ཅན་ཐམས་ཅད་དབུགས་འབྱིན་པ་དང་། སེམས་ཅན་ཐམས་ཅད་བསྐྱབ་པའི་སླད་དུ་གོ་ཆ་འཚལ་བ་དང་། མ་རྒལ་བ་རྣམས་སྒྲོལ་བ་དང་། མ་གྲོལ་བ་རྣམས་དགྲོལ་བ་དང་། དབུགས་མ་ཕྱིན་པ་རྣམས་དབུགས་དབྱུང་བ་དང་། ཡོངས་སུ་མྱ་ངན་ལས་མ་འདས་པ་རྣམས་ཡོངས་སུ་མྱ་ངན་ལས་བཟླའོ་ཞེས་སེམས་ཅན་ཐམས་ཅད་ཀྱི་དོན་དུ་ཁུར་ཆེན་པོ་ལེན་པ་དང་། འཇུག་པ་རླབས་པོ་ཆེ་ཆེན་པོ་ལ་རབ་ཏུ་གནས་པ་དང་། སངས་རྒྱས་ཀྱི་ཡེ་ཤེས་དཔག་ཏུ་མ་མཆིས་པ་ཐོས་ནས་ཡེ་ཤེས་དེ་ཡང་དག་པར་བསྒྲུབ་པའི་སླད་དུ་གོ་ཆ་འཚལ་བ་དང་། འཁོར་བའི་སྡུག་བསྔལ་གྱི་སྐྱོན་མང་པོ་དུ་མ་འཚལ་ཀྱང་ཡིད་ཡོངས་སུ་མི་སྐྱོ་ཞིང་བསྐལ་པ་གྲངས་མ་མཆིས་པར་འཁོར་ཡང་སེམས་ཞུམ་པར་མི་འགྱུར་བ་དེ་དག་དང་། བཅོམ་ལྡན་འདས་དེ་ལ་རིགས་ཀྱི་བུ་འམ། རིགས་ཀྱི་བུ་མོ་བྱང་ཆུབ་སེམས་དཔའི་ཐེག་པ་བ་གང་དག་ཁྱིམ་གྱི་གནས་ནས་མངོན་པར་བྱུང་སྟེ། བྱང་ཆུབ་ཀྱི་ཕྱོགས་ཀྱི་ཆོས་རྣམས་ཡང་དག་པར་སྒྲུབ་ཅིང་ཁྱིམ་ན་མི་གནས་པ་དག་དང་། གང་ཡང་ཁྱིམ་ན་གནས་ཤིང་བྱང་ཆུབ་ཀྱི་ཕྱོགས་ཀྱི་ཆོས་རྣམས་ཡང་དག་པར་སྒྲུབ་སྟེ། ཁྱིམ་གྱི་གནས་ནས་མངོན་པར་མི་འབྱུང་བ་དག་ཀྱང་མཆིས་ན། བཅོམ་ལྡན་འདས་ལྷ་དང་། མི་དང་། ལྷ་མ་ཡིན་དུ་བཅས་པའི་འཇིག་རྟེན་ལ་

ཐུགས་བསྐྱེ་བ་དང་། ཐེག་པ་ཆེན་པོ་ལ་འདི་རྗེས་སུ་གཟུང་བ་དང་། དཀོན་མཆོག་གསུམ་གྱི་རིགས་མི་འཆད་པར་བགྱི་བ་དང་། ཐམས་ཅད་མཁྱེན་པའི་ཡེ་ཤེས་ཡུན་རིང་དུ་གནས་པར་བགྱི་བའི་སླད་དུ་བཅོམ་ལྡན་འདས་ཀྱིས་བྱང་ཆུབ་སེམས་དཔའ་ཁྱིམ་པ་རྣམས་ཀྱི་བསླབ་པའི་ཡོན་ཏན་རྣམ་པར་གཞག་པ་དེ་ལེགས་པར་བཤད་དུ་གསོལ། བྱང་ཆུབ་སེམས་དཔའ་ཁྱིམ་པ་ཁྱིམ་གྱི་ས་ལ་གནས་ནས་ཇི་ལྟར་དེ་བཞིན་གཤེགས་པ་རྣམས་ཀྱི་བཀའ་བཞིན་བགྱིད་ཅིང་བྱང་ཆུབ་ཀྱི་ཕྱོགས་ཀྱི་ཆོས་རྣམས་ལས་མི་ཉམས། ཡོངས་སུ་མི་ཉམས་ཏེ། ཚེ་འདི་ལ་ཡང་ལས་ཁ་ན་མ་ཐོ་བ་མ་མཆིས་ཤིང་ཚེ་གཞན་དུ་ཡང་བྱེ་བྲག་ཏུ་མཆི་བར་འགྱུར་བ་དང་། བཅོམ་ལྡན་འདས་གང་ཡང་བྱང་ཆུབ་སེམས་དཔའ་ཁྱིམ་གྱི་གནས་ནས་མངོན་པར་བྱུང་སྟེ། སྡུག་པ་དང་། མི་སྡུག་པ་སྤངས་ནས་སྐྲ་དང་ཁ་སྤུ་བྲེགས་ཏེ། གོས་ངུར་སྨྲིག་བགོས་ཏེ། ཡང་དག་པར་དད་པས་ཁྱིམ་ནས་ཁྱིམ་མ་ལགས་པར་རབ་ཏུ་བྱུང་བ་དེ་དག་ཇི་ཙམ་དུ་གདམས་པ་དང་། རྗེས་སུ་བསྟན་པ་གཉིས་ཀྱིས་ཆོས་སྤྱོད་པ་དང་། དགེ་བ་སྤྱོད་པ་ཡང་དག་པར་རབ་ཏུ་བཤད་དུ་གསོལ། བྱང་ཆུབ་སེམས་དཔའ་ཁྱིམ་པ་དང་། རབ་ཏུ་བྱུང་བས་ཇི་ལྟར་གནས་པར་བགྱི། ཇི་ལྟར་བསྒྲུབ་པར་བགྱི། དེ་སྐད་ཅེས་གསོལ་པ་དང་། བཅོམ་ལྡན་འདས་ཀྱིས་ཁྱིམ་བདག་དྲག་ཤུལ་ཅན་ལ་འདི་སྐད་ཅེས་བཀའ་སྩལ་ཏོ། །ཁྱིམ་བདག་ལེགས་སོ་ལེགས་སོ། །ཁྱོད་ང་ལ་དོན་འདི་འདྲི་བར་སེམས་པ་ནི་ཁྱོད་ཀྱི་ཚུལ་དང་འཐུན་པའོ། །དེའི་ཕྱིར་ལེགས་པར་རབ་ཏུ་ཉོན་ལ་ཡིད་ལ་ཟུང་ཤིག་དང་། བྱང་ཆུབ་སེམས་དཔའ་ཁྱིམ་པ་དང་། རབ་ཏུ་བྱུང་བས་ཇི་ལྟར་བསླབ་པའི་ཡོན་ཏན་ཡང་དག་པར་གཟུང་ཞིང་སྤྱོད་པ་མཆོག་ལ་གནས་པར་བྱ་བ་དང་། ཇི་ལྟར་བསྒྲུབ་པར་བྱ་བ་ངས་ཁྱོད་ལ་བཤད་དོ། །བཅོམ་ལྡན་འདས་དེ་བཞིན་ནོ་ཞེས་གསོལ་ནས་ཁྱིམ་བདག་དྲག་ཤུལ་ཅན་བཅོམ་ལྡན་འདས་ཀྱི་ལྟར་ཉན་པ་དང་། བཅོམ་ལྡན་འདས་ཀྱིས་དེ་ལ་འདི་སྐད་ཅེས་བཀའ་སྩལ་ཏོ། །ཁྱིམ་བདག་འདི་ལ་བྱང་ཆུབ་སེམས་དཔའ་ཁྱིམ་པ་ཁྱིམ་ན་གནས་པས་སངས་རྒྱས་ལ་སྐྱབས་སུ་འགྲོ་བར་བྱའོ། །ཆོས་ལ་སྐྱབས་སུ་འགྲོ་བར་བྱའོ། །དགེ་འདུན་ལ་

སྐྱབས་སུ་འགྲོ་བར་བྱའོ། །དེ་གསུམ་ལ་སྐྱབས་སུ་སོང་བའི་དགེ་བའི་རྩ་བ་དེ་བླ་ན་མེད་པ་ཡང་དག་པར་རྫོགས་པའི་བྱང་ཆུབ་ཏུ་ཡོངས་སུ་བསྔོ་བར་བྱའོ། །ཁྱིམ་བདག་ཇི་ལྟར་ན་བྱང་ཆུབ་སེམས་དཔའ་ཁྱིམ་པ་སངས་རྒྱས་ལ་སྐྱབས་སུ་སོང་བ་ཡིན་ཞེ་ན། ཁྱིམ་བདག་འདི་ལ་བྱང་ཆུབ་སེམས་དཔའ་ཁྱིམ་པ་སངས་རྒྱས་ཀྱི་སྐུ་སྐྱེས་བུ་ཆེན་པོའི་མཚན་སུམ་ཅུ་རྩ་གཉིས་ཀྱིས་ལེགས་པར་བརྒྱན་པ་ཡོངས་སུ་བསྒྲུབ་པར་བྱའོ་སྙམ་དུ་སེམས་མངོན་པར་འདུ་བྱེད་དེ། དགེ་བའི་རྩ་བ་གང་དག་གིས་སྐྱེས་བུ་ཆེན་པོའི་མཚན་སུམ་ཅུ་རྩ་གཉིས་ཡང་དག་པར་འགྲུབ་པར་འགྱུར་བའི་དགེ་བའི་རྩ་བ་དེ་དག་ཡང་དག་པར་བསྒྲུབ་པའི་ཕྱིར་བརྩོན་འགྲུས་རྩོམ་པ་དེ་ལྟ་བུ་ནི་ཁྱིམ་བདག་བྱང་ཆུབ་སེམས་དཔའ་སངས་རྒྱས་ལ་སྐྱབས་སུ་སོང་བ་ཡིན་ནོ། །ཁྱིམ་བདག་ཇི་ལྟར་ན་བྱང་ཆུབ་སེམས་དཔའ་ཁྱིམ་པ་ཆོས་ལ་སྐྱབས་སུ་སོང་བ་ཡིན་ཞེ་ན། ཁྱིམ་བདག་འདི་ལ་བྱང་ཆུབ་སེམས་དཔའ་ཁྱིམ་པ་ཆོས་ལ་གུས་པ་དང་བཅས་ཤིང་རི་མོ་བྱེད་པ་དང་བཅས་པ། ཆོས་དོན་དུ་གཉེར་བ། ཆོས་འདོད་པ། ཆོས་ཀྱི་ཀུན་དགའ་ལ་དགའ་ཞིང་མོས་པ། ཆོས་ལ་གཞོལ་བ། ཆོས་ལ་འབབ་པ། ཆོས་ལ་བབ་པ། ཆོས་སྲུང་བ། ཆོས་སྲིད་ཅིང་གནས་པ། ཆོས་ཀྱི་གྲགས་པ་དང་། ཆོས་ཀྱི་སྤྱོད་པ་ལ་གནས་པ། ཆོས་ཀྱི་དབང་དུ་གྱུར་པ། ཆོས་ཡོངས་སུ་ཚོལ་བ། ཆོས་ཀྱི་སྟོབས་དང་ལྡན་པ། ཆོས་ཀྱི་སྦྱིན་པའི་མཚོན་ཆ་དང་ལྡན་པ། ཆོས་ཀྱི་བྱ་བ་བྱེད་པ་དེ་འདི་ལྟ་བུའི་ཆོས་དང་ལྡན་པས་བདག་བླ་ན་མེད་པ་ཡང་དག་པར་རྫོགས་པའི་བྱང་ཆུབ་མངོན་པར་རྫོགས་པར་སངས་རྒྱས་ནས་ལྷ་དང་། མི་དང་། ལྷ་མ་ཡིན་དུ་བཅས་པའི་འཇིག་རྟེན་ལ་ཆོས་ཀྱིས་ཆོས་ཀྱི་བགོ་བཤའ་བྱའོ་སྙམ་དུ་དྲན་པ་རབ་ཏུ་འཐོབ་སྟེ། ཁྱིམ་བདག་དེ་ལྟར་ན་བྱང་ཆུབ་སེམས་དཔའ་ཁྱིམ་པ་ཆོས་ལ་སྐྱབས་སུ་སོང་བ་ཡིན་ནོ། །ཁྱིམ་བདག་ཇི་ལྟར་ན་བྱང་ཆུབ་སེམས་དཔའ་ཁྱིམ་པ་དགེ་འདུན་ལ་སྐྱབས་སུ་སོང་བ་ཡིན་ཞེ་ན། ཁྱིམ་བདག་འདི་ལ་བྱང་ཆུབ་སེམས་དཔའ་ཁྱིམ་པ་དགེ་འདུན་ལ་སྐྱབས་སུ་སོང་བ་ནི་གལ་ཏེ་དགེ་སློང་རྒྱུན་དུ་ཞུགས་པ་འམ། ལན་ཅིག་ཕྱིར་འོང་བ་འམ། ཕྱིར་མི་འོང་བ་འམ། དགྲ་བཅོམ་པ་འམ། སོ་

སོའི་སྐྱེ་བོ་འམ། ཉན་ཐོས་ཀྱི་ཐེག་པ་པ་འམ། རང་སངས་རྒྱས་ཀྱི་ཐེག་པ་པ་འམ་ཐེག་པ་ཆེན་པོ་བ་བདག་མཐོང་ན་དེ་དེ་ལ་གུས་པ་དང་བཅས། ཞེ་ས་དང་བཅས་ཤིང་ལྷང་བར་བསྙེན་པ། བཀའ་གློ་བདེ་ཞིང་འཐུན་པར་འཛིན་པ་ཡིན་ཏེ། དེ་ཡང་དག་པར་སོང་བ་དང་། ཡང་དག་པར་ཞུགས་པ་དེ་དག་ལ་བསྙེན་བཀུར་བྱས་པས་འདི་ལྟར་བདག་བླ་ན་མེད་པ་ཡང་དག་པར་རྫོགས་པའི་བྱང་ཆུབ་མངོན་པར་རྫོགས་པར་སངས་རྒྱས་ནས་ཀྱང་ཉན་ཐོས་ཀྱི་ཡོན་ཏན་ཡོངས་སུ་བསྒྲུབ་པ་དང་། རང་སངས་རྒྱས་ཀྱི་ཡོན་ཏན་ཡོངས་སུ་བསྒྲུབ་པའི་ཕྱིར་ཆོས་བསྟན་ཏོ་སྙམ་དུ་དྲན་པ་རབ་ཏུ་འཐོབ་སྟེ། དེ་དེ་དག་ལ་གུས་པ་དང་བཅས་ཤིང་ཞེ་ས་དང་བཅས་པ་ཡིན་གྱི་དེ་དག་ལ་མི་དགའ་བར་ནི་མི་བྱེད་དེ། དེ་ལྟར་ན་ཁྱིམ་བདག་བྱང་ཆུབ་སེམས་དཔའ་ཁྱིམ་པ་དགེ་འདུན་ལ་སྐྱབས་སུ་སོང་བ་ཡིན་ནོ། །ཁྱིམ་བདག་གཞན་ཡང་བྱང་ཆུབ་སེམས་དཔའ་ཁྱིམ་པ་ཆོས་བཞི་དང་ལྡན་ན་སངས་རྒྱས་ལ་སྐྱབས་སུ་སོང་བ་ཡིན་ཏེ། བཞི་གང་ཞེ་ན། བྱང་ཆུབ་ཀྱི་སེམས་མི་འདོར་བ་དང་། དམ་བཅས་པ་མི་འཇིག་པ་དང་། སྙིང་རྗེ་ཆེན་པོ་ཡོངས་སུ་མི་གཏོང་བ་དང་། ཐེག་པ་གཞན་ལ་མི་དམིགས་པ་སྟེ། ཁྱིམ་བདག་བྱང་ཆུབ་སེམས་དཔའ་ཁྱིམ་པ་ཆོས་བཞི་པོ་དེ་དག་དང་ལྡན་ན་སངས་རྒྱས་ལ་སྐྱབས་སུ་སོང་བ་ཡིན་ནོ། །ཁྱིམ་བདག་གཞན་ཡང་བྱང་ཆུབ་སེམས་དཔའ་ཁྱིམ་པ་ཆོས་བཞི་དང་ལྡན་ན་ཆོས་ལ་སྐྱབས་སུ་སོང་བ་ཡིན་ཏེ། བཞི་གང་ཞེ་ན། ཆོས་སྨྲ་བའི་གང་ཟག་རྣམས་ལ་བརྟེན་ཅིང་བསྙེན་ཏེ་བསྙེན་བཀུར་བྱེད་ཅིང་བསྙི་སྣང་དུ་བྱས་ནས་ཆོས་ཉན་པ་དང་། ཆོས་ཐོས་པ་དང་། ཚུལ་བཞིན་དུ་སོ་སོར་རྟོག་པ་དང་། ཇི་ལྟར་ཐོས་པའི་ཆོས་རྣམས་དང་ཇི་ལྟར་ཁོང་དུ་ཆུད་པ་རྣམས་གཞན་དག་ལ་ཡང་སྟོན་ཅིང་ཡང་དག་པར་རབ་ཏུ་འཆད་པ་དང་། ཆོས་ཀྱི་སྦྱིན་པ་ལས་བྱུང་བའི་དགེ་བའི་རྩ་བ་དེ་བླ་ན་མེད་པ་ཡང་དག་པར་རྫོགས་པའི་བྱང་ཆུབ་ཏུ་ཡོངས་སུ་བསྔོ་བ་སྟེ། ཁྱིམ་བདག་བྱང་ཆུབ་སེམས་དཔའ་ཁྱིམ་པ་ཆོས་བཞི་པོ་དེ་དག་དང་ལྡན་ན་ཆོས་ལ་སྐྱབས་སུ་སོང་བ་ཡིན་ནོ། །ཁྱིམ་བདག་གཞན་ཡང་བྱང་ཆུབ་སེམས་དཔའ་ཁྱིམ་པ་ཆོས་བཞི་དང་ལྡན་ན་དགེ་འདུན་ལ་སྐྱབས་སུ་སོང་

བ་ཡིན་ཏེ། བཞི་གང་ཞེ་ན། ཉན་ཐོས་ཀྱི་ཐེག་པ་པ་ཡང་དག་པར་སྐྱོན་མེད་པ་ལ་ཞུགས་པ་རྣམས་ཐམས་ཅད་མཁྱེན་པ་ཉིད་ཀྱི་སེམས་ལ་འཛུད་པ་དང་། གང་ཟང་ཟིང་གིས་སྡུད་པར་བྱེད་པ་དེ་དག་ཆོས་ཀྱིས་བསྡུ་བ་ལ་སྦྱོར་བ་དང་། བྱང་ཆུབ་སེམས་དཔའ་ཕྱིར་མི་ལྡོག་པའི་དགེ་འདུན་ལ་རྟེན་གྱི་ཉན་ཐོས་ཀྱི་དགེ་འདུན་ལ་རྟེན་པ་མ་ཡིན་པ་དང་། ཉན་ཐོས་ཀྱི་ཡོན་ཏན་ཡང་ཡོངས་སུ་ཚོལ་ལ། དེའི་རྣམ་པར་གྲོལ་བ་ལ་མོས་པ་ཡང་མ་ཡིན་པ་སྟེ། ཁྱིམ་བདག་བྱང་ཆུབ་སེམས་དཔའ་ཁྱིམ་པ་ཆོས་བཞི་པོ་དེ་དག་དང་ལྡན་ན་དགེ་འདུན་ལ་སྐྱབས་སུ་སོང་བ་ཡིན་ནོ། །ཁྱིམ་བདག་གཞན་ཡང་བྱང་ཆུབ་སེམས་དཔའ་ཁྱིམ་པ་དེ་བཞིན་གཤེགས་པའི་སྐུ་གཟུགས་མཐོང་ནས་སངས་རྒྱས་རྗེས་སུ་དྲན་པ་རབ་ཏུ་ཐོབ་པ་ནི་སངས་རྒྱས་ལ་སྐྱབས་སུ་སོང་བ་ཡིན་ནོ། །ཆོས་ཐོས་ནས་ཆོས་རྗེས་སུ་དྲན་པ་རབ་ཏུ་ཐོབ་པ་ནི་ཆོས་ལ་སྐྱབས་སུ་སོང་བ་ཡིན་ནོ། །དེ་བཞིན་གཤེགས་པའི་ཉན་ཐོས་ཀྱི་དགེ་འདུན་མཐོང་ནས་བྱང་ཆུབ་ཀྱི་སེམས་རྗེས་སུ་དྲན་པ་ནི་དགེ་འདུན་ལ་སྐྱབས་སུ་སོང་བ་ཡིན་ནོ། །ཁྱིམ་བདག་གཞན་ཡང་བྱང་ཆུབ་སེམས་དཔའ་ཁྱིམ་པ་ཁྱིམ་ན་གནས་པ་སངས་རྒྱས་དང་འགྲོགས་པར་སློན་ཅིང་སྦྱིན་པ་སྦྱིན་པ་ནི་སངས་རྒྱས་ལ་སྐྱབས་སུ་སོང་བ་ཡིན་ནོ། །དམ་པའི་ཆོས་ཡང་དག་པར་བསྲུང་བའི་ཕྱིར་སྦྱིན་པ་སྦྱིན་པ་ནི་ཆོས་ལ་སྐྱབས་སུ་སོང་བ་ཡིན་ནོ། །སྦྱིན་པ་དེ་བླ་ན་མེད་པ་ཡང་དག་པར་རྫོགས་པའི་བྱང་ཆུབ་ཏུ་ཡོངས་སུ་བསྔོ་བ་ནི་དགེ་འདུན་ལ་སྐྱབས་སུ་སོང་བ་ཡིན་ནོ། །ཁྱིམ་བདག་གཞན་ཡང་བྱང་ཆུབ་སེམས་དཔའ་ཁྱིམ་པ་ཁྱིམ་ན་གནས་པ་ནི་སྐྱེས་བུ་དམ་པའི་ལས་རྣམས་བྱེད་ཅིང་སྐྱེས་བུ་ངན་པའི་ལས་རྣམས་མི་བྱེད་དོ། །ཁྱིམ་བདག་སྐྱེས་བུ་དམ་པའི་ལས་ཡིན་གྱི་སྐྱེས་བུ་ངན་པའི་ལས་མ་ཡིན་པ་རྣམས་གང་ཞེ་ན། ཁྱིམ་བདག་འདི་ལ་བྱང་ཆུབ་སེམས་དཔའ་ཁྱིམ་པ་ཆོས་ཀྱིས་ལོངས་སྤྱོད་ཚོལ་གྱི་ཆོས་མ་ཡིན་པས་མི་ཚོལ་ལོ། །འཐུན་པས་ཚོལ་གྱི་མི་འཐུན་པས་མ་ཡིན་ནོ། །ཡང་དག་པས་འཚོ་བ་ཡིན་གྱི་ལོག་པས་འཚོ་བ་མ་ཡིན་ཏེ། དེ་ཆོས་ཀྱིས་ལོངས་སྤྱོད་ཐོབ་པ་དེ་དག་གིས་གཞན་ལ་འཚེ་བར་མི་བྱེད་དེ། མི་རྟག་པའི་འདུ་ཤེས་སྒོམ་པ་མང་ཞིང་སྙིང་པོ་ལེན་

ཏོ། འདི་ལྟ་སྟེ། ཕ་མ་ལ་བསྙེན་བཀུར་བྱེད་པ་དང་། བུ་དང་། ཆུང་མ་དང་། བྲན་ཕོ་དང་། བྲན་མོ་དང་། ལས་བྱེད་པ་དང་། ཉེ་ཤས་འཚོ་བ་རྣམས་ཡང་དག་པར་ཡོངས་སྐྱོང་དང་། མཛའ་བཤེས་དང་། བློན་པོ་དང་། ཉེ་དུ་དང་། སྣག་གི་གཉེན་མཚམས་རྣམས་ལ་བཀུར་སྟི་དང་། གང་དུ་ཡང་ཆོས་ལ་འཛུད་པས་གཏོང་བ་འཕེལ་བར་བྱེད་དོ། །ཁྱིམ་བདག་གཞན་ཡང་བྱང་ཆུབ་སེམས་དཔའ་ཁྱིམ་པ་ནི་འདི་ལྟ་སྟེ། སེམས་ཅན་ཐམས་ཅད་ཀྱི་ཕུང་པོ་ལྔའི་ཁུར་ཁྱེར་བས་ཁུར་བླངས་བཀུར་བའི་ཕྱིར་བརྩོན་འགྲུས་རྩོམ་མོ། །འདི་ལྟ་སྟེ། ཉན་ཐོས་དང་། རང་སངས་རྒྱས་ཀྱི་ཐེག་པ་མི་འདོར་བས་ཁུར་བླངས་པ་བཀུར་བའི་ཕྱིར་བརྩོན་འགྲུས་རྩོམ་མོ། །སེམས་ཅན་ཡོངས་སུ་སྨིན་པར་བྱ་བས་ཡོངས་སུ་མི་སྐྱོ་བ། བདག་བདེ་བ་ལ་མི་ཆགས་པ། སེམས་ཅན་ཐམས་ཅད་བདེ་བ་ཐོབ་པ་བྱེད་པ། རྙེད་པ་དང་། མ་རྙེད་པ་དང་། གྲགས་པ་དང་། མ་གྲགས་པ་དང་། བསྟོད་པ་དང་། སྨད་པ་དང་། བདེ་བ་དང་། སྡུག་བསྔལ་གྱིས་མི་བསྐྱོད་པས་དེ་འཇིག་རྟེན་གྱི་ཆོས་ལས་ཡང་དག་པར་འདའ་བ་དང་། རྙེད་པ་དང་། ཡོངས་སྤྱོད་ཕུན་སུམ་ཚོགས་པས་མི་སླེམས་པ་དང་། རྙེད་པ་དང་། གྲགས་པ་དང་བརྗོད་པའི་སྒྲའི་སླན་པ་མེད་པ་ལ་ཡི་མི་ཆད་པ་དང་། ཤིན་ཏུ་བརྟགས་ཏེ་ལས་བྱེད་པ་དང་། ཡང་དག་པར་སྒྲུབ་པ་ཀུན་ཏུ་སྤྱང་བ་དང་། ལོག་པར་སྒྲུབ་པ་ལ་ཡིད་མི་མོས་པ་དང་། མི་གནས་པའི་གློས་འབྱུང་བ་མཐོང་བ་དང་། ཤིང་བལ་གྱི་འདབ་བ་ལྟ་བུའི་སེམས་མེད་དེ། ཇི་ལྟར་དམ་བཅས་པ་ཡོངས་སུ་རྫོགས་པ་བྱེད་པ་དང་། གཞན་གྱི་བྱ་བ་བྱེད་པ་དང་། རང་གི་བྱ་བ་ཡོངས་སུ་འདོར་བ་དང་། གཞན་ལ་བྱས་པ་ལ་ལན་དུ་ཕན་འདོགས་པར་མི་རེ་བ་དང་། གནོད་པ་བྱས་པ་ལ་ཞ་མི་ལྡོན་པ་དང་། བྱས་པ་གཟོ་བ་དང་། བྱས་པ་ཚོར་བ་དང་། ལེགས་པར་བྱ་བའི་ལས་བྱེད་པ་དང་། དབུལ་པོ་རྣམས་ལ་ལོངས་སྤྱོད་དག་པར་འགྱེད་པ་དང་། སྟོབས་དང་ལྡན་པ་རྣམས་ལ་ང་རྒྱལ་བཅག་པ་དང་། འཇིགས་པ་རྣམས་མི་འཇིགས་པར་དབུགས་འབྱིན་པ་དང་། མྱ་ངན་གྱིས་ཉམ་ཐག་པ་རྣམས་ལ་མྱ་ངན་གྱི་ཟུག་རྔུ་

སེལ་བ་དང་། མཐུ་ཆུང་བ་རྣམས་ལ་བཟོད་ཅིང་དང་དུ་ལེན་པ་དང་། ང་རྒྱལ་ལས་ཀྱང་ང་རྒྱལ་རྣམ་པར་སྤོང་བ་དང་བླ་མ་རྣམས་ལ་གུས་པ་དང་། མང་དུ་ཐོས་པ་རྣམས་ལ་སྟེན་པ་དང་། མཁས་པ་རྣམས་ལ་ཀུན་འདྲི་བ་དང་། ལྟ་བ་དྲང་བ་དང་། གཡོ་མེད་པར་སྤྱོད་པ་དང་། སྒྱུ་མེད་པ་དང་། བཅོས་མ་མེད་པར་སེམས་ཅན་ཐམས་ཅད་ལ་བྱམས་པ་དང་། དགེ་བ་གང་ཡིན་ཞེས་ཚོལ་བས་མི་ངོམས་པ་དང་། མང་དུ་ཐོས་པ་ལ་ཚོག་མི་ཤེས་པར་བྱེད་པ་དང་། བརྩམས་པ་རྣམས་ལ་ཡི་དམ་བརྟན་པ་དང་། འཕགས་པའི་སྐྱེ་བོ་དང་འགྲོགས་པ་དང་། འཕགས་པ་མ་ཡིན་པའི་སྐྱེ་བོ་རྣམས་ལ་ཆེར་སྙིང་རྗེ་བ་དང་། མཛའ་བ་བརྟན་པ་དང་། མཛའ་བ་དང་། མི་མཛའ་བ་ལ་སེམས་སྙོམས་པ་དང་། སངས་རྒྱས་ཀྱི་ཆོས་ཐམས་ཅད་ལ་སློབ་དཔོན་གྱི་དཔེ་མཁྱུད་མེད་པ་དང་། ཇི་ལྟར་ཐོས་པའི་ཆོས་རྣམས་རབ་ཏུ་སྟོན་པ་དང་། ཐོས་པའི་དོན་རྗེས་སུ་སྒོམ་པ་དང་། འདོད་པ་ལ་དགའ་ཞིང་རྩེ་བ་ཐམས་ཅད་ལ་མི་རྟག་པར་འདུ་ཤེས་པ་དང་། ལུས་ལ་མི་གཙང་བར་འདུ་ཤེས་པ་དང་། སྲོག་ལ་ཟིལ་པའི་ཐིགས་པ་ལྟར་འདུ་ཤེས་པ་དང་། ལོངས་སྤྱོད་ལ་སྒྱུ་མ་དང་། སྨིག་རྒྱུ་ལྟ་བུར་འདུ་ཤེས་པ་དང་། བུ་དང་ཆུང་མ་ལ་སེམས་ཅན་དམྱལ་བ་མནར་མེད་པར་འདུ་ཤེས་པ་དང་། ཞིང་དང་ཁྱིམ་གྱི་ལས་ཀྱི་མཐའ་དང་གོས་རྣམ་པ་སྣ་ཚོགས་ལོངས་སུ་འཛིན་པ་ལ་ཕོངས་པའི་སྡུག་པར་འདུ་ཤེས་པ་དང་། ལོངས་སུ་ཚོལ་བ་ལ་དགེ་བའི་རྩ་བ་རྣམ་པར་འཇིག་པར་འདུ་ཤེས་པ་དང་། ཁྱིམ་གྱི་གནས་ལ་གཤེད་མ་ལྟ་བུར་འདུ་ཤེས་པ་དང་། མཛའ་བཤེས་དང་། བློན་པོ་དང་། ཉེ་དུ་དང་། སྣག་གི་གཉེན་མཚམས་རྣམས་ལ་སེམས་ཅན་དམྱལ་བའི་སྲུངས་མར་འདུ་ཤེས་པ་དང་། ཉིན་དང་མཚན་དུ་བྱེ་བྲག་ཏུ་སྦྱར་བ་ཅི་ཡོད་ཅེས་ཡོངས་སུ་འཛལ་བར་འདུ་ཤེས་པ་དང་། སྙིང་པོ་མེད་པའི་ལུས་ལས་སྙིང་པོ་བླང་བར་འདུ་ཤེས་པ་དང་། སྙིང་པོ་མེད་པའི་སྲོག་ལས་སྙིང་པོ་བླང་བར་འདུ་ཤེས་པ་དང་། སྙིང་པོ་མེད་པའི་ལོངས་སྤྱོད་རྣམས་ལས་སྙིང་པོ་བླང་བར་འདུ་ཤེས་པ་ཡིན་ནོ། །དེ་ལ་སྙིང་པོ་མེད་པའི་ལུས་ལས་སྙིང་པོ་བླང་བར་འདུ་ཤེས་པ་

གང་ཞེ་ན། གང་གཞན་གྱི་བྱའོ་ཅོག་བྱ་བར་སྨྲོ་བ་དང་། བླ་མ་རྣམས་ལ་གུས་
པར་སྨྲ་བ་དང་། ཕྱག་འཚལ་བ་དང་། ལྡང་བ་དང་། ཐལ་མོ་སྦྱོར་བ་དང་།
འདུད་པའི་ལས་བྱེད་པ་སྟེ། འདི་ནི་སྙིང་པོ་མེད་པའི་ལུས་ལས་སྙིང་པོ་བླང་བར་
འདུ་ཤེས་པ་ཞེས་བྱའོ། །དེ་ལ་སྙིང་པོ་མེད་པའི་སྲོག་ལས་སྙིང་པོ་བླང་བར་འདུ་
ཤེས་པ་གང་ཞེ་ན། གང་སྟོན་བྱས་པའི་དགེ་བའི་རྩ་བ་རྣམས་ཡོངས་སུ་མི་ཉམས་ལ་
གོང་དུ་ཡང་རྣམ་པར་འཕེལ་བར་བྱེད་པ་སྟེ། འདི་ནི་སྙིང་པོ་མེད་པའི་སྲོག་ལས་
སྙིང་པོ་བླང་བར་འདུ་ཤེས་པ་ཞེས་བྱའོ། །དེ་ལ་སྙིང་པོ་མེད་པའི་ལོངས་སྤྱོད་རྣམས་
ལས་སྙིང་པོ་བླང་བར་འདུ་ཤེས་པ་གང་ཞེ་ན། གང་སེར་སྣའི་སེམས་ཆར་གཅོད་
ཅིང་གཏོང་བ་ཆེན་པོའི་སེམས་འཕེལ་བར་བྱེད་ཅིང་སྦྱིན་པ་ཡང་དག་པར་འགྲེད་པ་སྟེ།
འདི་ནི་སྙིང་པོ་མེད་པའི་ལོངས་སྤྱོད་རྣམས་ལས་སྙིང་པོ་བླང་བར་འདུ་ཤེས་པ་ཞེས་
བྱའོ། །ཁྱིམ་བདག་དེ་ལྟར་ན་བྱང་ཆུབ་སེམས་དཔའ་ཁྱིམ་པ་གང་འདི་ལྟ་བུའི་སྐྱེས་
བུ་དམ་པའི་ལས་འདི་དག་བྱེད་ཀྱི། སྐྱེས་བུ་ངན་པའི་ལས་ནི་མ་ཡིན་ནོ། །དེ་
ལྟར་བྱེད་ན་དེ་བཞིན་གཤེགས་པ་རྣམས་ཀྱིས་ཉེས་པར་བརྗོད་པ་མ་ཡིན་ཏེ། རིགས་
པར་སྨྲ་བ་ཡིན། ཆོས་སྨྲ་བ་ཡིན་ནོ། །འདི་ལྟ་སྟེ། སྟོན་བླ་ན་མེད་པ་ཡང་
དག་པར་རྫོགས་པའི་བྱང་ཆུབ་ཏུ་དམ་བཅས་པ་ཡང་མི་ཉམས་ཡོངས་སུ་མི་ཉམས་པ་
ཡིན་ནོ། །ཁྱིམ་བདག་གཞན་ཡང་བྱང་ཆུབ་སེམས་དཔའ་ཁྱིམ་པ་ནི་བསླབ་པའི་
གཞི་ཐམས་ཅད་ཡོངས་སུ་བཟུང་བ་ཡིན་ཏེ། འདི་ལྟ་སྟེ། བསླབ་པའི་གཞི་ལྔ་
ཡོངས་སུ་བཟུང་ནས་དེས་སྲོག་གཅོད་པ་སྤང་བར་བྱ་སྟེ། དབྱུག་པ་དོར་བ་དང་།
མཚོན་ཆ་དོར་བ་དང་། ང་ཚ་ཤེས་པ་དང་། སྙིང་རྗེ་དང་ལྡན་པ་དང་། སྲོག་
ཆགས་འབྱུང་པོ་ཐམས་ཅད་ལ་མི་འཚེ་བའི་རང་བཞིན་ཅན་དང་། སེམས་ཅན་
ཐམས་ཅད་ལ་སེམས་སྙོམས་པ་དང་། རྟག་ཏུ་བྱམས་པ་ལ་གནས་པར་བྱའོ། །
དེས་མ་བྱིན་པར་ལེན་པ་སྤང་བར་བྱ་སྟེ། བདག་གི་ལོངས་སྤྱོད་ཀྱིས་ཆོག་ཤེས་པ་
དང་། གཞན་གྱི་ལོངས་སྤྱོད་ལ་མངོན་པར་དགའ་བ་མེད་པ་དང་། ཆགས་
སེམས་དང་བརྣབ་སེམས་མེད་པ་དང་། གཞན་གྱི་ནོར་ལ་འདོད་པ་མེད་པ་དང་།

ཐ་ན་རྡྭ་དང་ལོ་མ་ཙམ་ཡང་མ་བྱིན་པར་མི་བླང་བར་བྱའོ། །དེས་འདོད་པ་ལ་ལོག་པར་གཡེམ་པ་སྤང་བར་བྱ་སྟེ། རང་གི་ཆུང་མས་ཆོག་པར་འཛིན་པ་དང་། གཞན་གྱི་ཆུང་མ་ལ་འདོད་པ་མེད་པ་དང་། མ་ཆགས་པའི་མིག་གིས་བལྟ་བ་དང་། ཡིད་བྱུང་བའི་ཡིད་དང་། འདོད་པ་དག་ནི་ཤིན་ཏུ་སྡུག་བསྔལ་བའོ་སྙམ་དུ་མ་ཆགས་པ་ཡིད་ལ་བྱེད་པ་ལ་བརྩོན་པར་བྱའོ། །དེ་གང་གི་ཚེ་རང་གི་ཆུང་མ་ལ་འདོད་པའི་རྣམ་པར་རྟོག་པ་བྱུང་བ་དེའི་ཚེ་ཡང་ཉོན་མོངས་པའི་དབང་དུ་གྱུར་པས་ན་དེས་རང་གི་ཆུང་མ་ལ་མི་སྡུག་པར་རྗེས་སུ་བལྟ་བ་དང་། སྐྲག་པའི་ཡིད་ཀྱིས་འདོད་པ་བསྟེན་པར་བྱའི། ཞེན་པས་ཟིན་བཞིན་དུ་ནི་མ་ཡིན་པ་དང་། མི་རྟག་པ་དང་། སྡུག་བསྔལ་བ་དང་། བདག་མེད་པ་དང་། མི་གཙང་བར་འདུ་ཤེས་པས་དེས་ཅི་ནས་བདག་གིས་ཡིད་ཀྱི་མགུ་ལ་ཡང་འདོད་པ་ལ་སྤྱོད་པར་མི་བྱ་ན། མཚན་གཉིས་སྤྲད་པ་འམ། ཡན་ལག་མ་ཡིན་པར་འཇུག་པ་ལྟ་ཅི་སྨོས་ཏེ། བདག་གིས་དེ་ལྟར་མི་བྱའོ་སྙམ་མོ། །དེས་བརྫུན་དུ་སྨྲ་བ་སྤང་བར་བྱ་སྟེ། བདེན་པར་སྨྲ་བ་དང་། ཡང་དག་པར་སྨྲ་བ་དང་། ཇི་སྐད་སྨྲས་པ་དེ་བཞིན་དུ་བྱེད་པ་དང་། མི་སླུ་བ་དང་། བསམ་པ་ཕུན་སུམ་ཚོགས་པ་དང་། དྲན་པ་དང་ཤེས་བཞིན་དང་ལྡན་པར་བྱ་སྟེ། ཇི་ལྟར་མཐོང་བ་དང་། ཐོས་པ་སྨྲ་བ་དང་། ཆོས་རྗེས་སུ་སྲུང་བར་གྱུར་པ་དེས་ལུས་དང་སྲོག་གི་ཕྱིར་ཡང་ཤེས་བཞིན་དུ་བརྫུན་སྨྲ་བར་མི་བྱའོ། །དེས་འབྲུའི་ཆང་དང་སྦྱར་བའི་ཆང་མྱོས་པར་འགྱུར་བའི་བཏུང་བ་སྤང་བར་བྱ་སྟེ། དེར་རོ་བ་མེད་པ་དང་། མྱོས་པ་མེད་པ་དང་། འཁྲུལ་པ་མེད་པ་དང་། ཀྱིག་མ་འཆལ་པ་དང་། མི་འཕྱུར་བ་དང་། མི་གྲོད་པ་དང་། མི་གཡེང་བ་དང་། དྲན་པ་ཉེ་བར་གནས་པ་དང་། ཤེས་བཞིན་དང་ལྡན་པར་བྱ་སྟེ། དེ་ནས་བདོག་པ་ཐམས་ཅད་ཡོངས་སུ་གཏོང་བའི་བློ་འཇུག་ཅིང་ཟས་འདོད་པ་རྣམས་ལ་ཟས། སྐོམ་འདོད་པ་རྣམས་ལ་སྐོམ་སྦྱིན་པ་སྦྱིན་པར་བྱའོ་སྙམ་ན་དེས་གཞན་དག་ལ་ཆང་ཡང་སྦྱིན་ཏེ། འདི་སྙམ་དུ་འདི་ནི་སྦྱིན་པའི་ཕ་རོལ་ཏུ་ཕྱིན་པའི་དུས་ཡིན་ཏེ། གང་ཅི་འདོད་པ་དེ་ལ་དེ་སྦྱིན་པའི་དུས་ལ་བབ་ཀྱིས་བདག་གིས་འདི་

ལྟར་བྱ་སྟེ། གང་དང་གང་ལ་འདི་ལྟར་ཆང་ཡང་བྱིན་ནས་གང་འདི་འཁྲུལ་པ་མེད་
པའི་སྤྱོད་པ་ལ་དེ་དང་དེ་དག་དྲན་པ་དང་ཤེས་བཞིན་ཡང་དག་པར་འཛིན་དུ་གཞུག་གོ་
སླམ་པའི་འདུ་ཤེས་བསྐྱེད་པར་བྱའོ། །དེ་ཅིའི་ཕྱིར་ཞེ་ན། བསམ་པ་ཐམས་ཅད་
ཡོངས་སུ་རྫོགས་པར་བྱེད་པ་ནི་བྱང་ཆུབ་སེམས་དཔའི་སྦྱིན་པའི་ཕ་རོལ་ཏུ་ཕྱིན་པ་
ཡོངས་སུ་སྤྱོད་པ་ཡིན་ནོ། །ཁྱིམ་བདག་དེ་ལྟར་ན་བྱང་ཆུབ་སེམས་དཔའ་ཁྱིམ་པ་
གཞན་དག་ལ་ཆང་བྱིན་ཡང་དེ་བཞིན་གཤེགས་པ་རྣམས་ཀྱིས་ཉེས་པར་བརྗོད་པ་མ་
ཡིན་ནོ། །ཁྱིམ་བདག་བྱང་ཆུབ་སེམས་དཔའ་ཁྱིམ་པ་དེས་བསླབ་པའི་གཞི་ལྔ་
བཟུང་བའི་དགེ་བའི་རྩ་བ་ཡང་བླ་ན་མེད་པ་ཡང་དག་པར་རྫོགས་པའི་བྱང་ཆུབ་ཏུ་
ཡོངས་སུ་བསྔོ་བར་བྱའོ། །དེས་བསླབ་པའི་གཞི་ལྔ་པོ་དེ་དག་ཀྱང་ཤིན་ཏུ་བསྲུང་
བར་བྱའོ། །གང་དུ་ཡང་དེས་ཕྲ་མ་མི་བྱ་ཞིང་བྱེ་བ་རྣམས་ཀྱི་བསྡུམས་བྱའོ། །
དེས་ངག་རྩུབ་པོ་ཡང་མི་སྨྲ་བར་བྱ་ཞིང་དེས་ངག་འཇམ་པོར་སྨྲ་བ་དང་། ཚིག་
མཉེན་པ་དང་། གསོང་པོར་སྨྲ་བར་བྱའོ། །ཚིག་ཀྱལ་པ་ཡང་སྨྲ་བར་མི་བྱ་ཞིང་།
དུས་སུ་སྨྲ་བ་དང་། ཡང་དག་པར་སྨྲ་བ་དང་། དོན་སྨྲ་བ་དང་། ཆོས་སྨྲ་བ་
དང་། རིགས་པ་སྨྲ་བ་དང་། འདུལ་བ་སྨྲ་བ་དང་། ལན་ལེགས་པར་
འདེབས་པ་དང་། ཇི་སྐད་སྨྲས་པ་དེ་བཞིན་བྱེད་པར་བྱའོ། །དེས་བརྣབ་སེམས་
སུ་མི་བྱ་ཞིང་སེམས་ཅན་ཐམས་ཅད་ལ་ཕན་པ་དང་བདེ་བ་བསམ་པར་བྱའོ། །གནོད་
སེམས་སུ་མི་བྱ་ཞིང་རྟག་ཏུ་བཟོད་པའི་སྟོབས་ཀྱི་གོ་ཆ་བགོ་བར་བྱའོ། །དེས་ཡང་
དག་པར་བལྟ་བར་བྱ་ཞིང་ལོག་པ་ཕྱིན་ཅི་ལོག་ཏུ་ལྟ་བ་ཐམས་ཅད་དང་བྲལ་བར་
བྱའོ། །ལྷར་སངས་རྒྱས་ལ་བསམ་པ་རྗེས་སུ་སོང་ཞིང་ལྷ་གཞན་མི་འཛིན་པར་
བྱའོ། །ཁྱིམ་བདག་གཞན་ཡང་བྱང་ཆུབ་སེམས་དཔའ་ཁྱིམ་པ་གྲོང་ངམ། གྲོང་
ཁྱེར་རམ། གྲོང་རྡལ་ལམ། ལྗོངས་སམ། ལྗོངས་ཀྱི་ཕྱོགས་གང་ན་གནས་
པ་དེར་དེས་སེམས་ཅན་རྣམས་ལ་ཆོས་ཀྱི་གཏམ་བརྗོད་པར་བྱ་སྟེ། གང་དག་མ་
དད་པ་དེ་དག་ནི་དད་པ་ལ་གཟུད་པར་བྱ། སེམས་ཅན་གང་དག་མི་གུས་ཤིང་ཕར་མི་
འཛིན་པ། མར་མི་འཛིན་པ། དགེ་སྦྱོང་དུ་མི་འཛིན་པ། བྲམ་ཟེར་མི་འཛིན་

པ། རིགས་ཀྱི་གཙོ་བོ་ལ་རིམ་གྲོ་མི་བྱེད་པ། ཚུལ་དང་མི་ལྡན་ཞིང་མཚམས་ལས་འདས་པ་དེ་དག་བླ་མ་ལ་གུས་པ་དང་། ཆོས་སྤྱོད་པ་ལ་གཟུད་པར་བྱའོ། །སེམས་ཅན་གང་དག་ཐོས་པ་ཆུང་བ་དེ་དག་མང་དུ་ཐོས་པ་ལ་སྦྱར་བར་བྱའོ། །སེར་སྣ་ཅན་རྣམས་ནི་གཏོང་བ་ལ། ཚུལ་ཁྲིམས་འཆལ་བ་རྣམས་ནི་ཚུལ་ཁྲིམས་ལ། གནོད་སེམས་ཅན་རྣམས་ནི་བཟོད་པ་དང་ངེས་པ་ལ། ལེ་ལོ་ཅན་རྣམས་ནི་བརྩོན་འགྲུས་རྩོམ་པ་ལ། བརྗེད་ངས་པ་རྣམས་ནི་དྲན་པ་དང་ཤེས་བཞིན་ལ། འཆལ་བའི་ཤེས་རབ་ཅན་རྣམས་ནི་ཤེས་རབ་ལ་གཟུད་པར་བྱའོ། །སེམས་ཅན་དབུལ་པོ་རྣམས་ལ་ལོངས་སྤྱོད་ཡང་དག་པར་བགོ་བར་བྱའོ། །སེམས་ཅན་ནད་པ་རྣམས་ལ་སྨན་སྦྱིན་པ་བྱའོ། །སེམས་ཅན་མགོན་མེད་པ་རྣམས་ཀྱི་མགོན་བྱའོ། །སྐྱབས་མེད་པ་རྣམས་ཀྱི་སྐྱབས་དང་། དཔུང་གཉེན་མེད་པ་རྣམས་ཀྱི་དཔུང་གཉེན་བྱའོ། །ངེས་ལྟོངས་དང་ལྟོངས་ཀྱི་ཕྱོགས་དེ་དག་ཐམས་ཅད་དང་ཇི་ལྟར་འཐུན་པར་སེམས་ཅན་འགའ་ཡང་ལོག་པར་ལྟུང་བར་མི་འགྲོ་བ་དེ་ལྟར་ཆོས་ཀྱིས་བསྲུང་བར་བྱའོ། །ཁྲིམ་བདག་གལ་ཏེ་བྱང་ཆུབ་སེམས་དཔའ་ཁྲིམ་པས་ལན་གཅིག་ལན་གཉིས་ལན་གསུམ་ནས་ལན་བདུན་གྱི་བར་དུ་རྗེས་སུ་བསྟན་པས་སེམས་ཅན་རྣམས་ཡོན་ཏན་དག་ལ་བཀོད་པ་ལས་ཡོན་ཏན་གང་ཡང་རུང་བ་ལ་གནས་པར་མ་གྱུར་ན་ཁྲིམ་བདག་དེའི་ཚེ་བྱང་ཆུབ་སེམས་དཔའ་ཁྲིམ་པ་དེས་སེམས་ཅན་དེ་དག་ལ་སྙིང་རྗེ་ཆེན་པོ་བསྐྱེད་དེ། དེས་ཐམས་ཅད་མཁྱེན་པ་ཉིད་ཀྱི་གོ་ཆ་བསྲ་བ་ཡང་བགོ་ཞིང་ཚིག་འདི་སྐད་ཅེས་ཇི་སྲིད་དུ་སེམས་ཅན་གདུལ་དཀའ་བ་དམུ་རྒོད་དེ་དག་ཡོངས་སུ་སྨིན་པར་མ་གྱུར་པ་དེ་སྲིད་དུ་བདག་བླ་ན་མེད་པ་ཡང་དག་པར་རྫོགས་པའི་བྱང་ཆུབ་ཏུ་མངོན་པར་རྫོགས་པར་འཚང་མི་རྒྱའོ་ཞེས་བརྗོད་པར་བྱའོ། །དེ་ཅིའི་ཕྱིར་ཞེ་ན། བདག་གིས་ནི་དེ་དག་གི་ཕྱིར་གོ་ཆ་བགོས་ཏེ། སེམས་ཅན་དྲང་པོ་རྣམས་ཀྱི་ཕྱིར་མ་ཡིན། གཡོ་མེད་པ་རྣམས་ཀྱི་ཕྱིར་མ་ཡིན། སྒྱུ་མེད་པ་རྣམས་ཀྱི་ཕྱིར་མ་ཡིན། ཚུལ་ཁྲིམས་དང་ལྡན་པ་རྣམས་ཀྱི་ཕྱིར་མ་ཡིན་ཏེ། ཡོན་ཏན་དང་ལྡན་པ་རྣམས་ཀྱི་ཕྱིར་བདག་གི་གོ་ཆ་མ་བགོས་ཀྱིས། ཅི་ནས་བདག་གི་རྩོལ་བ་དོན་ཡོད་པར་འགྱུར་

བ་དང་། སེམས་ཅན་གྱིས་བདག་མཐོང་མ་ཐག་ཏུ་དགའ་བ་དང་། དད་པ་ཐོབ་
པར་འགྱུར་བ་དེ་ལྟར་བྱའོ། །དེ་ལྟར་བསྒྲུབ་བོ། །དེ་ལྟར་བརྩོན་འགྲུས་བརྩམ་
པར་བྱའོ་སྙམ་མོ། །ཁྱིམ་བདག་གལ་ཏེ་གྲོང་ངམ། གྲོང་ཁྱེར་རམ། གྲོང་
རྡལ་ལམ། ལྗོངས་སམ། ལྗོངས་ཀྱི་ཕྱོགས་གང་ན་གནས་པའི་བྱང་ཆུབ་སེམས་
དཔའ་དེས་ཕྱོགས་དེར་མ་བསྐུལ་ཏམ། དྲན་པར་མ་བྱས་ཏེ་སེམས་ཅན་རྣམས་ངན་
འགྲོ་གང་ཡང་རུང་བ་ཞིག་ཏུ་སྐྱེས་པར་གྱུར་ན་བྱང་ཆུབ་སེམས་དཔའ་དེ་ནི་དེ་བཞིན་
གཤེགས་པ་རྣམས་ཀྱིས་སྨད་པ་ཡིན་ནོ། །ཁྱིམ་བདག་འདི་ལྟ་སྟེ་དཔེར་ན་གྲོང་ངམ།
གྲོང་ཁྱེར་རམ། གྲོང་རྡལ་ལམ། ལྗོངས་སམ། ལྗོངས་ཀྱི་ཕྱོགས་གང་ན་
སྨན་པ་མཁས་པ་ཞིག་གནས་པ་དེས་ཐ་ན་སེམས་ཅན་འགའ་ཞིག་གི་དུག་ཞི་བར་མ་
ནུས་ཏེ་འཆི་བའི་དུས་བྱེད་པར་གྱུར་ན་སྨན་པ་དེ་སྐྱེ་བོ་མང་པོས་སྨད་པར་འགྱུར་
རོ། །ཁྱིམ་བདག་དེ་བཞིན་དུ་གྲོང་ངམ། གྲོང་ཁྱེར་རམ། གྲོང་རྡལ་ལམ།
ལྗོངས་སམ། ལྗོངས་ཀྱི་ཕྱོགས་གང་ན་བྱང་ཆུབ་སེམས་དཔའ་གནས་པ་དེས་དེའི་
ཕྱོགས་སུ་ཐ་ན་སེམས་ཅན་འགའ་ཙམ་ལ་ཡང་མ་བསྐུལ་ཏམ་དྲན་པར་མ་བྱས་ཏེ་ངན་
འགྲོ་གང་ཡང་རུང་བ་ཞིག་ཏུ་སྐྱེས་པར་གྱུར་ན་བྱང་ཆུབ་སེམས་དཔའ་དེ་དེ་བཞིན་
གཤེགས་པ་རྣམས་ཀྱིས་སྨད་པ་ཡིན་ནོ། །ཁྱིམ་བདག་དེ་བས་ན་འདི་ལ་བྱང་ཆུབ་
སེམས་དཔའ་ཁྱིམ་པ་ཅི་ནས་གྲོང་ངམ། གྲོང་ཁྱེར་རམ། གྲོང་རྡལ་ལམ།
ལྗོངས་སམ། ལྗོངས་ཀྱི་ཕྱོགས་གང་ན་གནས་པ་དེས་བདག་གིས་སེམས་ཅན་
འགའ་ཡང་ལོག་པར་ལྟུང་བར་འགྲོ་བར་མི་འགྱུར་བ་དེ་ལྟར་བྱའོ། །དེ་ལྟར་བསྒྲུབ་
བོ། །དེ་ལྟར་བརྩོན་འགྲུས་བརྩམ་མོ་སྙམ་པའི་གོ་ཆ་དེ་ལྟ་བུ་བགོ་བར་བྱའོ། །
ཁྱིམ་བདག་གཞན་ཡང་བྱང་ཆུབ་སེམས་དཔའ་ཁྱིམ་པ་ཁྱིམ་ན་གནས་པས་ཁྱིམ་ན་
གནས་པའི་ཉེས་པ་ལ་མཁས་པར་བྱའོ། །དེས་འདི་ལྟར་སོ་སོར་བསླབ་པར་བྱ་སྟེ།
ཁྱིམ་ཞེས་བྱ་བ་འདི་ནི་དགེ་བའི་རྩ་བ་རྣམས་འཇོམས་པར་བྱེད་པ། འབྱུང་བ་སུན་
འབྱིན་པ། དགེ་བའི་སྡོང་པོ་འཇིལ་བར་བྱེད་པ་སྟེ། དེའི་ཕྱིར་ཁྱིམ་ཞེས་
བྱའོ། །ཁྱིམ་ན་གནས་པ་ཞེས་བྱ་བ་འདི་ནི་ཉོན་མོངས་པ་ཐམས་ཅད་ཀྱི་གནས།

མི་དགེ་བའི་རྩ་བ་ལ་རྣམ་པར་རྟོག་པ་རྣམས་ཀྱི་གནས། བྱིས་པ་སོ་སོའི་སྐྱེ་བོ་མ་དུལ་བ་མ་སྨྲས་པ་རྣམས་ཀྱི་གནས། མི་དགེ་བ་སྤྱོད་པ་རྣམས་ཀྱི་གནས། སྐྱེ་བོ་ངན་པ་འདུས་པ་ཡིན་ཏེ། དེའི་ཕྱིར་ཁྱིམ་ན་གནས་པ་ཞེས་བྱའོ། །ཁྱིམ་ན་གནས་པ་ཞེས་བྱ་བ་འདི་ནི་སྡུག་བསྔལ་གྱི་ཆོས་ཐམས་ཅད་ཀྱི་གནས་ཞེས་བརྗོད་པའོ། །འདི་ནི་སྔོན་གོམས་པར་བྱས་པའི་དགེ་བའི་རྩ་བ་རྣམས་ཉམས་པར་བྱེད་པ་སྟེ། དེའི་ཕྱིར་ཁྱིམ་ན་གནས་པ་ཞེས་བྱའོ། །ཁྱིམ་ཞེས་བྱ་བ་འདི་ནི་དེར་གནས་ནས་བྱ་བའི་མི་རིགས་པ་བྱེད་པའོ། །དེར་གནས་ནས་ཕ་མ་དང་། དགེ་སྦྱོང་དང་། བྲམ་ཟེ་ལ་གུས་པར་མི་འགྱུར་བ་ཡིན་ཏེ། དེའི་ཕྱིར་ཁྱིམ་ཞེས་བྱའོ། །ཁྱིམ་ཞེས་བྱ་བ་འདི་ནི་སྲིད་པའི་འཁྲི་ཤིང་ལ་མངོན་པར་དགའ་བའི་ཕྱིར་མྱ་ངན་དང་། སྨྲེ་སྔགས་འདོན་པ་དང་། སྡུག་བསྔལ་བ་དང་། ཡིད་མི་བདེ་བ་དང་། འཁྲུག་པ་རྣམས་འབྱུང་སྟེ། དེའི་ཕྱིར་ཁྱིམ་ཞེས་བྱའོ། །ཁྱིམ་ཞེས་བྱ་བ་འདི་ནི་གསད་པ་དང་། བཅིང་བ་དང་། བརྡེག་པ་དང་། བསྡིགས་པ་དང་། འཚེ་བ་དང་། མི་སྙན་པ་དང་། གཤེ་བ་དང་། ངན་དུ་བརྗོད་པ་དང་། ངན་དུ་བྱ་བའི་ཚིག་གི་ལམ་རྣམས་འདུ་བ་སྟེ། དེའི་ཕྱིར་ཁྱིམ་ཞེས་བྱའོ། །ཁྱིམ་ཞེས་བྱ་བ་འདི་ནི་དགེ་བའི་རྩ་བ་མ་བྱས་པ་མི་འཛུགས་པའོ། །དགེ་བའི་རྩ་བ་བྱས་པ་རྣམས་རྣམ་པར་འཇིག་པའོ། །མཁས་པ་རྣམས་དང་། སངས་རྒྱས་དང་། སངས་རྒྱས་ཀྱི་ཉན་ཐོས་ཐམས་ཅད་ཀྱིས་སྨད་པའོ། །འདི་ལ་གནས་པ་ནི་ངན་འགྲོར་འགྲོ་བར་འགྱུར་རོ། །འདི་ལ་གནས་པ་ནི་འདོད་ཆགས་ཀྱིས་འགྲོ་བ་མ་ཡིན་པར་འགྲོ་བའོ། །ཞེ་སྡང་དང་། འཇིགས་པ་དང་། གཏི་མུག་གིས་འགྲོ་བ་མ་ཡིན་པར་འགྲོ་བ་སྟེ། དེའི་ཕྱིར་ཁྱིམ་ཞེས་བྱའོ། །འདི་ནི་ཚུལ་ཁྲིམས་ཀྱི་ཕུང་པོ་ཀུན་མི་སྲུང་བའོ། །ཏིང་ངེ་འཛིན་གྱི་ཕུང་པོ་འདོར་བའོ། །ཤེས་རབ་ཀྱི་ཕུང་པོ་ལ་མི་འཇུག་པའོ། །རྣམ་པར་གྲོལ་བའི་ཕུང་པོ་མི་འཐོབ་པའོ། །རྣམ་པར་གྲོལ་བའི་ཡེ་ཤེས་མཐོང་བའི་ཕུང་པོ་མི་སྐྱེད་པ་སྟེ། དེའི་ཕྱིར་ཁྱིམ་ཞེས་བྱའོ། །ཁྱིམ་ན་གནས་པ་ནི་ཕ་དང་། མ་དང་། བུ་དང་། ཆུང་མ་དང་། བྲན་ཕོ་དང་།

བྲན་མོ་དང་། ལས་བྱེད་པ་དང་། ཞོ་ཤས་འཚོ་བ་དང་། མཛའ་བཤེས་དང་། བློན་པོ་དང་། ཉེ་དུ་དང་། སྡུག་གི་གཉེན་མཚམས་དང་། གཡོག་ཡོངས་སུ་འཛིན་པ་ལ་སྲིད་པ་ཡིན་ནོ། །ཁྲིམ་ན་གནས་པ་འདི་ནི་རྒྱ་མཚོ་ལ་ཆུ་ཕྲན་ལྟར་དགང་དཀའ་བའོ། །ཁྲིམ་ན་གནས་པ་ནི་མེ་ལ་ཤིང་ལྟར་ཚོག་མི་ཤེས་པའོ། །ཁྲིམ་ན་གནས་པ་ནི་ཐུག་པ་མེད་པའི་རྩོལ་གྱིས་རླུང་མར་ལྟར་ཐུག་པ་མེད་པར་རྣམ་པར་རྟོག་པའོ། །ཁྲིམ་ན་གནས་པ་ནི་འཇིག་པས་བྱེ་མའི་གྲོང་ཁྱེར་ལྟར་འཇིག་པའོ། །ཁྲིམ་ན་གནས་པ་ནི་ཁ་ཟས་བཟང་པོ་དུག་དང་འདྲེས་པ་ལྟར་འདྲེས་པའོ། །ཁྲིམ་ན་གནས་པ་ནི་མི་མཛའ་བ་བཞིན་དུ་འཁྲུན་པ་མ་ཡིན་པས་རྟག་ཏུ་སྡུག་བསྔལ་བའོ། །ཁྲིམ་ན་གནས་པ་ནི་འཕགས་པའི་ཆོས་སྒྲུབ་པ་ལ་བར་ཆད་བྱེད་པའོ། །ཁྲིམ་ན་གནས་པ་ནི་ཕན་ཚུན་རྩེན་གྱིས་འཐབ་པའོ། །ཁྲིམ་ན་གནས་པ་ནི་གཅིག་ལ་གཅིག་གནོད་པར་སེམས་པས་རྟག་ཏུ་མི་འཁྲུན་པའོ། །ཁྲིམ་ན་གནས་པ་ནི་ལེགས་པར་བྱས་པ་དང་། ཉེས་པར་བྱས་པའི་ལས་ཀྱི་མཐའ་ལ་སྨྲོར་བས་གནོད་པ་མང་བའོ། །ཁྲིམ་ན་གནས་པ་ནི་ལས་ཀྱི་མཐའ་ཐུག་པ་མེད་པས་རྟག་ཏུ་བརྩོན་པའོ། །ཁྲིམ་ན་གནས་པ་ནི་ཡུན་རིང་པོ་ནས་བསགས་པ་རྣམ་པར་འཇིག་པའི་ཆོས་ཅན་གྱི་ཕྱིར་མི་རྟག་པའོ། །ཁྲིམ་ན་གནས་པ་ནི་དངོས་པོ་ཀུན་དུ་ཚོལ་ཞིང་ཡོངས་སུ་སྲུང་བས་སྡུག་བསྔལ་བའོ། །ཁྲིམ་ན་གནས་པ་ནི་དགྲ་ལྟར་མི་མཛའ་བས་རྟག་ཏུ་བག་ཚ་བའོ། །ཁྲིམ་ན་གནས་པ་ནི་ཕྱིན་ཅི་ལོག་གིས་ཟིན་པས་བག་མེད་པའོ། །ཁྲིམ་ན་གནས་པ་ནི་རང་གི་དཔྱོད་པས་རྣམ་པར་བསྒྲུབས་ཏེ། ངོ་བོ་ཉིད་ཀྱིས་སྟོང་པས་གར་མཁན་གྱི་ཆོན་དང་འདྲའོ། །ཁྲིམ་ན་གནས་པ་ནི་མྱུར་དུ་ཕན་ཚུན་འགྱེས་པས་མཐར་རྒྱུད་ཅིང་འགྱུར་བའོ། །ཁྲིམ་ན་གནས་པ་ནི་སྐྱེ་བོ་བློ་བུར་དུ་འདུས་པས་རྟག་ཏུ་ངོ་བོ་ཉིད་མེད་པའི་ཕྱིར་སྒྱུ་མ་ལ་ལྟ་བ་དང་མཚུངས་སོ། ཁྲིམ་ན་གནས་པ་ནི་ཕུན་སུམ་ཚོགས་པ་ཐམས་ཅད་ཀྱང་མཐར་རྒྱུད་པར་འགྱུར་བས་རྨི་ལམ་དང་མཚུངས་སོ། །ཁྲིམ་ན་གནས་པ་ནི་མྱུར་དུ་འབྲལ་བས་ཟིལ་པའི་ཐིགས་པ་དང་མཚུངས་སོ། །ཁྲིམ་ན་གནས་པ་ནི་རོ་བྲོ་བ་ཆུང་དུ་ཡོངས་སུ་འཛལ་བས་སྦྲང་རྩིའི་ཐིགས་པ་དང་མཚུངས་

སོ། །ཁྱིམ་ན་གནས་པ་ནི་གཟུགས་དང་། སྒྲ་དང་། དྲི་དང་། རོ་དང་། རེག་དང་། ཆོས་ཀྱིས་ཡོངས་སུ་གཟིར་བས་ཚེར་མའི་དྲ་བ་དང་མཚུངས་སོ། །ཁྱིམ་ན་གནས་པ་ནི་མི་དགེ་བ་ལ་རྣམ་པར་རྟོག་པས་ཡོངས་སུ་མི་སྐྱོ་བའི་ཕྱིར་ཁ་ཁབ་ཙམ་གྱི་སྲོག་ཆགས་དང་མཚུངས་སོ། །ཁྱིམ་ན་གནས་པ་ནི་གཅིག་ལ་གཅིག་འདྲིད་པས་སྲོག་རྣམ་པར་འཇིག་པའོ། །ཁྱིམ་ན་གནས་པ་ནི་སེམས་རྙོག་པ་ཅན་དུ་བྱེད་པས་རྟག་ཏུ་འཁྲུག་པའོ། །ཁྱིམ་ན་གནས་པ་ནི་རྒྱལ་པོ་དང་། ཆོམ་རྐུན་དང་། མེ་དང་། ཆུ་དང་། བགོ་སྐལ་ལ་སྤྱོད་པས་རྣམ་པར་འཇོམས་པའི་ཕྱིར་ཐུན་མོང་བའོ། །ཁྱིམ་ན་གནས་པ་ནི་ཉེས་དམིགས་མང་བས་རོ་བྲོ་བ་ཆུང་བའོ། །ཁྱིམ་བདག་དེ་ལྟར་བྱང་ཆུབ་སེམས་དཔའ་ཁྱིམ་པ་ཁྱིམ་ན་གནས་པས་ཁྱིམ་ན་གནས་པའི་ཉེས་པ་ལ་མཁས་པར་བྱའོ། ཁྱིམ་བདག་གཞན་ཡང་བྱང་ཆུབ་སེམས་དཔའ་ཁྱིམ་པ་ཁྱིམ་ན་གནས་པས་སྦྱིན་པ་དང་། དུལ་བ་དང་། ཡང་དག་པར་སྡོམ་པ་དང་། ངེས་པ་མང་དུ་བྱའོ། །དེས་ཡང་འདི་ལྟར་བརྟག་པར་བྱ་སྟེ། གང་བྱིན་པ་དེ་ནི་བདག་གི་ཡིན་ནོ། ཁྱིམ་ན་བཞག་པ་དེ་ནི་བདག་གི་མ་ཡིན་ནོ། །གང་བྱིན་པ་དེ་ནི་སྙིང་པོ་ཅན་ནོ། །གང་ཁྱིམ་ན་བཞག་པ་དེ་ནི་སྙིང་པོ་མེད་པའོ། །གང་བྱིན་པ་དེ་ནི་གཞན་དུ་བདེ་བའོ། །གང་ཁྱིམ་ན་བཞག་པ་དེ་ནི་ད་ལྟར་བྱུང་བ་ན་བདེ་བའོ། །གང་བྱིན་པ་དེ་ནི་ཡང་བསྲུང་བར་བྱ་བ་མ་ཡིན་པའོ། །གང་ཁྱིམ་ན་བཞག་པ་དེ་ནི་བསྲུང་བར་བྱ་བའོ། །གང་བྱིན་པ་དེ་ནི་སྲེད་པ་ཟད་པར་འགྱུར་བའོ། །གང་ཁྱིམ་ན་བཞག་པ་དེ་ནི་སྲེད་པ་རྣམ་པར་འཕེལ་བའོ། །གང་བྱིན་པ་དེ་ནི་བདག་གི་བ་མེད་པའོ། །གང་ཁྱིམ་ན་བཞག་པ་དེ་ནི་བདག་གི་བ་དང་བཅས་པའོ། །གང་བྱིན་པ་དེ་ནི་ཡོངས་སུ་མི་འཛིན་པའོ། །གང་ཁྱིམ་ན་བཞག་པ་དེ་ནི་འཛིན་པ་དང་བཅས་པའོ། །གང་བྱིན་པ་དེ་ནི་འཇིགས་པ་མེད་པའོ། །གང་ཁྱིམ་ན་བཞག་པ་དེ་ནི་འཇིགས་པ་དང་བཅས་པའོ། །གང་བྱིན་པ་དེ་ནི་བྱང་ཆུབ་ཀྱི་ལམ་ཉེ་བར་སྟོན་པའོ། །གང་ཁྱིམ་ན་བཞག་པ་དེ་ནི་བདུད་ཀྱི་ཕྱོགས་ཉེ་བར་སྟོན་པའོ། །གང་བྱིན་པ་དེ་ནི་ཟད་མི་ཤེས་པའོ། །གང་ཁྱིམ་ན་བཞག་པ་དེ་ནི་ཟད་པར་འགྱུར་

པའོ། །གང་བྱིན་པ་དེ་ནི་བདེ་བའོ། །གང་ཁྱིམ་ན་བཞག་པ་དེ་ནི་ཀུན་ཏུ་བསྲུང་
དགོས་པས་སྡུག་བསྔལ་བའོ། །གང་བྱིན་པ་དེ་ནི་ཉོན་མོངས་པ་སྤོང་བར་འགྱུར་
བའོ། །གང་ཁྱིམ་ན་ཡོད་པ་དེ་ནི་ཉོན་མོངས་པ་འཕེལ་བར་བྱེད་པའོ། །གང་བྱིན་
པ་དེ་ནི་ལོངས་སྤྱོད་ཆེན་པོར་འགྱུར་བའོ། །གང་ཁྱིམ་ན་བཞག་པ་དེ་ནི་ལོངས་སྤྱོད་
ཆེན་པོར་མི་འགྱུར་བའོ། །གང་བྱིན་པ་དེ་ནི་སྐྱེས་བུ་དམ་པའི་ལས་སོ། །གང་
ཁྱིམ་ན་བཞག་པ་དེ་ནི་སྐྱེས་བུ་ངན་པའི་ལས་སོ། །གང་བྱིན་པ་དེ་ནི་སངས་རྒྱས་
ཐམས་ཅད་ཀྱིས་བསྔགས་པའོ། །གང་ཁྱིམ་ན་བཞག་པ་དེ་ནི་བྱིས་པའི་སྐྱེ་བོས་
བསྔགས་པའོ་སྙམ་དུ་བརྟག་པར་བྱའོ། །ཁྱིམ་བདག་དེ་ལྟར་བྱང་ཆུབ་སེམས་དཔའ་
ཁྱིམ་པས་སྙིང་པོ་བླང་བར་བྱའོ། །ཁྱིམ་བདག་གཞན་ཡང་བྱང་ཆུབ་སེམས་དཔའ་
ཁྱིམ་པས་སློང་བ་མཐོང་ན་འདུ་ཤེས་གསུམ་བསྐྱེད་པར་བྱ་སྟེ། གསུམ་གང་ཞེ་ན།
དགེ་བའི་བཤེས་གཉེན་དུ་འདུ་ཤེས་པ་དང་། ཚེ་རྗེས་ནས་ལོངས་སྤྱོད་ཆེན་པོར་
འགྱུར་བར་འདུ་ཤེས་པ་དང་། བྱང་ཆུབ་ཀྱི་ལམ་ཉེ་བར་སྟོན་པར་འདུ་ཤེས་པ་སྟེ།
ཁྱིམ་བདག་བྱང་ཆུབ་སེམས་དཔའ་ཁྱིམ་པས་སློང་བ་མཐོང་ན་འདུ་ཤེས་གསུམ་པོ་དེ་
དག་བསྐྱེད་པར་བྱའོ། །ཁྱིམ་བདག་གཞན་ཡང་བྱང་ཆུབ་སེམས་དཔའ་ཁྱིམ་པས་
སློང་བ་མཐོང་ན་འདུ་ཤེས་གསུམ་བསྐྱེད་པར་བྱ་སྟེ། གསུམ་གང་ཞེ་ན། སེར་
སྣ་ཆོར་གཅད་པའི་འདུ་ཤེས་དང་། བཏོག་པ་ཐམས་ཅད་ཡོངས་སུ་གཏོང་བའི་འདུ་
ཤེས་དང་། ཐམས་ཅད་མཁྱེན་པའི་ཡེ་ཤེས་ལ་ལྟ་བའི་འདུ་ཤེས་ཏེ། ཁྱིམ་བདག་
བྱང་ཆུབ་སེམས་དཔའ་ཁྱིམ་པས་སློང་བ་མཐོང་ན་འདུ་ཤེས་གསུམ་པོ་དེ་དག་བསྐྱེད་
པར་བྱའོ། །ཁྱིམ་བདག་གཞན་ཡང་བྱང་ཆུབ་སེམས་དཔའ་ཁྱིམ་པས་སློང་བ་མཐོང་
ན་འདུ་ཤེས་གསུམ་བསྐྱེད་པར་བྱ་སྟེ། གསུམ་གང་ཞེ་ན། དེ་བཞིན་གཤེགས་
པའི་བཀའ་བཞིན་དུ་བྱ་བའི་འདུ་ཤེས་དང་། བདུད་ཆོར་གཅད་པའི་འདུ་ཤེས་དང་།
རྣམ་པར་སྨིན་པ་ལ་རེ་བ་མེད་པའི་འདུ་ཤེས་ཏེ། ཁྱིམ་བདག་བྱང་ཆུབ་སེམས་དཔའ་
ཁྱིམ་པས་སློང་བ་མཐོང་ན་འདུ་ཤེས་གསུམ་པོ་དེ་དག་བསྐྱེད་པར་བྱའོ། ཁྱིམ་བདག་
གཞན་ཡང་བྱང་ཆུབ་སེམས་དཔའ་ཁྱིམ་པས་སློང་བ་མཐོང་ན་འདུ་ཤེས་གསུམ་བསྐྱེད་

པར་བྱ་སྟེ། གསུམ་གང་ཞེ་ན། སློང་བ་ལ་གཡོག་ཏུ་འདུ་ཤེས་པ་དང་། བསྡུ་བའི་དངོས་པོས་མི་གཏོང་བར་འདུ་ཤེས་པ་དང་། དམ་པ་མ་ཡིན་པ་ཡོངས་སུ་འཛིན་པ་ལས་འབྱུང་བར་འདུ་ཤེས་པ་སྟེ། ཁྱིམ་བདག་བྱང་ཆུབ་སེམས་དཔའ་ཁྱིམ་པས་སློང་བ་མཐོང་ན་འདུ་ཤེས་གསུམ་པོ་དེ་དག་བསྐྱེད་པར་བྱའོ། །ཁྱིམ་བདག་གཞན་ཡང་བྱང་ཆུབ་སེམས་དཔའ་ཁྱིམ་པས་སློང་བ་མཐོང་ན་འདུ་ཤེས་གསུམ་བསྐྱེད་པར་བྱ་སྟེ། གསུམ་གང་ཞེ་ན། འདོད་ཆགས་དང་བྲལ་བའི་འདུ་ཤེས་དང་། བྱམས་པ་བསྒོམ་པའི་འདུ་ཤེས་དང་། གཏི་མུག་ལ་མི་འཇུག་པའི་འདུ་ཤེས་ཏེ། ཁྱིམ་བདག་བྱང་ཆུབ་སེམས་དཔའ་ཁྱིམ་པས་སློང་བ་མཐོང་ན་འདུ་ཤེས་གསུམ་པོ་དེ་དག་བསྐྱེད་པར་བྱའོ། །དེ་ཅིའི་ཕྱིར་ཞེ་ན། ཁྱིམ་བདག་འདི་ལྟར་བྱང་ཆུབ་སེམས་དཔའ་ཁྱིམ་པས་སློང་བ་མཐོང་ན་འདོད་ཆགས་དང་། ཞེ་སྡང་དང་། གཏི་མུག་སྲབ་མོར་འགྱུར་རོ། །ཁྱིམ་བདག་ཇི་ལྟར་བྱང་ཆུབ་སེམས་དཔའ་ཁྱིམ་པས་སློང་བ་མཐོང་ན་འདོད་ཆགས་དང་། ཞེ་སྡང་དང་། གཏི་མུག་སྲབ་མོར་འགྱུར་ཞེ་ན། གང་དེའི་དངོས་པོ་ལ་བཏང་སྙོམས་ཤིང་ཡོངས་སུ་གཏོང་བ་འདི་ནི་དེའི་འདོད་ཆགས་སྲབ་པའོ། །གང་སློང་བ་དེ་དག་ལ་བྱམས་པ་ཉེ་བར་སྒྲུབ་པ་འདི་ནི་དེའི་ཞེ་སྡང་སྲབ་པའོ། །གང་དངོས་པོ་བྱིན་ནས་བླ་ན་མེད་པ་ཡང་དག་པར་རྫོགས་པའི་བྱང་ཆུབ་ཏུ་ཡོངས་སུ་བསྔོ་བ་འདི་ནི་དེའི་གཏི་མུག་སྲབ་པའོ། །ཁྱིམ་བདག་དེ་ལྟར་ན་བྱང་ཆུབ་སེམས་དཔའ་ཁྱིམ་པས་སློང་བ་མཐོང་ན་འདོད་ཆགས་དང་། ཞེ་སྡང་དང་། གཏི་མུག་སྲབ་མོར་འགྱུར་རོ། །ཁྱིམ་བདག་གཞན་ཡང་བྱང་ཆུབ་སེམས་དཔའ་ཁྱིམ་པས་སློང་བ་མཐོང་ན་ཕ་རོལ་ཏུ་ཕྱིན་པ་དྲུག་བསྒོམ་པ་ཡོངས་སུ་རྫོགས་པར་འགྱུར་ཏེ། ཁྱིམ་བདག་འདི་ལ་བྱང་ཆུབ་སེམས་དཔའ་ཁྱིམ་པས་དངོས་པོ་གང་ཡང་རུང་བ་ཞིག་བཏང་ནས་མ་ཐག་ཏུ་དངོས་པོ་དེ་ལ་སེམས་ཀྱིས་འཛིན་པར་མི་བྱེད་དེ། དེ་ལྟར་ན་དེའི་སྦྱིན་པའི་ཕ་རོལ་ཏུ་ཕྱིན་པ་བསྒོམ་པ་ཡོངས་སུ་རྫོགས་པར་འགྱུར་རོ། །གང་བྱང་ཆུབ་ཀྱི་སེམས་ལ་བརྟེན་ནས་ཡོངས་སུ་གཏོང་སྟེ། དེ་ལྟར་ན་དེའི་ཚུལ་ཁྲིམས་ཀྱི་ཕ་རོལ་ཏུ་ཕྱིན་པ་བསྒོམ་པ་ཡོངས་སུ་རྫོགས་པར་འགྱུར་

རོ། །གང་སློང་བ་དེ་དག་ལ་བྱམས་པ་ཉེ་བར་སྒྲུབ་སྟེ་མི་ཁྲོ་ཞིང་གནོད་སེམས་མི་
བྱེད་དེ། དེ་ལྟར་ན་དེའི་བཟོད་པའི་ཕ་རོལ་ཏུ་ཕྱིན་པ་བསྒོམ་པ་ཡོངས་སུ་རྫོགས་པར་
འགྱུར་རོ། །གལ་ཏེ་བྱིན་ན་ཅི་སྙུད་སྙམ་དུ་འདི་ལྟར་སེམས་གཡོ་བས་ཞུམ་པ་མེད་
དེ་དེ་ལྟར་ན་དེའི་བརྩོན་འགྲུས་ཀྱི་ཕ་རོལ་ཏུ་ཕྱིན་པ་བསྒོམ་པ་ཡོངས་སུ་རྫོགས་པར་
འགྱུར་རོ། །གང་སློང་བ་ལ་བྱིན་ཏེ་བྱིན་ནས་ཀྱང་གདུང་བ་མེད་ཅིང་འགྱོད་པ་མེད་
པ་ཡིན། གང་དུ་ཡང་དགའ་ཞིང་རབ་ཏུ་མགུ་སྟེ་བདེ་བ་དང་ཡིད་བདེ་བ་སྐྱེད་ཅིང་
གང་བྱང་ཆུབ་ཀྱི་སེམས་ལ་གནས་ནས་གཏོང་སྟེ། དེ་ལྟར་ན་དེའི་བསམ་གཏན་གྱི་
ཕ་རོལ་ཏུ་ཕྱིན་པ་བསྒོམ་པ་ཡོངས་སུ་རྫོགས་པར་འགྱུར་རོ། །བྱིན་ནས་ཀྱང་གང་
ཆོས་ཐམས་ཅད་མི་དམིགས་ཤིང་རྣམ་པར་སྨིན་པ་ལ་མི་རེ་སྟེ། ཇི་ལྟར་མཁས་པ་དེ་
དག་ཆོས་གང་ལ་ཡང་མངོན་པར་མ་ཞེན་པ་དེ་ལྟར་མངོན་པར་ཞེན་པ་མེད་པས་བླ་ན་
མེད་པ་ཡང་དག་པར་རྫོགས་པའི་བྱང་ཆུབ་ཏུ་ཡོངས་སུ་སྔོ་སྟེ། དེ་ལྟར་ན་དེའི་ཤེས་
རབ་ཀྱི་ཕ་རོལ་ཏུ་ཕྱིན་པ་བསྒོམ་པ་ཡོངས་སུ་རྫོགས་པར་འགྱུར་རོ། །ཁྱིམ་བདག་དེ་
ལྟར་ན་བྱང་ཆུབ་སེམས་དཔའ་ཁྱིམ་པས་སློང་བ་མཐོང་ན་ཕ་རོལ་ཏུ་ཕྱིན་པ་དྲུག་བསྒོམ་
པ་ཡོངས་སུ་རྫོགས་པར་འགྱུར་རོ།། །།བམ་པོ་གཉིས་པ། ཁྱིམ་བདག་གཞན་
ཡང་བྱང་ཆུབ་སེམས་དཔའ་ཁྱིམ་པ་ཁྱིམ་ན་གནས་པས་རྗེས་སུ་ཆགས་པ་དང་ཁོང་ཁྲོ་
བ་མེད་པས་འཇིག་རྟེན་གྱི་ཆོས་བརྒྱད་ལ་མཉམ་པ་ཉིད་ཐོབ་པར་བྱའོ། །དེས་ལོངས་
སྤྱོད་རྙེད་དམ། ཆུང་མ་རྙེད་དམ། བུ་རྙེད་དམ། ནོར་རྙེད་དམ། འབྲུ་
རྙེད་ཀྱང་ཁེངས་པར་ཡང་མི་བྱ། དགའ་བར་ཡང་མི་བྱ། ཐམས་ཅད་མ་འབྱོར་
ཀྱང་དེས་ཞུམ་པར་ཡང་མི་བྱ། ཡི་མུག་པར་ཡང་མི་བྱའི། དེས་འདི་ལྟར་བརྟག
པར་བྱ་སྟེ། འདུས་བྱས་ཐམས་ཅད་ནི་སྒྱུ་མ་བྱས་པ། རྣམ་པར་བསྒྲུབས་པས་སོ་
སོར་ཉེ་བར་གནས་པའི་མཚན་ཉིད་དོ། །འདི་ལྟ་སྟེ། ཕ་མ་དང་། བུ་དང་།
ཆུང་མ་དང་། བྲན་ཕོ་དང་། བྲན་མོ་དང་། ལས་བྱེད་པ་དང་། ཞོ་ཤས་
འཚོ་བ་དང་། མཛའ་བ་ཤེས་དང་། བློན་པོ་དང་། ཉེ་དུ་དང་། སྣག་གི་
གཉེན་མཚམས་དེ་དག་ནི་ལས་ཀྱི་རྣམ་པར་སྨིན་པས་གྲུབ་པ་ཡིན་ཏེ། དེ་དག་ཀྱང་

བདག་གི་མ་ཡིན། བདག་ཀྱང་དེ་དག་གི་མ་ཡིན་ནོ། །དེ་ཅིའི་ཕྱིར་ཞེ་ན། ཕ་མ་ལ་སོགས་པ་དེ་དག་ནི་བདག་གི་མགོན་ནམ། སྐྱབས་སམ། དཔུང་གཉེན་ནམ། གནས་སམ། གླིང་ངམ། བདག་གམ། བདག་གི་བ་མ་ཡིན་ནོ། །གང་བདག་གི་ཟིན་པའི་ཕུང་པོ་དང་། ཁམས་དང་། སྐྱེ་མཆེད་དེ་དག་ཀྱང་བདག་མ་ཡིན། བདག་གི་མ་ཡིན་ན། གང་བདག་གི་ཕ་མ་ལ་སོགས་པ་དེ་དག་བདག་དང་བདག་གིར་འགྱུར་བ་དང་། བདག་ཀྱང་དེ་དག་གི་ཡིན་པ་ལྟ་སྨོས་ཀྱང་ཅི་དགོས། དེ་ཅིའི་ཕྱིར་ཞེ་ན། བདག་ཀྱང་ལས་བདག་གིར་བྱ་བ། ལས་ཀྱི་བགོ་སྐལ་ལ་སྤྱོད་པ་ཡིན་ཏེ། ལས་དགེ་བའམ། སྡིག་པའམ། གང་དང་གང་བྱས་པ་དེ་དང་དེ་ཉིད་ཀྱིས་བགོ་སྐལ་ལ་སྤྱོད་པར་འགྱུར་རོ། །དེ་དང་དེ་ཉིད་ཀྱི་འབྲས་བུ་སོ་སོར་མྱོང་ངོ་། །དེ་དང་དེ་ཉིད་ཀྱི་རྣམ་པར་སྨིན་པ་ལ་སྤྱོད་དོ། །འདི་དག་ཀྱང་ལས་བདག་གིར་བྱ་བ། ལས་ཀྱི་བགོ་སྐལ་ལ་སྤྱོད་པ་ཡིན་ཏེ། ལས་དགེ་བའམ། སྡིག་པའམ། གང་དང་གང་བྱས་པ་དེ་དང་དེ་ཉིད་ཀྱི་བགོ་སྐལ་ལ་སྤྱོད་པར་འགྱུར། དེ་དང་དེ་ཉིད་ཀྱི་རྣམ་པར་སྨིན་པ་སོ་སོར་མྱོང་བར་འགྱུར། དེ་དང་དེ་ཉིད་ཀྱི་འབྲས་བུ་སོ་སོར་མྱོང་བར་འགྱུར་རོ། །དེ་དག་གི་ཕྱིར་བདག་མི་དགེ་བའི་ལས་མངོན་པར་འདུ་བྱ་བ་ནི་བདག་གི་ཆ་མ་ཡིན་ཏེ། འདི་དག་ནི་ཚེ་འདི་ལ་བདེ་བའི་བདག་གིར་བྱ་བ་ཡིན་གྱི། ཚེ་གཞན་ལ་བདེ་བའི་བདག་གིར་བྱ་བ་མ་ཡིན་ནོ། །བདག་གི་གང་ཡིན་པ་དེ་ལ་བདག་འཛུག་པར་བྱ་སྟེ། འདི་ལྟ་སྟེ། སྦྱིན་པ་དང་། དུལ་བ་དང་། ཡང་དག་པར་སྡོམ་པ་དང་། བཟོད་པ་དང་། ངེས་པ་དང་། བརྩོན་འགྲུས་དང་། བག་ཡོད་པ་དང་། བྱང་ཆུབ་ཀྱི་ཡན་ལག་སྤུད་ཅིང་མངོན་པར་སྒྲུབ་པའི་དགེ་བ་དེ་ནི་བདག་གི་ཡིན་ཏེ། གང་དུ་བདག་འགྲོ་བར་འགྱུར་བའི་ལམ་དེར་འདི་དག་ཀྱང་འགྲོ་བར་འགྱུར་རོ་སྙམ་སྟེ། དེ་སྒྲོག་གི་ཕྱིར་རམ། བུ་དང་ཆུང་མའི་ཕྱིར་ཡང་སྡིག་པའི་ལས་མངོན་པར་འདུ་མི་བྱེད་དོ། །ཁྱིམ་བདག་བྱང་ཆུབ་སེམས་དཔའ་ཁྱིམ་པ་ཁྱིམ་ན་གནས་པ་དེས་རང་གི་ཆུང་མ་ལ་འདུ་ཤེས་གསུམ་བསྐྱེད་པར་བྱ་སྟེ། གསུམ་གང་ཞེ་ན། མི་རྟག་པའི་འདུ་

ཞེས་དང་། མི་བརྟན་པའི་འདུ་ཤེས་དང་། འགྱུར་བའི་འདུ་ཤེས་ཏེ། ཁྱིམ་བདག་བྱང་ཆུབ་སེམས་དཔའ་ཁྱིམ་པས་རང་གི་ཆུང་མ་ལ་འདུ་ཤེས་གསུམ་པོ་དེ་དག་བསྐྱེད་པར་བྱའོ། །ཁྱིམ་བདག་གཞན་ཡང་བྱང་ཆུབ་སེམས་དཔའ་ཁྱིམ་པས་རང་གི་ཆུང་མ་ལ་འདུ་ཤེས་གསུམ་བསྐྱེད་པར་བྱ་སྟེ། གསུམ་གང་ཞེ་ན། འདི་ནི་དགའ་ཞིང་རྩེ་བའི་གྲོགས་ཡིན་གྱི། འདི་འཇིག་རྟེན་ཕ་རོལ་གྱི་གྲོགས་ནི་མ་ཡིན་ནོ། །འདི་ནི་བཟའ་བ་དང་བཏུང་བའི་གྲོགས་ཡིན་གྱི། འདི་ལས་ཀྱི་རྣམ་པར་སྨིན་པ་མྱོང་བའི་གྲོགས་ནི་མ་ཡིན་ནོ། །འདི་ནི་བདེ་བའི་གྲོགས་ཡིན་གྱི། འདི་སྡུག་བསྔལ་གྱི་གྲོགས་ནི་མ་ཡིན་ནོ་སྙམ་པ་སྟེ། ཁྱིམ་བདག་བྱང་ཆུབ་སེམས་དཔའ་ཁྱིམ་པས་རང་གི་ཆུང་མ་ལ་འདུ་ཤེས་གསུམ་པོ་དེ་དག་བསྐྱེད་པར་བྱའོ། །ཁྱིམ་བདག་གཞན་ཡང་བྱང་ཆུབ་སེམས་དཔའ་ཁྱིམ་པས་རང་གི་ཆུང་མ་ལ་འདུ་ཤེས་གསུམ་བསྐྱེད་པར་བྱ་སྟེ། གསུམ་གང་ཞེ་ན། མི་གཙང་བར་འདུ་ཤེས་པ་དང་། བྲིད་པར་འདུ་ཤེས་པ་དང་། མི་འཐུན་པར་འདུ་ཤེས་པའོ། །ཁྱིམ་བདག་གཞན་ཡང་བྱང་ཆུབ་སེམས་དཔའ་ཁྱིམ་པས་རང་གི་ཆུང་མ་ལ་འདུ་ཤེས་གསུམ་བསྐྱེད་པར་བྱ་སྟེ། གསུམ་གང་ཞེ་ན། དགྲར་འདུ་ཤེས་པ་དང་། གཤེད་མར་འདུ་ཤེས་པ་དང་། ཕྱིར་རྒོལ་བར་འདུ་ཤེས་པའོ། །ཁྱིམ་བདག་གཞན་ཡང་བྱང་ཆུབ་སེམས་དཔའ་ཁྱིམ་པས་རང་གི་ཆུང་མ་ལ་འདུ་ཤེས་གསུམ་བསྐྱེད་པར་བྱ་སྟེ། གསུམ་གང་ཞེ་ན། ཤ་ཟ་མོར་འདུ་ཤེས་པ་དང་། སྲིན་མོར་འདུ་ཤེས་པ་དང་། གཟུགས་མི་སྡུག་པར་འདུ་ཤེས་པའོ། །ཁྱིམ་བདག་གཞན་ཡང་བྱང་ཆུབ་སེམས་དཔའ་ཁྱིམ་པས་རང་གི་ཆུང་མ་ལ་འདུ་ཤེས་གསུམ་བསྐྱེད་པར་བྱ་སྟེ། གསུམ་གང་ཞེ་ན། དགང་དཀའ་བར་འདུ་ཤེས་པ་དང་། གཉེན་དུ་འདུ་ཤེས་པ་དང་། བྱས་པ་མི་གཟོ་བར་འདུ་ཤེས་པའོ། །ཁྱིམ་བདག་གཞན་ཡང་བྱང་ཆུབ་སེམས་དཔའ་ཁྱིམ་པས་རང་གི་ཆུང་མ་ལ་འདུ་ཤེས་གསུམ་བསྐྱེད་པར་བྱ་སྟེ། གསུམ་གང་ཞེ་ན། སེམས་ཅན་དམྱལ་བར་འགྲོ་བར་འདུ་ཤེས་པ་དང་། དུད་འགྲོའི་སྐྱེ་གནས་སུ་འགྲོ་བར་འདུ་ཤེས་པ་དང་། གཤིན་རྗེའི་འཇིག་རྟེན་དུ་འགྲོ་བར་འདུ་ཤེས་པའོ། །ཁྱིམ་བདག

གཞན་ཡང་བྱང་ཆུབ་སེམས་དཔའ་ཁྱིམ་པས་རང་གི་ཆུང་མ་ལ་འདུ་ཤེས་གསུམ་བསྐྱེད་པར་བྱ་སྟེ། གསུམ་གང་ཞེ་ན། ཁུར་དུ་འདུ་ཤེས་པ་དང་། སྲིད་པར་འདུ་ཤེས་པ་དང་། སྲིད་པ་ཡོངས་སུ་འཛིན་པར་འདུ་ཤེས་པའོ། །ཁྱིམ་བདག་གཞན་ཡང་བྱང་ཆུབ་སེམས་དཔའ་ཁྱིམ་པས་རང་གི་ཆུང་མ་ལ་འདུ་ཤེས་གསུམ་བསྐྱེད་པར་བྱ་སྟེ། གསུམ་གང་ཞེ་ན། བདག་གི་བ་མ་ཡིན་པར་འདུ་ཤེས་པ་དང་། ཡོངས་སུ་འཛིན་པ་མེད་པར་འདུ་ཤེས་པ་དང་། བརྙན་མར་འདུ་ཤེས་པའོ། །ཁྱིམ་བདག་གཞན་ཡང་བྱང་ཆུབ་སེམས་དཔའ་ཁྱིམ་པས་རང་གི་ཆུང་མ་ལ་འདུ་ཤེས་གསུམ་བསྐྱེད་པར་བྱ་སྟེ། གསུམ་གང་ཞེ་ན། ལུས་ཀྱིས་ཉེས་པར་སྤྱོད་པའི་གནས་སུ་འདུ་ཤེས་པ་དང་། ངག་གིས་ཉེས་པར་སྤྱོད་པའི་གནས་སུ་འདུ་ཤེས་པ་དང་། ཡིད་ཀྱིས་ཉེས་པར་སྤྱོད་པའི་གནས་སུ་འདུ་ཤེས་པའོ། །ཁྱིམ་བདག་གཞན་ཡང་བྱང་ཆུབ་སེམས་དཔའ་ཁྱིམ་པས་རང་གི་ཆུང་མ་ལ་འདུ་ཤེས་གསུམ་བསྐྱེད་པར་བྱ་སྟེ། གསུམ་གང་ཞེ་ན། འདོད་པའི་རྣམ་པར་རྟོག་པའི་གནས་སུ་འདུ་ཤེས་པ་དང་། གནོད་སེམས་ཀྱི་རྣམ་པར་རྟོག་པའི་གནས་སུ་འདུ་ཤེས་པ་དང་། རྣམ་པར་འཚེ་བའི་རྣམ་པར་རྟོག་པའི་གནས་སུ་འདུ་ཤེས་པའོ། །ཁྱིམ་བདག་གཞན་ཡང་བྱང་ཆུབ་སེམས་དཔའ་ཁྱིམ་པས་རང་གི་ཆུང་མ་ལ་འདུ་ཤེས་གསུམ་བསྐྱེད་པར་བྱ་སྟེ། གསུམ་གང་ཞེ་ན། ཁྲི་མོན་དུ་འདུ་ཤེས་པ་དང་། གསོད་པར་འདུ་ཤེས་པ་དང་། འཆིང་བར་འདུ་ཤེས་པའོ། །ཁྱིམ་བདག་གཞན་ཡང་བྱང་ཆུབ་སེམས་དཔའ་ཁྱིམ་པས་རང་གི་ཆུང་མ་ལ་འདུ་ཤེས་གསུམ་བསྐྱེད་པར་བྱ་སྟེ། གསུམ་གང་ཞེ་ན། ཚུལ་ཁྲིམས་ཀྱི་བར་དུ་གཅོད་པར་འདུ་ཤེས་པ་དང་། ཏིང་ངེ་འཛིན་གྱི་བར་དུ་གཅོད་པར་འདུ་ཤེས་པ་དང་། ཤེས་རབ་ཀྱི་བར་དུ་གཅོད་པར་འདུ་ཤེས་པའོ། །ཁྱིམ་བདག་གཞན་ཡང་བྱང་ཆུབ་སེམས་དཔའ་ཁྱིམ་པས་རང་གི་ཆུང་མ་ལ་འདུ་ཤེས་གསུམ་བསྐྱེད་པར་བྱ་སྟེ། གསུམ་གང་ཞེ་ན། ཕོག་ཅོར་འདུ་ཤེས་པ་དང་། སླིར་འདུ་ཤེས་པ་དང་། རྒྱུར་འདུ་ཤེས་པའོ། །ཁྱིམ་བདག་གཞན་ཡང་བྱང་ཆུབ་སེམས་དཔའ་ཁྱིམ་པས་རང་གི་ཆུང་མ་ལ་འདུ་ཤེས་གསུམ་བསྐྱེད་

པར་བྱ་སྟེ། གསུམ་གང་ཞེ་ན། ཡམས་ཀྱི་ནད་དུ་འདུ་ཤེས་པ་དང་། གནོད་
པར་འདུ་ཤེས་པ་དང་། ནད་འགོ་བར་འདུ་ཤེས་པའོ། །ཁྱིམ་བདག་གཞན་ཡང་
བྱང་ཆུབ་སེམས་དཔའ་ཁྱིམ་པས་རང་གི་ཆུང་མ་ལ་འདུ་ཤེས་གསུམ་བསྐྱེད་པར་བྱ་སྟེ།
གསུམ་གང་ཞེ་ན། འཐབ་པར་འདུ་ཤེས་པ་དང་། བྱུར་དུ་འདུ་ཤེས་པ་དང་།
སེར་བར་འདུ་ཤེས་པའོ། །ཁྱིམ་བདག་གཞན་ཡང་བྱང་ཆུབ་སེམས་དཔའ་ཁྱིམ་པས་
རང་གི་ཆུང་མ་ལ་འདུ་ཤེས་གསུམ་བསྐྱེད་པར་བྱ་སྟེ། གསུམ་གང་ཞེ་ན། ནད་
དུ་འདུ་ཤེས་པ་དང་། རྒ་བར་འདུ་ཤེས་པ་དང་། འཆི་བར་འདུ་ཤེས་པའོ། །
ཁྱིམ་བདག་གཞན་ཡང་བྱང་ཆུབ་སེམས་དཔའ་ཁྱིམ་པས་རང་གི་ཆུང་མ་ལ་འདུ་ཤེས་
གསུམ་བསྐྱེད་པར་བྱ་སྟེ། གསུམ་གང་ཞེ་ན། བདུད་དུ་འདུ་ཤེས་པ་དང་།
བདུད་ལ་རྗེན་པར་འདུ་ཤེས་པ་དང་། འཇིགས་པར་འདུ་ཤེས་པའོ། །ཁྱིམ་བདག་
གཞན་ཡང་བྱང་ཆུབ་སེམས་དཔའ་ཁྱིམ་པས་རང་གི་ཆུང་མ་ལ་འདུ་ཤེས་གསུམ་བསྐྱེད་
པར་བྱ་སྟེ། གསུམ་གང་ཞེ་ན། མྱ་ངན་དུ་འདུ་ཤེས་པ་དང་། སྨྲེ་སྔགས་
འདོན་པར་འདུ་ཤེས་པ་དང་། སྡུག་བསྔལ་བ་དང་། ཡིད་མི་བདེ་བ་དང་།
འཁྲུག་པར་འདུ་ཤེས་པའོ། །ཁྱིམ་བདག་གཞན་ཡང་བྱང་ཆུབ་སེམས་དཔའ་ཁྱིམ་
པས་རང་གི་ཆུང་མ་ལ་འདུ་ཤེས་གསུམ་བསྐྱེད་པར་བྱ་སྟེ། གསུམ་གང་ཞེ་ན།
སྲུང་མོ་ཆེན་མོར་འདུ་ཤེས་པ་དང་། ཆུ་སྲིན་ཆེན་མོར་འདུ་ཤེས་པ་དང་། བྱི་ལ་
ཆེན་མོར་འདུ་ཤེས་པའོ། །ཁྱིམ་བདག་གཞན་ཡང་བྱང་ཆུབ་སེམས་དཔའ་ཁྱིམ་པས་
རང་གི་ཆུང་མ་ལ་འདུ་ཤེས་གསུམ་བསྐྱེད་པར་བྱ་སྟེ། གསུམ་གང་ཞེ་ན། སྦྲུལ་
ནག་མོར་འདུ་ཤེས་པ་དང་། ཆུ་སྲིན་བྱིས་པ་གསོད་དུ་འདུ་ཤེས་པ་དང་།
མདངས་འཕྲོག་མར་འདུ་ཤེས་པའོ། །ཁྱིམ་བདག་གཞན་ཡང་བྱང་ཆུབ་སེམས་
དཔའ་ཁྱིམ་པས་རང་གི་ཆུང་མ་ལ་འདུ་ཤེས་གསུམ་བསྐྱེད་པར་བྱ་སྟེ། གསུམ་གང་
ཞེ་ན། མགོན་མེད་པར་འདུ་ཤེས་པ་དང་། སྐྱབས་མེད་པར་འདུ་ཤེས་པ་དང་།
གནས་མེད་པར་འདུ་ཤེས་པའོ། །ཁྱིམ་བདག་གཞན་ཡང་བྱང་ཆུབ་སེམས་དཔའ་
ཁྱིམ་པས་རང་གི་ཆུང་མ་ལ་འདུ་ཤེས་གསུམ་བསྐྱེད་པར་བྱ་སྟེ། གསུམ་གང་ཞེ་ན།

གང་བར་འདུ་ཤེས་པ་དང་། བྲི་བར་འདུ་ཤེས་པ་དང་། ན་བར་འདུ་ཤེས་པའོ། །ཁྱིམ་བདག་གཞན་ཡང་བྱང་ཆུབ་སེམས་དཔའ་ཁྱིམ་པས་རང་གི་ཆུང་མ་ལ་འདུ་ཤེས་གསུམ་བསྐྱེད་པར་བྱ་སྟེ། གསུམ་གང་ཞེ་ན། ཆོམ་རྐུན་དུ་འདུ་ཤེས་པ་དང་། བཙོན་སྲུངས་སུ་འདུ་ཤེས་པ་དང་། སེམས་ཅན་དམྱལ་བའི་སྲུངས་མར་འདུ་ཤེས་པའོ། །ཁྱིམ་བདག་གཞན་ཡང་བྱང་ཆུབ་སེམས་དཔའ་ཁྱིམ་པས་རང་གི་ཆུང་མ་ལ་འདུ་ཤེས་གསུམ་བསྐྱེད་པར་བྱ་སྟེ། གསུམ་གང་ཞེ་ན། ཆུ་བོར་འདུ་ཤེས་པ་དང་། སྦྲུར་བར་འདུ་ཤེས་པ་དང་། མདུད་པར་འདུ་ཤེས་པའོ། །ཁྱིམ་བདག་གཞན་ཡང་བྱང་ཆུབ་སེམས་དཔའ་ཁྱིམ་པས་རང་གི་ཆུང་མ་ལ་འདུ་ཤེས་གསུམ་བསྐྱེད་པར་བྱ་སྟེ། གསུམ་གང་ཞེ་ན། འདམ་དུ་འདུ་ཤེས་པ་དང་། ཆགས་པར་འདུ་ཤེས་པ་དང་། གློང་དུ་འདུ་ཤེས་པའོ། །ཁྱིམ་བདག་གཞན་ཡང་བྱང་ཆུབ་སེམས་དཔའ་ཁྱིམ་པས་རང་གི་ཆུང་མ་ལ་འདུ་ཤེས་གསུམ་བསྐྱེད་པར་བྱ་སྟེ། གསུམ་གང་ཞེ་ན། ཐག་པར་འདུ་ཤེས་པ་དང་། ཁོང་སྤྲིལ་དུ་འདུ་ཤེས་པ་དང་། རློང་དུ་འདུ་ཤེས་པའོ། །ཁྱིམ་བདག་གཞན་ཡང་བྱང་ཆུབ་སེམས་དཔའ་ཁྱིམ་པས་རང་གི་ཆུང་མ་ལ་འདུ་ཤེས་གསུམ་བསྐྱེད་པར་བྱ་སྟེ། གསུམ་གང་ཞེ་ན། མེ་མ་མུར་དུ་འདུ་ཤེས་པ་དང་། ཛྭ་མེའི་སྦྲོན་མ་ལྟ་བུར་འདུ་ཤེས་པ་དང་། ཆུ་གྲི་ལྟ་བུར་འདུ་ཤེས་པའོ། །ཁྱིམ་བདག་གཞན་ཡང་བྱང་ཆུབ་སེམས་དཔའ་ཁྱིམ་པས་རང་གི་ཆུང་མ་ལ་འདུ་ཤེས་གསུམ་བསྐྱེད་པར་བྱ་སྟེ། གསུམ་གང་ཞེ་ན། དོན་མེད་པར་འདུ་ཤེས་པ་དང་། ཚེར་མར་འདུ་ཤེས་པ་དང་། དུག་ཏུ་འདུ་ཤེས་པའོ། །ཁྱིམ་བདག་གཞན་ཡང་བྱང་ཆུབ་སེམས་དཔའ་ཁྱིམ་པས་རང་གི་ཆུང་མ་ལ་འདུ་ཤེས་གསུམ་བསྐྱེད་པར་བྱ་སྟེ། གསུམ་གང་ཞེ་ན། ལྷག་པར་སྒྲོ་འདོགས་པར་འདུ་ཤེས་པ་དང་། ལྷག་པར་ཀུན་དུ་གོས་པར་བྱེད་པར་འདུ་ཤེས་པ་དང་། ལྷག་པར་ཆགས་པར་འདུ་ཤེས་པའོ། །ཁྱིམ་བདག་གཞན་ཡང་བྱང་ཆུབ་སེམས་དཔའ་ཁྱིམ་པས་རང་གི་ཆུང་མ་ལ་འདུ་ཤེས་གསུམ་བསྐྱེད་པར་བྱ་སྟེ། གསུམ་གང་ཞེ་ན། ཤར་གཅེར་བར་འདུ་ཤེས་པ་དང་། ཆད་པས་གཅོད་པར་འདུ་ཤེས་པ

དང་། མཚོན་ཆ་འཛིན་པར་འདུ་ཤེས་པའོ། །ཁྱིམ་བདག་གཞན་ཡང་བྱང་ཆུབ་སེམས་དཔའ་ཁྱིམ་པས་རང་གི་ཆུང་མ་ལ་འདུ་ཤེས་གསུམ་བསྐྱེད་པར་བྱ་སྟེ། གསུམ་གང་ཞེ་ན། འབྲིད་པར་འདུ་ཤེས་པ་དང་། རྩོད་པར་འདུ་ཤེས་པ་དང་། མཚང་འདྲུ་བར་འདུ་ཤེས་པའོ། །ཁྱིམ་བདག་གཞན་ཡང་བྱང་ཆུབ་སེམས་དཔའ་ཁྱིམ་པས་རང་གི་ཆུང་མ་ལ་འདུ་ཤེས་གསུམ་བསྐྱེད་པར་བྱ་སྟེ། གསུམ་གང་ཞེ་ན། མི་སྡུག་པ་དང་ཕྲད་པར་འདུ་ཤེས་པ་དང་། སྡུག་པ་དང་བྲལ་བར་འདུ་ཤེས་པ་དང་། ཉམ་ང་བར་འདུ་ཤེས་པའོ། །མདོར་ན་ཐབ་མོའི་དྲི་མར་འདུ་ཤེས་པ་དང་། ཐབ་མོ་རྙོག་པ་ཐམས་ཅད་དུ་འདུ་ཤེས་པ་དང་། གནོད་པ་ཐམས་ཅད་ཀྱི་རྒྱུར་གྱུར་པར་འདུ་ཤེས་པ་དང་། མི་དགེ་བ་ཐམས་ཅད་ཀྱི་རྩ་བར་འདུ་ཤེས་བསྐྱེད་པར་བྱའོ། །ཁྱིམ་བདག་བྱང་ཆུབ་སེམས་དཔའ་ཁྱིམ་པ་ཁྱིམ་ན་གནས་པས་འདི་ལྟ་བུའི་འདུ་ཤེས་ཡིད་ལ་བྱེད་པས་རང་གི་ཆུང་མ་ལ་བརྟག་པར་བྱའོ། །ཁྱིམ་བདག་གཞན་ཡང་བྱང་ཆུབ་སེམས་དཔའ་ཁྱིམ་པས་བུ་ལ་ལྷག་པར་སྡུག་པའི་སེམས་བསྐྱེད་པར་མི་བྱའོ། །ཁྱིམ་བདག་གལ་ཏེ་དེས་བུ་ལ་ལྷག་པར་སྡུག་པའི་སེམས་བསྐྱེད་ལ་དེ་བཞིན་དུ་སེམས་ཅན་གཞན་ལ་མ་ཡིན་ན་དེས་སྤྱོ་བ་གསུམ་གྱིས་རང་གི་སེམས་ལ་སྤྱོ་བར་བྱ་སྟེ། གསུམ་གང་ཞེ་ན། བྱང་ཆུབ་ནི་སེམས་སྙོམས་པའི་བྱང་ཆུབ་སེམས་དཔའི་ཡིན་གྱི། སེམས་མི་སྙོམས་པའི་མ་ཡིན་ནོ། །བྱང་ཆུབ་ནི་ཡང་དག་པར་སྦྱོར་བའི་བྱང་ཆུབ་སེམས་དཔའི་ཡིན་གྱི། ལོག་པའི་སྦྱོར་བའི་ནི་མ་ཡིན་ནོ། །བྱང་ཆུབ་ནི་ཐ་དད་པ་མེད་པར་སྤྱོད་པའི་བྱང་ཆུབ་སེམས་དཔའི་ཡིན་གྱི། ཐ་དད་དུ་སྤྱོད་པའི་ནི་མ་ཡིན་པ་སྟེ། སྤྱོ་བ་གསུམ་པོ་དེ་དག་གིས་རང་གི་སེམས་ལ་སྤྱོས་ནས་བུ་དེ་ལ་མི་སྡུག་པའི་འདུ་ཤེས་བསྐྱེད་པར་བྱའོ། །འདི་ནི་མི་སྡུག་པ་སྟེ། བདག་གི་སྙིང་དུ་སྡུག་པ་མ་ཡིན་ན། གང་བདག་གིས་དེའི་དོན་དུ་བུ་དེ་ལ་ནི་ལྷག་པར་སྡུག་པ་སྐྱེད་ལ། སེམས་ཅན་གཞན་ལ་ནི་དེ་ལྟ་མ་ཡིན་ན། སངས་རྒྱས་ཀྱིས་བཀའ་སྩལ་པའི་བསླབ་པ་དང་འགལ་བར་འགྱུར་རོ། །བདག་གིས་དེའི་ཕྱིར་དགེ་བའི་རྩ་བ་ལ་ཡང་གནོད་པར་བྱས། སྒྲོག་ལ་ཡང་བག་མེད་དེ་གནོད་པར་གྱུར་པས་འདི་ནི་བདག་ལ་གནོད་པ་

བྱེད་པའོ། །བདག་དེའི་ཕྱིར་བྱང་ཆུབ་ཀྱི་ལམ་དང་མི་འཐུན་པའི་ལམ་ལ་སྤྱོད་པས་
འདི་ནི་བདག་ལ་ཕྱིར་རྒོལ་བའོ་སྙམ་དུ་འདུ་ཤེས་གསུམ་པོ་དེ་དག་བསྐྱེད་པར་
བྱའོ། །དེས་བུ་དེ་རྒྱུར་བྱས་ཏེ། ཇི་ལྟ་ཇི་ལྟ་བུར་བུ་དེ་ལ་སྡུག་པར་སེམས་པ་དང་
ལྡན་པ་བཞིན་དུ་སེམས་ཅན་ཐམས་ཅད་ལ་བྱམས་པ་བསྐྱེད་པ་དང་། བདག་ཕངས་
པར་སེམས་པ་དང་ལྡན་པ་བཞིན་དུ་བྱམས་པ་བསྐྱེད་པ་དེ་ལྟ་དེ་ལྟ་བུར་དེས་
སེམས་བསྐྱེད་པར་བྱའོ། །དེས་ཡང་འདི་ལྟར་འདི་ཡང་གུད་ནས་འོངས་ལ་བདག་
ཀྱང་གུད་ནས་འོངས་མོད་ཀྱི། སེམས་ཅན་ཐམས་ཅད་ཀྱང་སྔོན་བདག་གི་བུར་གྱུར་
ལ་བདག་ཀྱང་སེམས་ཅན་ཐམས་ཅད་ཀྱི་བུར་གྱུར་ཏེ། འདི་ལ་ནི་བདག་གིའམ།
གཞན་གྱིའམ། སུའི་སེམས་ཅན་གང་ཡང་མེད་དོ་སྙམ་དུ་ཚུལ་བཞིན་བརྟག་པར་
བྱའོ། །དེ་ཅིའི་ཕྱིར་ཞེ་ན། མི་འཐུན་པའི་ཕྱིར་ཏེ། འགྲོ་བ་ལྔ་རྣམས་སུ་མཐོང་
བ་ལས་ཀྱང་མི་མཐོང་བར་འགྱུར་བས་བདག་ནི་ཇི་ལྟར་སུ་དང་ཡང་མཐོང་བ་འམ་མི་
མཐོང་བར་མི་འགྱུར་བ་དེ་ལྟར་བྱའོ། །དེ་ཅིའི་ཕྱིར་ཞེ་ན། མི་མཐོང་བ་བཟུང་ན་
ནི་ཐམས་ཅད་ཀྱི་ཐམས་ཅད་དུ་བྱེད་མི་འདོད་པར་འགྱུར། མཐོང་བ་བཟུང་ན་ནི་ཧ་
ཅང་བྱེད་འདོད་པར་འགྱུར་ཏེ། རྗེས་སུ་ཆགས་པ་དང་། ཁོང་ཁྲོ་བའི་སེམས་
གཉིས་ཀྱིས་ནི་ཆོས་མཉམ་པ་ཉིད་ཁོང་དུ་ཆུད་པར་བྱེད་མི་ནུས་སོ། །དེ་ཅིའི་ཕྱིར་ཞེ་
ན། མི་མཉམ་པར་སྤྱོད་པ་ནི་མི་མཉམ་པར་འགྲོ་བར་འགྱུར། མཉམ་པར་སྤྱོད་
པ་ནི་མཉམ་པར་འགྱུར་བའོ། །དེ་ལ་བདག་གིས་ནི་མི་མཉམ་པར་སྤྱོད་པ་མི་བྱའི་
སེམས་ཅན་ཐམས་ཅད་ལ་མཉམ་པར་སྤྱོད་ན་ཐམས་ཅད་མཁྱེན་པ་ཉིད་ཁོང་དུ་ཆུད་པར་
འགྱུར་རོ། །ཁྱིམ་བདག་དེ་ལྟར་བྱང་ཆུབ་སེམས་དཔའ་ཁྱིམ་པས་དངོས་པོ་གང་ལ་
ཡང་བདག་གི་སྙམ་དུ་ཡོངས་སུ་བཟུང་བར་མི་བྱ། ཆགས་པར་མི་བྱའོ། །གཡོ་
དང་སྲེད་པའི་བག་ལ་ཉལ་མི་བྱའོ། །ཁྱིམ་བདག་གལ་ཏེ་བྱང་ཆུབ་སེམས་དཔའ་
ཁྱིམ་པའི་དྲུང་དུ་སློང་མོ་པ་འོངས་ལ་དངོས་པོ་ཞིག་བསླངས་པ་ལས་གལ་ཏེ་དེས་
དངོས་པོ་མ་བཏང་ན་དེས་འདི་ལྟར་དངོས་པོ་འདི་བཏང་ཡང་རུང་། མ་བཏང་ཡང་
རུང་སྟེ། བདག་ནི་དངོས་པོ་འདི་དང་གདོན་མི་ཟ་བར་འབྲལ་བར་ཡང་འགྱུར།

མི་འདོད་བཞིན་དུ་འཆི་བར་ཡང་འགྱུར་ཞིང་དངོས་པོ་འདིས་ཀྱང་བདག་འདོར།
བདག་གིས་ཀྱང་དངོས་པོ་འདི་འདོར་གྱི། དངོས་པོ་འདི་བཏང་ལ་ཡིད་དགའ་བ་
དང་། སྙིང་པོ་བླངས་ཏེ་འཆི་བའི་དུས་བྱའོ། །འདི་ཡོངས་སུ་བཏང་ན་བདག་
འཆི་བའི་དུས་ཀྱི་ཚེ་སེམས་ཀུན་ནས་ཟིན་ཏེ་གནས་པར་མི་འགྱུར། འདིས་ནི་བདག་
འཆི་བའི་དུས་ཀྱི་ཚེ་དགའ་བ་དང་། མཆོག་ཏུ་དགའ་བ་དང་རངས་པ་དང་།
འགྱོད་པ་མེད་པ་སྐྱེ་བར་འགྱུར་སྙམ་དུ་སེམས་ངེས་པར་བསམ་པར་བྱའོ། །གལ་ཏེ་
དེ་ལྟར་བསམས་ཀྱང་དངོས་པོ་དེ་གཏོང་མ་ནུས་ན། དེས་སྙིང་བ་ལ་ཀུན་གོ་བར་བྱ་
བ་གསུམ་གྱིས་གོ་བར་བྱ་སྟེ། བདག་ནི་ད་དུང་དུ་མཐུ་ཆུང་ཞིང་དགེ་བའི་རྩ་བ་
ཡོངས་སུ་མ་སྨིན་ཏེ། ཐེག་པ་ཆེན་པོ་ལ་ལས་དང་པོ་པ་དང་། བདག་ནི་མི་
གཏོང་བ་ལ་སེམས་ཀྱི་དབང་དུ་གྱུར་པ་དང་། བདག་ནི་ཉེ་བར་ལེན་པའི་ལྟ་བ་དང་
བཅས་པ་དང་། བདག་ཏུ་འཛིན་པ་དང་། བདག་གིར་འཛིན་པ་ལ་གནས་པ་
ལགས་ཀྱིས། སྐྱེས་བུ་དམ་པ་བཟོད་པར་མཛོད་ཅིང་ཡོངས་སུ་གདུང་བར་མི་མཛད་
དུ་གསོལ། །ཇི་ལྟར་ཁྱོད་དང་སེམས་ཅན་ཐམས་ཅད་ཀྱི་བསམ་པ་ཡོངས་སུ་རྫོགས་
པར་འགྱུར་བ་དེ་ལྟར་བདག་གིས་བགྱིའོ། །དེ་ལྟར་བསྒྲུབ་པོ། །དེ་ལྟར་བརྩོན་
འགྲུས་བརྩམ་མོ་ཞེས་ཁྲིམ་བདག་དེ་ལྟར་བྱང་ཆུབ་སེམས་དཔའ་ཁྲིམ་པས་སྙིང་བ་ལ་
ཀུན་གོ་བར་བྱ་བ་གསུམ་གྱིས་གོ་བར་བྱའོ། །ཁྲིམ་བདག་གཞན་ཡང་བྱང་ཆུབ་
སེམས་དཔའ་ཁྲིམ་པ་ཁྲིམ་ན་གནས་པས་རྟག་ཏུ་རྒྱུན་མི་འཆད་པར་ཡོངས་སུ་བསྔོ་བ་
ལ་མཁས་པར་བྱ་སྟེ། གལ་ཏེ་དེ་སྟོན་པ་འདས་པའི་གསུང་རབ་ཡོད་ལ་སངས་
རྒྱས་འབྱུང་བ་ཡང་མེད། ཆོས་སྟོན་པ་ཡང་མེད། འཕགས་པའི་དགེ་འདུན་དང་
ཕྲད་པ་ཡང་མེད་པར་གྱུར་ན། དེས་ཕྱོགས་བཅུའི་སངས་རྒྱས་ཐམས་ཅད་ལ་ཕྱག་
བྱས་ཏེ། གང་དེ་དག་གི་སྔོན་གྱི་སྤྱོད་པ་དང་མཚུངས་པར་སྤྱོད་པ་དང་། དགེ་བ་
སྤྱོད་པ་དང་། བསམ་པ་དང་། ལྷག་པའི་བསམ་པ་ཕུན་སུམ་ཚོགས་པ་དང་།
བྱང་ཆུབ་ཐོབ་པ་རྣམས་ཀྱི་སངས་རྒྱས་ཀྱི་ཆོས་ཐམས་ཅད་ཡོངས་སུ་གྲུབ་པ་དེ་དེས་
རྗེས་སུ་དྲན་པར་བྱ། རྗེས་སུ་ཡི་རང་བར་བྱའོ། །དེས་ཡང་འདི་ལྟར་ཉིན་ལན་

གསུམ་མཚན་ལན་གསུམ་དུ་ལུས་ཀྱི་ལས་ཡོངས་སུ་དག་པ་དང་། ངག་གི་ལས་ཡོངས་སུ་དག་པ་དང་། ཡིད་ཀྱི་ལས་ཡོངས་སུ་དག་པ་དང་། གཙང་བ་དང་། བསམ་པ་དག་པ་དང་། བྱམས་པ་བསྒོམ་པ་ལ་མཁས་པ་དང་། གོས་གཙང་མ་དང་། ངོ་ཚ་ཤེས་ཤིང་ཁྲེལ་ཡོད་པས་ལེགས་པར་བརྒྱན་པ་དང་། བསོད་ནམས་ཀྱི་ཚོགས་དགེ་བའི་རྩ་བ་བསགས་པ་དང་། མཛེས་པ་དང་། བྱང་ཆུབ་ཀྱི་སེམས་ལ་རབ་ཏུ་དགའ་བ་དང་། ངེས་པ་དང་། འགྲོགས་ན་བདེ་བ་དང་། ལེགས་པར་བྱ་བའི་ལས་བྱེད་པ་དང་། གུས་པ་དང་བཅས་པ་དང་། བཀའ་བློ་བདེ་བ་དང་། ང་རྒྱལ་དང་། རྒྱགས་པ་དང་། དྲེགས་པ་ཡང་དག་པར་ཆད་པས་མི་དགེ་བའི་ལས་ཀྱི་ཉེས་པ་ཐམས་ཅད་བཤགས་པ་དང་། ཕྱིན་ཆད་ཀྱང་བསྡམ་པ་དང་། བསོད་ནམས་ཐམས་ཅད་ཀྱི་རྗེས་སུ་ཡི་རང་བ་དང་། མཚན་བསགས་པ་རབ་ཏུ་རྫོགས་པར་བྱ་བ་དང་། སངས་རྒྱས་ཐམས་ཅད་ལ་ཆོས་ཀྱི་འཁོར་ལོ་རབ་ཏུ་བསྐོར་བར་གསོལ་བ་གདབ་པ་དང་། ཆོས་ཐམས་ཅད་གཟུང་བ་དང་། སངས་རྒྱས་ཀྱི་ཞིང་དཔག་ཏུ་མེད་པ་རྣམས་སུ་ཚེ་ཡོངས་སུ་བསྲུང་བའི་ཕྱིར་ཕུང་པོ་གསུམ་པའི་ཆོས་ཀྱི་རྣམ་གྲངས་ཁ་ཏོན་དུ་བྱའོ། །ཁྱིམ་བདག་གཞན་ཡང་བྱང་ཆུབ་སེམས་དཔའ་ཁྱིམ་པ་ཁྱིམ་ན་གནས་པས་ཡན་ལག་བརྒྱད་དང་ལྡན་པའི་བསྙེན་པར་གནས་པ་བླང་བར་བྱའོ། །དེས་དགེ་སྦྱོང་དང་བྲམ་ཟེ་ཚུལ་ཁྲིམས་དང་ལྡན་པ། ཡོན་ཏན་དང་ལྡན་པ། དགེ་བའི་ཆོས་དང་ལྡན་པ་རྣམས་ལ་བསྙེན་པར་བྱ། བསྟེན་པར་བྱ། བསྙེན་བཀུར་བྱའོ། །དེ་དག་ལ་བསྙེན་ཅིང་བསྟེན་ཏེ། བསྙེན་བཀུར་བྱེད་ཅིང་། སྤྱོད་པ་འཁྲུལ་པ་མེད་པར་རང་གི་ཉེས་པ་མཐོང་བར་བྱའོ། །དེས་དགེ་སྦྱོང་གི་སྤྱོད་པ་ལས་ཉམས་པའི་དགེ་སློང་མཐོང་ན་ཡང་མི་གུས་པའི་བག་ཙུང་ཟད་ཀྱང་མི་བྱ་སྟེ། འདི་ལྟར་བཅོམ་ལྡན་འདས་དེ་བཞིན་གཤེགས་པ་དགྲ་བཅོམ་པ་ཡང་དག་པར་རྫོགས་པའི་སངས་རྒྱས་རྟོག་པ་མེད་པ། ཉོན་མོངས་པའི་རྟོག་པ་ཐམས་ཅད་དང་བྲལ་བ་དེའི་དུར་སྨྲིག་ནི་ཚུལ་ཁྲིམས་ཀྱིས་ཡོངས་སུ་བསྒོས་པ། ཏིང་ངེ་འཛིན་དང་། ཤེས་རབ་དང་། རྣམ་པར་གྲོལ་བ་དང་།

རྣམ་པར་གྲོལ་བའི་ས་མཐོང་བས་ཡོངས་སུ་བསྔོས་པ་འདི་དག་ཡིན་ཏེ། འདི་ནི་འཕགས་པ་རྣམས་ཀྱི་དྲང་སྲོང་གི་རྒྱལ་མཚན་ཡིན་ནོ་སྙམ་དུ་སེམས་བསྐྱེད་པར་བྱའོ། །དེས་དེ་དག་ལ་རབ་ཏུ་གུས་པ་བསྐྱེད་ནས་དགེ་སློང་དེ་ལ་སྙིང་རྗེ་ཆེན་པོ་བསྐྱེད་པར་བྱའོ། །སྡིག་པའི་སྤྱོད་པ་འདི་ནི་མ་ལེགས་སོ། །ཀུན་ནས་ཉོན་མོངས་པའི་སྤྱོད་པ་འདི་ནི་མ་ལེགས་སོ། །འདི་ལྟར་བཅོམ་ལྡན་འདས་དེ་བཞིན་གཤེགས་པ་དགྲ་བཅོམ་པ་ཡང་དག་པར་རྫོགས་པའི་སངས་རྒྱས་དུལ་བ། ཞི་བ། སྲུས་པ། ཅང་ཤེས་པ་དེའི་དྲང་སྲོང་གི་རྒྱལ་མཚན་བགོས་ཀྱང་འདི་ནི་མ་བྱུང་། མ་ཞི། མ་སྲུས། མ་དུལ་བ་སྟེ། ཅང་ཤེས་པ་མ་ཡིན་པའི་སྤྱོད་པ་སྤྱོད་དོ། །བཅོམ་ལྡན་འདས་དེས་མ་བསླབས་པ་ལ་མ་བཀླས་ཤིག་ཅེས་གསུངས་པས་ན་འདིས་ཉེས་པ་མ་ཡིན། ཉོན་མོངས་པ་གང་གིས་མི་དགེ་བ་འདི་དག་སྐྱོན་པའི་ཉོན་མོངས་པས་ཉེས་པའོ། །སངས་རྒྱས་བཅོམ་ལྡན་འདས་རྣམས་ཀྱི་བསྟན་པ་ནི་འབྱུང་བ་དང་བཅས་པ་ཡིན་པས་གང་ཉོན་མོངས་པ་འདི་དག་ཁོང་དུ་ཆུད་ནས་ཚུལ་བཞིན་སོ་སོར་རྟོག་ན་དང་པོའི་འབྲས་བུ་ཐོབ་པར་འགྱུར་ཏེ། དེ་བླ་ན་མེད་པ་ཡང་དག་པར་རྫོགས་པའི་བྱང་ཆུབ་ཏུ་ངེས་པར་འགྱུར་བའི་གནས་ཡོད་དོ། །དེ་ཅིའི་ཕྱིར་ཞེ་ན། འདི་ལྟར་ཉོན་མོངས་པ་རྣམས་ནི་ཡེ་ཤེས་ཀྱིས་གསལ་བར་བྱ་བ་ཡིན་པས་ན་བཅོམ་ལྡན་འདས་ཀྱིས་ཀྱང་གང་ཟག་གིས་གང་ཟག་ལ་ཚོད་གཟུང་བར་མི་བྱ་སྟེ། གང་ཟག་གིས་གང་ཟག་ལ་ཚོད་བཟུང་ན་ཉམས་པར་འགྱུར་རོ་ཞེས་གསུངས་པས་དེ་བཞིན་གཤེགས་པ་ནི་རབ་ཏུ་མཁྱེན་པ། བདག་ནི་རབ་ཏུ་ཤེས་པ་མ་ཡིན་ནོ་སྙམ་ནས་དེས་དགེ་སློང་དེ་ལ་གནོད་སེམས་མེད་པ་དང་། ཞེ་སྡང་མེད་པ་དང་། ཁོང་ཁྲོ་བ་མེད་པ་དང་། ཁྲོ་བ་མེད་པ་ཡང་བསྐྱེད་པར་བྱའོ། །ཁྱིམ་བདག་གཞན་ཡང་བྱང་ཆུབ་སེམས་དཔའ་ཁྱིམ་པ་དེ་གཙུག་ལག་ཁང་དུ་འཇུག་པར་འདོད་ན་ཅང་ཤེས་ཀྱི་སེམས་དང་། ལས་སུ་རུང་བའི་སེམས་དང་། གུས་པ་དང་བཅས་པ་དང་། ཞེ་ས་དང་བཅས་པ་དང་། དད་པ་དང་བཅས་པ་དང་། རི་མོ་དང་བཅས་པས་གཙུག་ལག་ཁང་གི་སྒོར་འདུག་སྟེ། གཙུག་ལག་ཁང་ལ་ཡན་ལག་ལྔས་ཕྱག་བྱས་

ལ།  དེ་ནས་གདོད་བདག་གཙུག་ལག་ཁང་གི་ནང་དུ་འགྲོ་བར་བྱའོ།  །དེས་ཡང་འདི་ལྟར་བརྟག་པར་བྱ་སྟེ།  འདི་ནི་སྟོང་པ་ཉིད་ལ་གནས་པའི་གནས་སོ།  །མཚན་མ་མེད་པ་ལ་གནས་པ་དང་།  སྨོན་པ་མེད་པ་ལ་གནས་པ་དང་།  བྱམས་པ་དང་།  སྙིང་རྗེ་དང་།  དགའ་བ་དང་།  བཏང་སྙོམས་ལ་གནས་པའི་གནས་སོ།  །འདི་ནི་བསམ་གཏན་པ་རྣམས་ཀྱི་གནས་ཏེ།  གནས་ཐམས་ཅད་ཡང་དག་པར་ཆད་པ་རྣམས་ཀྱི་གནས་སོ།  །འདི་ནི་ཡང་དག་པར་སོང་བ་རྣམས་དང་། ཡང་དག་པར་ཞུགས་པ་རྣམས་ཀྱི་གནས་སོ།  །བདག་ཀྱང་རྟུལ་གྱི་གནས། ཁྲིམ་གྱི་གནས་ནས་མངོན་པར་བྱུང་སྟེ།  ནམ་ཞིག་ན་འདི་ལྟ་བུ་སྤྱོད་པར་འགྱུར། བདག་ཀྱང་ནམ་ཞིག་ན་གང་དགེ་འདུན་གྱི་ལས་དང་།  གསོ་སྦྱོང་གི་ལས་དང་། དགག་དབྱེའི་ལས་དང་།  འདུད་པའི་ལས་དེ་ལ་གནས་པར་འགྱུར་སྙམ་ནས་དེས་འདི་ལྟར་རབ་ཏུ་འབྱུང་བའི་སེམས་ལ་དགའ་བར་བྱའོ།  །བྱང་ཆུབ་སེམས་དཔའ་ཁྲིམ་ན་གནས་ཏེ་བླ་ན་མེད་པ་ཡང་དག་པར་རྫོགས་པའི་བྱང་ཆུབ་མངོན་པར་རྫོགས་པར་སངས་རྒྱས་པ་ནི་གང་ཡང་མེད་དེ།  དེ་དག་ཐམས་ཅད་ཀྱང་ཁྲིམ་གྱི་གནས་ནས་མངོན་པར་བྱུང་ནས་དགོན་པ་ལ་སེམས།  དགོན་པ་ལ་གཞོལ།  དགོན་པར་སོང་ནས་བླ་ན་མེད་པ་ཡང་དག་པར་རྫོགས་པའི་བྱང་ཆུབ་མངོན་པར་རྫོགས་པར་སངས་རྒྱས་སོ།  །ཚིགས་དེ་ཡང་ཡང་དག་པར་བསྒྲུབས་སོ།  །ཁྲིམ་ན་གནས་པ་ནི་ཀུན་དུ་གནོད་པ་སྡེ་རྟག་འབབ་པའོ།  །རབ་ཏུ་བྱུང་བ་ནི་སངས་རྒྱས་དང་། དེའི་ཉན་ཐོས་རྣམས་ཀྱིས་བསྔགས་པའོ།  །ཁྲིམ་ན་གནས་པ་ནི་ཉེས་པའི་སྐྱོན་ཆགས་པ་མང་བའོ།  །རབ་ཏུ་བྱུང་བ་ནི་ཡོན་ཏན་ཕུན་སུམ་ཚོགས་པ་མང་བའོ།  །ཁྲིམ་ན་གནས་པ་ནི་ཉམ་ང་བའོ།  །རབ་ཏུ་བྱུང་བ་ནི་བག་ཡངས་པའོ།  །ཁྲིམ་ན་གནས་པ་ནི་ཡོངས་སུ་འཛིན་པའི་དྲི་མ་ཅན་ནོ།  །རབ་ཏུ་བྱུང་བ་ནི་ཡོངས་སུ་འཛིན་པ་ལས་རྣམ་པར་གྲོལ་བའོ།  །ཁྲིམ་ན་གནས་པ་ནི་ཉེས་པར་སྤྱོད་པའི་གཞིའོ།  །རབ་ཏུ་བྱུང་བ་ནི་ལེགས་པར་སྤྱོད་པའི་གཞིའོ།  །ཁྲིམ་ན་གནས་པ་ནི་རྟུལ་གྱི་ནང་ན་གནས་པའོ།  །རབ་ཏུ་བྱུང་བ་ནི་རྟུལ་གྱི་ནང་ན་མི་གནས་

པའོ། །ཁྱིམ་ན་གནས་པ་ནི་འདོད་པའི་འདམ་དུ་བྱིང་བའོ། །རབ་ཏུ་བྱུང་བ་ནི་འདོད་པའི་འདམ་ནས་འབྱིན་པའོ། །ཁྱིམ་ན་གནས་པ་ནི་བྱིས་པའི་སྐྱེ་བོའི་ལུགས་པའོ། །རབ་ཏུ་བྱུང་བ་ནི་སྐྱེ་བོ་མཁས་པའི་ལུགས་པའོ། །ཁྱིམ་ན་གནས་པ་ནི་འཚོ་བ་སྒྲུབ་པར་དཀའ་བའོ། །རབ་ཏུ་བྱུང་བ་ནི་འཚོ་བ་སྒྲུབ་པར་སླ་བའོ། །ཁྱིམ་ན་གནས་པ་ནི་འགྲན་ཟླ་མང་བའོ། །རབ་ཏུ་བྱུང་བ་ནི་འགྲན་ཟླ་མེད་པའོ། །ཁྱིམ་ན་གནས་པ་ནི་ཕོངས་པ་མང་བའོ། །རབ་ཏུ་བྱུང་བ་ནི་ཕོངས་པ་མེད་པའོ། །ཁྱིམ་ན་གནས་པ་ནི་མྱ་ངན་གྱི་གནས་སོ། །རབ་ཏུ་བྱུང་བ་ནི་དགའ་བའོ། །ཁྱིམ་ན་གནས་པ་ནི་ངན་སོང་གི་ཐེམ་སྐས་སོ། །རབ་ཏུ་བྱུང་བ་ནི་མངོན་པར་མཐོ་བའི་ཐེམ་སྐས་སོ། །ཁྱིམ་ན་གནས་པ་ནི་བཅིངས་པའོ། །རབ་ཏུ་བྱུང་བ་ནི་ཐར་པའོ། །ཁྱིམ་ན་གནས་པ་ནི་འཇིགས་པ་དང་བཅས་པའོ། །རབ་ཏུ་བྱུང་བ་ནི་འཇིགས་པ་མེད་པའོ། །ཁྱིམ་ན་གནས་པ་ནི་ཆད་པ་དང་བཅས་པར་སྤྱོད་པའོ། །རབ་ཏུ་བྱུང་བ་ནི་ཆད་པ་མེད་པར་སྤྱོད་པའོ། །ཁྱིམ་ན་གནས་པ་ནི་མཚོན་ཆ་སྤྱོད་པ་དང་བཅས་པའོ། །རབ་ཏུ་བྱུང་བ་ནི་མཚོན་ཆ་མི་སྤྱོད་པའོ། །ཁྱིམ་ན་གནས་པ་ནི་ཡོངས་སུ་གདུང་བ་དང་བཅས་པའོ། །རབ་ཏུ་བྱུང་བ་ནི་ཡོངས་སུ་གདུང་བ་མེད་པའོ། །ཁྱིམ་ན་གནས་པ་ནི་ཀུན་དུ་ཚོལ་བས་སྡུག་བསྔལ་བའོ། །རབ་ཏུ་བྱུང་བ་ནི་ཀུན་དུ་ཚོལ་བ་མེད་པས་བདེ་བའོ། །ཁྱིམ་ན་གནས་པ་ནི་རྒོད་པའོ། །རབ་ཏུ་བྱུང་བ་ནི་ཉེ་བར་ཞི་བའོ། །ཁྱིམ་ན་གནས་པ་ནི་འཇུངས་པའོ། །རབ་ཏུ་བྱུང་བ་ནི་མ་འཇུངས་པའོ། །ཁྱིམ་ན་གནས་པ་ནི་ཞན་པའོ། །རབ་ཏུ་བྱུང་བ་ནི་མི་ཞན་པའོ། །ཁྱིམ་ན་གནས་པ་ནི་མ་རབས་སོ། །རབ་ཏུ་བྱུང་བ་ནི་ཡ་རབས་སོ། །ཁྱིམ་ན་གནས་པ་ནི་ཀུན་དུ་འབར་བའོ། །རབ་ཏུ་བྱུང་བ་ནི་འབར་བ་ཞི་བའོ། །ཁྱིམ་ན་གནས་པ་ནི་གཞན་གྱི་དོན་ཏོ། །རབ་ཏུ་བྱུང་བ་ནི་གཉི་གའི་དོན་ཏོ། །ཁྱིམ་ན་གནས་པ་ནི་དོན་ཆུང་བའོ། །རབ་ཏུ་བྱུང་བ་ནི་དོན་ཆེ་བའོ། །ཁྱིམ་ན་གནས་པ་ནི་གཟི་ཆུང་བའོ། །རབ་ཏུ་བྱུང་བ་ནི་གཟི་ཆེ་བའོ། །ཁྱིམ་ན་གནས་པ་ནི་ཀུན་ནས་ཉོན་མོངས་པས་སྡུག་བསྔལ་བའོ། །རབ་ཏུ་བྱུང་བ་ནི་མངོན་པར་བྱུང་བས་བདེ་

བའོ། །ཁྲིམས་ན་གནས་པ་ནི་ཚོར་མ་སྐྱེད་པའོ། །རབ་ཏུ་བྱུང་བ་ནི་ཚོར་མ་བསལ་བའོ། །ཁྲིམས་ན་གནས་པ་ནི་ཆོས་ཆུང་ངུ་དང་ལྡན་པའོ། །རབ་ཏུ་བྱུང་བ་ནི་ཆོས་ཆེན་པོ་དང་ལྡན་པའོ། །ཁྲིམས་ན་གནས་པ་ནི་འདུལ་བ་མ་ཡིན་པ་བྱེད་པའོ། །རབ་ཏུ་བྱུང་བ་ནི་འདུལ་བ་བྱེད་པའོ། །ཁྲིམས་ན་གནས་པ་ནི་འགྲོད་པའོ། །རབ་ཏུ་བྱུང་བ་ནི་མི་འགྲོད་པའོ། །ཁྲིམས་ན་གནས་པ་ནི་མཆི་མ་དང་ནུ་ཞོ་དང་ཁྲག་གི་རྒྱ་མཚོ་འཕེལ་བའོ། །རབ་ཏུ་བྱུང་བ་ནི་མཆི་མ་དང་ནུ་ཞོ་དང་ཁྲག་གི་རྒྱ་མཚོ་སྐེམས་པའོ། །ཁྲིམས་ན་གནས་པ་ནི་སངས་རྒྱས་དང་། རང་སངས་རྒྱས་དང་། ཉན་ཐོས་ཀྱིས་སྨད་པའོ། །རབ་ཏུ་བྱུང་བ་ནི་སངས་རྒྱས་དང་། རང་སངས་རྒྱས་དང་། ཉན་ཐོས་ཀྱིས་བསྔགས་པའོ། །ཁྲིམས་ན་གནས་པ་ནི་ཆོག་མི་ཤེས་པའོ། །རབ་ཏུ་བྱུང་བ་ནི་ཆོག་ཤེས་པའོ། །ཁྲིམས་ན་གནས་པ་ནི་བདུད་དགའ་བའོ། །རབ་ཏུ་བྱུང་བ་ནི་བདུད་མྱ་ངན་བྱེད་པའོ། །ཁྲིམས་ན་གནས་པ་ནི་སྡིག་པ་ཆེན་པོའི་མཐར་ཐུག་པར་འགྱུར་རོ། །རབ་ཏུ་བྱུང་བ་ནི་སྡིག་པ་ཐམས་ཅད་ཉེ་བར་ཞི་བའི་མཐར་ཐུག་པའོ། །ཁྲིམས་ན་གནས་པ་ནི་ཀུན་དུ་མི་ཐུལ་བའོ། །རབ་ཏུ་བྱུང་བ་ནི་ཀུན་དུ་ཐུལ་བའོ། །ཁྲིམས་ན་གནས་པ་ནི་བྲན་གྱི་ལས་བྱེད་པའོ། །རབ་ཏུ་བྱུང་བ་ནི་རྗེ་བོ་བྱེད་པའོ། །ཁྲིམས་ན་གནས་པ་ནི་འཁོར་བའི་མཐར་འགྱུར་བའོ། །རབ་ཏུ་བྱུང་བ་ནི་མྱ་ངན་ལས་འདས་པའི་མཐར་འགྱུར་བའོ། །ཁྲིམས་ན་གནས་པ་ནི་གཡང་ས་པའོ། །རབ་ཏུ་བྱུང་བ་ནི་གཡང་ས་ལས་འདས་པའོ། །ཁྲིམས་ན་གནས་པ་ནི་མུན་ནག་གོ །རབ་ཏུ་བྱུང་བ་ནི་སྣང་བའོ། །ཁྲིམས་ན་གནས་པ་ནི་དབང་པོ་ལ་དབང་མི་བྱེད་པའོ། །རབ་ཏུ་བྱུང་བ་ནི་དབང་པོ་ལ་དབང་བྱེད་པའོ། །ཁྲིམས་ན་གནས་པ་ནི་དྲེགས་པ་སྐྱེད་པའོ། །རབ་ཏུ་བྱུང་བ་ནི་དྲེགས་པ་འདུལ་བའོ། །ཁྲིམས་ན་གནས་པ་ནི་དམ་པ་མ་ཡིན་པ་སྐྱེད་པའོ། །རབ་ཏུ་བྱུང་བ་ནི་དམ་པ་སྐྱེད་པའོ། །ཁྲིམས་ན་གནས་པ་ནི་ངན་སོང་སྐྱེད་པའོ། །རབ་ཏུ་བྱུང་བ་ནི་བདེ་འགྲོ་སྐྱེད་པའོ། །ཁྲིམས་ན་གནས་པ་ནི་བལྟ་བར་མི་འོས་པའོ། །རབ་ཏུ་བྱུང་བ་ནི་བལྟ་བར་འོས་པའོ། །ཁྲིམས་ན་གནས་པ་ནི་རྩོམ་པ་ཆེན་པོའོ། །རབ་ཏུ་བྱུང་བ་ནི་རྩོམ་པ་

ཆུང་བའོ། །ཁྲིམས་ན་གནས་པ་ནི་འབྲས་བུ་ཆུང་བའོ། །རབ་ཏུ་བྱུང་བ་ནི་འབྲས་
བུ་ཆེ་བའོ། །ཁྲིམས་ན་གནས་པ་ནི་གྲུ་གྲུ་ཅན་ནོ། །རབ་ཏུ་བྱུང་བ་ནི་དྲང་
བའོ། །ཁྲིམས་ན་གནས་པ་ནི་ཡིད་མི་བདེ་བ་མང་བའོ། །རབ་ཏུ་བྱུང་བ་ནི་ཡིད་
བདེ་བ་དང་ལྡན་པའོ། །ཁྲིམས་ན་གནས་པ་ནི་ཟུག་རྔུ་དང་བཅས་པའོ། །རབ་ཏུ་
བྱུང་བ་ནི་ཟུག་རྔུ་ཕྱུང་བའོ། །ཁྲིམས་ན་གནས་པ་ནི་ན་བའོ། །རབ་ཏུ་བྱུང་བ་ནི་ནད་
མེད་པར་བྱེད་པའོ། །ཁྲིམས་ན་གནས་པ་ནི་ཆོས་རྒྱས་པར་བྱེད་པའོ། །རབ་ཏུ་བྱུང་
བ་ནི་ཆོས་དར་བར་བྱེད་པའོ། །ཁྲིམས་ན་གནས་པ་ནི་བག་མེད་པར་བྱེད་པའོ། །
རབ་ཏུ་བྱུང་བ་ནི་བག་ཡོད་པར་བྱེད་པའོ། །ཁྲིམས་ན་གནས་པ་ནི་འཆལ་པའི་ཤེས་
རབ་ཀྱི་འབྱུང་གནས་སོ། །རབ་ཏུ་བྱུང་བ་ནི་ཤེས་རབ་འཕེལ་བའོ། །ཁྲིམས་ན་
གནས་པ་ནི་ཤེས་རབ་ཀྱི་བར་ཆད་བྱེད་པའོ། །རབ་ཏུ་བྱུང་བ་ནི་ཤེས་རབ་ཀྱི་སྒྲོག་
བྱེད་པའོ། །ཁྲིམས་ན་གནས་པ་ནི་སླུ་བར་སོ་སོར་ཉེ་བར་གནས་པའོ། །རབ་ཏུ་
བྱུང་བ་ནི་མི་སླུ་བར་སོ་སོར་ཉེ་བར་གནས་པའོ། །ཁྲིམས་ན་གནས་པ་ནི་བྱེད་པ་མང་
བའོ། །རབ་ཏུ་བྱུང་བ་ནི་བྱེད་པ་ཉུང་བའོ། །ཁྲིམས་ན་གནས་པ་ནི་དུག་དང་བཅས་
པའི་བཏུང་བ་ལྟ་བུའོ། །རབ་ཏུ་བྱུང་བ་ནི་བདུད་རྩི་དང་བཅས་པའི་བཏུང་བ་ལྟ་
བུའོ། །ཁྲིམས་ན་གནས་པ་ནི་གནོད་པ་ཅན་ནོ། །རབ་ཏུ་བྱུང་བ་ནི་གནོད་པ་མེད་
པའོ། །ཁྲིམས་ན་གནས་པ་ནི་འདྲེས་པའོ། །རབ་ཏུ་བྱུང་བ་ནི་མ་འདྲེས་པའོ། །
ཁྲིམས་ན་གནས་པ་ནི་ཀིམ་པ་ཀའི་འབྲས་བུ་ལྟ་བུའོ། །རབ་ཏུ་བྱུང་བ་ནི་བདུད་རྩིའི་
འབྲས་བུ་ལྟ་བུའོ། །ཁྲིམས་ན་གནས་པ་ནི་མི་སྡུག་པ་དང་ཕྲད་པར་བྱེད་པའོ། །
རབ་ཏུ་བྱུང་བ་ནི་མི་སྡུག་པ་དང་འབྲལ་བར་བྱེད་པའོ། །ཁྲིམས་ན་གནས་པ་ནི་སྡུག་པ་
དང་འབྲལ་བར་བྱེད་པའོ། །རབ་ཏུ་བྱུང་བ་ནི་སྡུག་པ་དང་ཕྲད་པར་བྱེད་པའོ། །
ཁྲིམས་ན་གནས་པ་ནི་གཏི་མུག་གིས་ལྟི་བའོ། །རབ་ཏུ་བྱུང་བ་ནི་ཡེ་ཤེས་ཀྱིས་ཡང་
བའོ། །ཁྲིམས་ན་གནས་པ་ནི་སྒྲོར་བ་རྣམ་པར་འཇིག་པའོ། །རབ་ཏུ་བྱུང་བ་ནི་སྒྲོར་
བ་རྣམ་པར་སྒྲོང་བའོ། །ཁྲིམས་ན་གནས་པ་ནི་བསམ་པ་རྣམ་པར་འཇིག་པའོ། །
རབ་ཏུ་བྱུང་བ་ནི་བསམ་པ་རྣམ་པར་སྒྲོང་བའོ། །ཁྲིམས་ན་གནས་པ་ནི་ལྷག་པའི་

བསམ་པ་རྣམ་པར་འཛིན་པའོ། །རབ་ཏུ་བྱུང་བའི་ནི་ལྷག་པའི་བསམ་པ་རྣམ་པར་སྦྱོང་བའོ། །ཁྱིམ་ན་གནས་པ་ནི་དཔུང་གཉེན་མེད་པར་བྱེད་པའོ། །རབ་ཏུ་བྱུང་བ་ནི་དཔུང་གཉེན་བྱེད་པའོ། །ཁྱིམ་ན་གནས་པ་ནི་མགོན་མེད་པར་བྱེད་པའོ། །རབ་ཏུ་བྱུང་བ་ནི་མགོན་བྱེད་པའོ། །ཁྱིམ་ན་གནས་པ་ནི་གནས་མེད་པར་བྱེད་པའོ། །རབ་ཏུ་བྱུང་བ་ནི་གནས་བྱེད་པའོ། །ཁྱིམ་ན་གནས་པ་ནི་སྐྱབས་མེད་པར་བྱེད་པའོ། །རབ་ཏུ་བྱུང་བ་ནི་སྐྱབས་བྱེད་པའོ། །ཁྱིམ་ན་གནས་པ་ནི་གནོད་སེམས་མང་བའོ། །རབ་ཏུ་བྱུང་བ་ནི་བྱམས་པ་མང་བའོ། །ཁྱིམ་ན་གནས་པ་ནི་ཁུར་ཁྱེར་བའོ། །རབ་ཏུ་བྱུང་བ་ནི་ཁུར་བོར་བའོ། །ཁྱིམ་ན་གནས་པ་ནི་ཐུག་པ་མེད་པར་སྤྱོད་པའོ། །རབ་ཏུ་བྱུང་བ་ནི་སྤྱོད་པ་ཐམས་ཅད་མཐར་འབྱིན་པའོ། །ཁྱིམ་ན་གནས་པ་ནི་ཁ་ན་མ་ཐོ་བ་དང་བཅས་པའོ། །རབ་ཏུ་བྱུང་བ་ནི་ཁ་ན་མ་ཐོ་བ་མེད་པའོ། །ཁྱིམ་ན་གནས་པ་ནི་གདུང་བར་འགྱུར་བའོ། །རབ་ཏུ་བྱུང་བ་ནི་གདུང་བར་མི་འགྱུར་བའོ། །ཁྱིམ་ན་གནས་པ་ནི་ཉོན་མོངས་པ་དང་བཅས་པའོ། །རབ་ཏུ་བྱུང་བ་ནི་ཉོན་མོངས་པ་མེད་པའོ། །ཁྱིམ་ན་གནས་པ་ནི་ཟང་ཟིང་དང་བཅས་པའོ། །རབ་ཏུ་བྱུང་བ་ནི་ཟང་ཟིང་མེད་པའོ། །ཁྱིམ་ན་གནས་པ་ནི་མངོན་བའི་ང་རྒྱལ་དང་བཅས་པའོ། །རབ་ཏུ་བྱུང་བ་ནི་མངོན་པའི་ང་རྒྱལ་མེད་པའོ། །ཁྱིམ་ན་གནས་པ་ནི་ནོར་སྙིང་པོར་བྱེད་པའོ། །རབ་ཏུ་བྱུང་བ་ནི་ཡོན་ཏན་སྙིང་པོར་བྱེད་པའོ། །ཁྱིམ་ན་གནས་པ་ནི་ཡམས་ཀྱི་ནད་དོ། །རབ་ཏུ་བྱུང་བ་ནི་ཡམས་ཀྱི་ནད་ཞི་བར་བྱེད་པའོ། །ཁྱིམ་ན་གནས་པ་ནི་འབྲི་བའོ། །རབ་ཏུ་བྱུང་བ་ནི་འཕེལ་བའོ། །ཁྱིམ་ན་གནས་པ་ནི་རྙེད་པར་སླ་བའོ། །རབ་ཏུ་བྱུང་བ་ནི་བསྐལ་པ་བརྒྱ་སྟོང་དུ་ཡང་རྙེད་པར་དཀའ་བའོ། །ཁྱིམ་ན་གནས་པ་ནི་བྱ་སླ་བའོ། །རབ་ཏུ་བྱུང་བ་ནི་བྱ་དཀའ་བའོ། །ཁྱིམ་ན་གནས་པ་ནི་རྒྱུན་ཕྱོགས་སུ་འགྲོ་བའོ། །རབ་ཏུ་བྱུང་བ་ནི་རྒྱུན་ལས་བཟློག་སྟེ་འགྲོ་བའོ། །ཁྱིམ་ན་གནས་པ་ནི་ཆུ་བོའོ། །རབ་ཏུ་བྱུང་བ་ནི་གཟིངས་སོ། །ཁྱིམ་ན་གནས་པ་ནི་ཉོན་མོངས་པའི་ཆུ་བོའོ། །རབ་ཏུ་བྱུང་བ་ནི་ཟམ་པའོ། །ཁྱིམ་ན་གནས་པ་ནི་ཚུར་རོལ་གྱི་

ངོགས་སོ། །རབ་ཏུ་བྱུང་བ་ནི་ཕ་རོལ་གྱི་ངོགས་སོ། །ཁྱིམ་ན་གནས་པ་ནི་གླགས་པའོ། །རབ་ཏུ་བྱུང་བ་ནི་མ་གླགས་པའོ། །ཁྱིམ་ན་གནས་པ་ནི་ཤར་གཉེར་བའོ། །རབ་ཏུ་བྱུང་བ་ནི་ཤར་གཉེར་བ་ཞི་བའོ། །ཁྱིམ་ན་གནས་པ་ནི་རྒྱལ་པོའི་ནན་ཏུར་བཞིན་བྱེད་པའོ། །རབ་ཏུ་བྱུང་བ་ནི་སངས་རྒྱས་ཀྱི་བསྟན་པ་བཞིན་བྱེད་པའོ། །ཁྱིམ་ན་གནས་པ་ནི་ཉམ་ཐག་པའོ། །རབ་ཏུ་བྱུང་བ་ནི་ཉམ་ཐག་པ་མེད་པའོ། །ཁྱིམ་ན་གནས་པ་ནི་སྡུག་བསྔལ་འབྱུང་བའོ། །རབ་ཏུ་བྱུང་བ་ནི་བདེ་བ་འབྱུང་བའོ། །ཁྱིམ་ན་གནས་པ་ནི་སྒང་དུའོ། །རབ་ཏུ་བྱུང་བ་ནི་ཟབ་མོའོ། །ཁྱིམ་ན་གནས་པ་ནི་གྲོགས་མེད་པའོ། །རབ་ཏུ་བྱུང་བ་ནི་གྲོགས་དགོན་པའོ། །ཁྱིམ་ན་གནས་པ་ནི་ཆུང་མ་དང་འགྲོགས་པའོ། །རབ་ཏུ་བྱུང་བ་ནི་མོས་པ་དང་འགྲོགས་པའོ། །ཁྱིམ་ན་གནས་པ་ནི་རྒྱ་དང་འདྲ་བའོ། །རབ་ཏུ་བྱུང་བ་ནི་རྒྱ་དྲལ་བའོ། །ཁྱིམ་ན་གནས་པ་ནི་གཞན་ལ་གནོད་པ་བྱེད་པ་གཅེས་སུ་སྟི་བའོ། །རབ་ཏུ་བྱུང་བ་ནི་གཞན་ལ་ཕན་འདོགས་པ་གཅེས་སུ་སྟེ་བའོ། །ཁྱིམ་ན་གནས་པ་ནི་ཟང་ཟིང་གི་སྦྱིན་པ་ཆེད་ཆེར་འཛིན་པའོ། །རབ་ཏུ་བྱུང་བ་ནི་ཆོས་ཀྱི་སྦྱིན་པ་ཆེད་ཆེར་འཛིན་པའོ། །ཁྱིམ་ན་གནས་པ་ནི་བདུད་ཀྱི་རྒྱལ་མཚན་འཛིན་པའོ། །རབ་ཏུ་བྱུང་བ་ནི་སངས་རྒྱས་ཀྱི་རྒྱལ་མཚན་འཛིན་པའོ། །ཁྱིམ་ན་གནས་པ་ནི་སྡུག་བསྔལ་གྱི་གཞིའོ། །རབ་ཏུ་བྱུང་བ་ནི་སྡུག་བསྔལ་གྱི་གཞི་ཡང་དག་པར་འཇོམས་པའོ། །ཁྱིམ་ན་གནས་པ་ནི་ཕུང་པོ་རྣམ་པར་འཕེལ་བའོ། །རབ་ཏུ་བྱུང་བ་ནི་ཕུང་པོ་ཐམས་ཅད་ངེས་པར་འདོར་བའོ། །ཁྱིམ་ན་གནས་པ་ནི་ཐིབས་པོའོ། །རབ་ཏུ་བྱུང་བ་ནི་ཐིབས་པོ་ལས་ཐར་བ་ཡིན་ཏེ། ཁྱིམ་བདག་དེ་ལྟར་བྱང་ཆུབ་སེམས་དཔའ་ཁྱིམ་པས་རབ་ཏུ་བྱུང་བ་ལ་གཞོལ་བར་བྱའོ། །དེས་ཡང་འདི་ལྟར་གལ་ཏེ་བདག་གིས་ཉི་མ་དུ་མར་གང་གཱའི་ཀླུང་གི་བྱེ་མ་སྙེད་ཀྱི་མཆོད་སྦྱིན་བྱས་ཏེ་བདོག་པ་ཐམས་ཅད་ཡོངས་སུ་བཏང་བ་བྱས་པ་དེ་དག་ཐམས་ཅད་ནི་ལེགས་པར་བཤད་པའི་ཆོས་འདུལ་བ་ལ་རབ་ཏུ་འབྱུང་བའི་སེམས་ཀྱིས་ཟིལ་གྱིས་ནོན་ཏོ་སྙམ་དུ་སེམས་བསྐྱེད་པར་བྱའོ། །དེ་ཅིའི་ཕྱིར་ཞེ་ན། ཁྱིམ་བདག་མ་དད་པ་དང་།

བྱས་པ་མི་གཟོ་བ་དང་། ཆོམ་རྐུན་དང་། གདོལ་པ་དང་། རྒྱལ་པོའི་
བཀྲབས་པ་དང་། བློན་པོ་ཡང་སྦྱིན་པ་སྦྱིན་པར་བྱེད་དེ། ཟང་ཟིང་གི་སྦྱིན་པ་ནི་
དམན་པ་ཡིན་ནོ། །ཁྱིམ་བདག་བྱང་ཆུབ་སེམས་དཔའ་ཁྱིམ་པས་འདི་ལྟར་བདག་
གིས་སྦྱིན་པའི་སྙིང་པོས་ཆོག་པར་མི་བྱའི་བདག་གིས་ནི་ཚུལ་ཁྲིམས་དང་། ཐོས་པ་
དང་། ཚངས་པར་སྤྱོད་པ་ཡང་སྙིང་པོར་བྱའོ་སྙམ་དུ་སེམས་བསྐྱེད་པར་བྱའོ། །
དེ་གཙུག་ལག་ཁང་དུ་འོངས་ན་དེ་བཞིན་གཤེགས་པའི་མཆོད་མ་ལ་ཕྱག་བྱའོ། །དེ་
དག་ལ་ཕྱག་བྱས་ནས་འདུ་ཤེས་གསུམ་བསྐྱེད་པར་བྱ་སྟེ། གསུམ་གང་ཞེ་ན།
བདག་ཀྱང་འདི་འདྲ་བར་མཆོད་པའི་འོས་སུ་འགྱུར་བར་བྱ་བ་དང་། སེམས་ཅན་ལ་
སྙིང་བརྩེ་བའི་ཕྱིར་བདག་གི་ལུས་ཀྱང་བྱིན་གྱིས་བརླབ་པ་དང་། བདག་ཀྱང་ཇི་
ལྟར་མྱུར་དུ་བླ་ན་མེད་པ་ཡང་དག་པར་རྫོགས་པའི་བྱང་ཆུབ་མངོན་པར་རྫོགས་པར་
སངས་རྒྱས་ནས་སངས་རྒྱས་ཀྱི་བྱ་བ་བྱས་ཏེ་དེ་བཞིན་གཤེགས་པ་ཡོངས་སུ་མྱ་ངན་
ལས་འདས་པས་ཡོངས་སུ་མྱ་ངན་ལས་འདའ་བར་བྱ་བ་དེ་ལྟར་བསླབ་ཅིང་དེ་ལྟར་ནན་
ཏན་བྱའོ་སྙམ་པའོ། །དེ་གཙུག་ལག་ཁང་དུ་ཞུགས་ན་དེས་དགེ་སློང་མང་དུ་ཐོས་པ་
ནི་གང་། དགེ་སློང་ཆོས་བརྗོད་པ་ནི་གང་། དགེ་སློང་འདུལ་བ་འཛིན་པ་ནི་གང་།
དགེ་སློང་མ་མོ་འཛིན་པ་ནི་གང་། དགེ་སློང་བྱང་ཆུབ་སེམས་དཔའི་སྡེ་སྣོད་འཛིན་
པ་ནི་གང་། དགེ་སློང་དགོན་པ་པ་ནི་གང་། བསོད་སྙོམས་པ་ནི་གང་། ཕྱག་
དར་ཁྲོད་པ་དང་། འདོད་པ་ཆུང་བ་དང་། ཆོག་ཤེས་པ་དང་། རབ་ཏུ་དབེན་
པ་ནི་གང་། དགེ་སློང་རྣལ་འབྱོར་སྤྱོད་པ་ནི་གང་། དགེ་སློང་བསམ་གཏན་པ་ནི་
གང་། དགེ་སློང་བྱང་ཆུབ་སེམས་དཔའི་ཐེག་པ་པ་ནི་གང་། དགེ་སློང་ལག་གི་
བླ་ནི་གང་། དགེ་སློང་ཞལ་ཏ་བྱེད་པ་ནི་གང་། དགེ་སློང་དཔོན་སྣ་བྱེད་པ་ནི་གང་
ཡིན་ཞེས་དགེ་སློང་གི་དགེ་འདུན་གྱི་སྤྱོད་པ་ཐམས་ཅད་ལ་རྣམ་པར་བརྟག་པར་
བྱའོ། །དེས་དེ་དག་གི་སྤྱོད་པ་ལ་རྣམ་པར་བརྟགས་ནས་ཐམས་ཅད་དང་འཐུན་པར་
འཇུག་པའི་ཕྱིར་ཅི་རིགས་པར་འཐུན་པར་གནས་པར་བྱའོ། །དེས་གཞན་གྱི་མདུན་
དུ་སྤྱོད་པ་གཞན་བསྟན་པར་མི་བྱའོ། །དེ་ཅིའི་ཕྱིར་ཞེ་ན། གཙུག་ལག་ཁང་དུ་ནི་

གྲོང་གི་གསང་ངོ་། །གྲོང་དུ་ནི་གཙུག་ལག་ཁང་གི་གསང་ངོ་། །ངག་གི་ལས་ཞིན་དུ་བསྡམས་པ་དེས་གྲོང་དུ་གཙུག་ལག་ཁང་གི་གསང་དང་། གཙུག་ལག་ཁང་དུ་གྲོང་གི་གསང་བསླད་པར་མི་བྱའོ། །དགེ་སློང་གང་ཆོས་གོས་མཚང་བ་འམ། ལྷུང་བཟེད་མཚང་བ་འམ། ན་བའི་གསོས་སྨན་དང་ཡོ་བྱད་མཚང་བ་དེ་ལ་དེས་ཇི་ལྟར་གཞན་དག་གཞེ་བ་འམ། ཁྲོ་བ་སྐྱེད་པར་མི་འགྱུར་བ་དེ་ལྟར་སྦྱིན་བར་བྱའོ། །དེ་ཅིའི་ཕྱིར་ཞེ་ན། ལྷ་དང་མི་རྣམས་ཀྱི་ཀུན་དུ་སྦྱོར་བ་ནི་ཕྲག་དོག་དང་སེར་སྣ་ཡིན་ཏེ། དེ་བས་ན་སོ་སོའི་སྐྱེ་བོ་རྣམས་ལ་ནི་རབ་ཏུ་བསྲུང་བར་བྱའི་དགྲ་བཅོམ་པ་ལ་ནི་མ་ཡིན་ནོ། །དེ་ཅིའི་ཕྱིར་ཞེ་ན། སོ་སོའི་སྐྱེ་བོ་རྣམས་ལས་ནི་ཉེས་པ་སྐྱེའི་དགྲ་བཅོམ་པ་རྣམས་ལས་ནི་མ་ཡིན་ནོ། །དེ་བས་ན་མང་དུ་ཐོས་པ་ལ་བསྟེན་ཏེ་ཐོས་པ་ཡོངས་སུ་བཙལ་བ་ལ་བརྩོན་པར་བྱའོ། །ཆོས་བརྗོད་པ་ལ་བསྟེན་ཏེ་རྣམ་པར་ངེས་པའི་གཏམ་ལ་བརྩོན་པར་བྱའོ། །འདུལ་བ་འཛིན་པ་ལ་བསྟེན་ཏེ་ཉེས་པ་འདུལ་བ་དང་། ཉོན་མོངས་པ་འདུལ་བ་ལ་བརྩོན་པར་བྱའོ། །མ་མོ་འཛིན་པ་ལ་བསྟེན་ཏེ་ལུས་དང་ངག་དང་ཡིད་སྡོམ་པ་ལ་བརྩོན་པར་བྱའོ། །བྱང་ཆུབ་སེམས་དཔའི་སྡེ་སྣོད་འཛིན་པ་ལ་བསྟེན་ཏེ་ཕ་རོལ་དུ་ཕྱིན་པ་དྲུག་དང་། ཐབས་ལ་མཁས་པ་ལ་བརྩོན་པར་བྱའོ། །དགོན་པ་པ་ལ་བསྟེན་ཏེ་རབ་ཏུ་དབེན་པ་ལ་བརྩོན་པར་བྱའོ། །བསོད་སྙོམས་པ་ལ་བསྟེན་ཏེ་རྙེད་པ་དང་། མ་རྙེད་པ་དང་། གྲགས་པ་དང་། མ་གྲགས་པ་དང་། བསྟོད་པ་དང་། སྨད་པ་དང་། བདེ་བ་དང་། སྡུག་བསྔལ་གྱིས་མི་སྒྱུལ་བ་ལ་བརྩོན་པར་བྱའོ། །ཕྱག་དར་ཁྲོད་པ་ལ་བསྟེན་ཏེ་ཆོས་གོས་ཀྱིས་ཆོ་བ་དང་། རྒྱན་ལ་མངོན་པར་མི་དགའ་བ་ལ་བརྩོན་བར་བྱའོ། །འདོད་པ་ཆུང་བ་ལ་བསྟེན་ཏེ་འདོད་པ་ཆུང་བ་ལ་བརྩོན་པར་བྱའོ། །ཆོག་ཤེས་པ་ལ་བསྟེན་ཏེ་ཆོག་ཤེས་པ་ལ་བརྩོན་པར་བྱའོ། །རབ་ཏུ་དབེན་པ་ལ་བསྟེན་ཏེ་རབ་ཏུ་དབེན་པ་ལ་བརྩོན་པར་བྱའོ། །རྣལ་འབྱོར་སྤྱོད་པ་ལ་བསྟེན་ཏེ་ནང་གི་སེམས་ཀྱི་ཞི་གནས་དང་ལྷག་མཐོང་ཚུལ་བཞིན་ཡིད་ལ་བྱེད་པ་ནང་དུ་ཡང་དག་འཇོག་པ་ལ་བརྩོན་པར་བྱའོ། །བསམ་གཏན་པ་ལ་བསྟེན་ཏེ་ཉོན་མོངས་པ་བསལ་བ་ལ་བརྩོན་

པར་བྱའོ། །བྱང་ཆུབ་སེམས་དཔའི་ཐེག་པ་པ་ལ་བསྟེན་ཏེ་སྦྱིན་པ་དང་། སྙན་པར་སྨྲ་བ་དང་། དོན་སྤྱོད་པ་དང་། དོན་འཐུན་པ་སྟེ་བསྡུ་བའི་དངོས་པོ་བཞི་པོ་རྣམས་ལ་བརྩོན་པར་བྱའོ། །ལག་གི་བླ་ལ་བསྟེན་ཏེ་ཇི་ལྟར་དངོས་པོ་ཡོངས་སུ་གཏོང་བར་སྦྲོ་བ་ལ་བརྩོན་པར་བྱའོ། །ཞལ་ཏ་བྱེད་པ་ལ་བསྟེན་ཏེ་བྱའོ་ཅོག་བྱེད་པ་ལ་བརྩོན་པར་བྱའོ། །དཔོན་སྣ་བྱེད་པ་ལ་བསྟེན་ཏེ་ཡིད་ཡོངས་སུ་མི་སྐྱོ་བར་བྱའོ། །ཁྱིམ་བདག་དེ་ལྟར་བྱང་ཆུབ་སེམས་དཔའ་ཁྱིམ་པ་ཁྱིམ་ན་གནས་པས་སྤྱོད་པ་ཇི་ལྟ་བ་བཞིན་དུ་རྗེས་སུ་འཇུག་པ་ལ་བརྩོན་པར་བྱའོ། །དགེ་སློང་གང་ཡང་དག་པར་སྐྱོན་མེད་པ་ལ་ཞུགས་ཆོས་གོས་ཀྱིས་སྡུད་པ་འམ། ལྷུང་བཟེད་ཀྱིས་སྡུད་པ་བྱེད་པ་ན། དགེ་སློང་དེ་བླ་ན་མེད་པ་ཡང་དག་པར་རྫོགས་པའི་བྱང་ཆུབ་ཡང་དག་པར་འཛིན་དུ་གཞུག་གོ །དེ་ཅིའི་ཕྱིར་ཞེ་ན། གང་ཟང་ཟིང་གི་སྡུད་པས་ཆོས་ཀྱི་བསྡུ་བ་སྐྱེད་པའི་གནས་ཡོད་པའི་ཕྱིར་རོ། །ཁྱིམ་བདག་དེ་ལྟར་བྱང་ཆུབ་སེམས་དཔའ་ཁྱིམ་པས་དགེ་སྦྱོང་གི་སྤྱོད་པ་ལ་མཁས་པར་བྱའོ། །དེས་ཡང་དགེ་སློང་མི་འདུམ་པ་རྣམས་ཀྱི་བསྡུམས་ཀྱང་བྱའོ། །དམ་པའི་ཆོས་རབ་ཏུ་རྣམ་པར་འཇིག་པ་ན་དེས་སྲོག་ཀྱང་ཡོངས་སུ་གཏང་ཞིང་དམ་པའི་ཆོས་ཀུན་དུ་གཟུང་བར་བྱའོ། །ཁྱིམ་བདག་གང་བྱང་ཆུབ་སེམས་དཔའ་ཁྱིམ་པས་དགེ་སློང་ན་བ་ཞིག་མཐོང་ན་དེས་རང་གི་ཤ་དང་ཁྲག་གིས་ཀྱང་དགེ་སློང་དེ་ནད་དེ་ལས་གསོ་བར་བྱའོ། །ཁྱིམ་བདག་གཞན་ཡང་བྱང་ཆུབ་སེམས་དཔའ་ཁྱིམ་པ་གཏོང་ཞིང་སྦྱིན་པས་གཞན་དག་འགྲོན་དུ་གཉེར་བར་བྱ་སྟེ། བྱིན་ནས་ཀྱང་འགྱོད་པའི་སེམས་མི་བསྐྱེད་དོ། །དེ་དགེ་བའི་རྩ་བ་ཐམས་ཅད་ཀྱི་སྔོན་དུ་ཡང་བྱང་ཆུབ་ཀྱི་སེམས་འགྲོ་བར་བྱའོ། །ཁྱིམ་བདག་དེ་ལྟར་ན་བྱང་ཆུབ་སེམས་དཔའ་ཁྱིམ་པ་ཁྱིམ་གྱི་ས་ལ་གནས་པ་དེ་བཞིན་གཤེགས་པ་རྣམས་ཀྱི་བཀའ་བཞིན་བྱེད་པ་ཡིན་ཏེ། བྱང་ཆུབ་ཀྱི་ཕྱོགས་ཀྱི་ཆོས་རྣམས་ལས་མི་ཉམས། ཡོངས་སུ་མི་ཉམས་སོ། །འདི་ལ་ཡང་ཁ་ན་མ་ཐོ་བའི་ལས་མེད་ཅིང་གཞན་དུ་ཡང་བྱེ་བྲག་ཏུ་འགྲོ་བར་འགྱུར་རོ། །དེ་ནས་ཁྱིམ་བདག་དྲག་ཤུལ་ཅན་དང་། ཁྱིམ་བདག་གཞན་དེ་དག་གིས་མགྲིན་གཅིག་ཏུ་བཅོམ་ལྡན་འདས་ཀྱིས་གསུངས་པ་ལ་

མངོན་པར་བསྟོད་ནས་བཅོམ་ལྡན་འདས་ལ་འདི་སྐད་ཅེས་གསོལ་ཏོ། །ཇི་ཙམ་དུ་
བཅོམ་ལྡན་འདས་ཀྱིས་ཁྱིམ་ན་གནས་པའི་ཉེས་པ་དང་། སྡོམ་པ་དང་། སྤྱོད་པ་
དང་རབ་ཏུ་བྱུང་བའི་ཡོན་ཏན་གྱི་ཕན་ཡོན་འདི་དག་ལེགས་པར་གསུངས་པ་ནི་ངོ་
མཚར་ཏོ། །བཅོམ་ལྡན་འདས་བདག་ཅག་ཀྱང་འདིར་ཁྱིམ་ན་གནས་པ་ལ་ཉེས་པའི་
སྐྱོན་ཆགས་པ་ཇི་སྙེད་པ་དང་། རབ་ཏུ་བྱུང་བའི་ཡོན་ཏན་དང་ཕན་ཡོན་མཐའ་ཡས་
པ་མངོན་སུམ་དུ་གྱུར་ན། བཅོམ་ལྡན་འདས་བདག་ཅག་རྣམས་རབ་ཏུ་ཕྱུང་སྟེ།
བདེ་བར་གཤེགས་པས་ལེགས་པར་བཤད་པའི་ཆོས་འདུལ་བ་ལ་བསྙེན་པར་རྫོགས་
པར་མཛད་དུ་གསོལ། དེ་སྐད་ཅེས་གསོལ་པ་དང་། བཅོམ་ལྡན་འདས་ཀྱིས་
ཁྱིམ་བདག་དེ་དག་ལ་འདི་སྐད་ཅེས་བཀའ་སྩལ་ཏོ། །ཁྱིམ་བདག་རྣམས་རབ་ཏུ་
བྱུང་བ་ནི་འབྱུང་བར་དཀའ་སྟེ། སྤྱོད་པ་ནི་ཤིན་ཏུ་རྣམ་པར་དག་པར་བསྒྲུབ་པར་
དཀའོ། །དེ་སྐད་ཅེས་བཀའ་སྩལ་པ་དང་། བཅོམ་ལྡན་འདས་ལ་ཁྱིམ་བདག་དེ་
དག་གིས་འདི་སྐད་ཅེས་གསོལ་ཏོ། །བཅོམ་ལྡན་འདས་རབ་ཏུ་བྱུང་བ་ཡང་འབྱུང་
བར་དཀའ་བ་ལགས་མོད་ཀྱི། འོན་ཀྱང་བཅོམ་ལྡན་འདས་ཀྱིས་བདག་ཅག་རབ་ཏུ་
འབྱུང་བའི་སླད་དུ་སྐབས་དབྱེ་བར་གསོལ། བདག་ཅག་བཅོམ་ལྡན་འདས་ཀྱི་
བསྟན་པ་ལ་ནན་ཏན་གྱིས་བསྒྲུབ་པར་འཚལ་ལོ། །བཅོམ་ལྡན་འདས་ཀྱིས་ཁྱིམ་
བདག་དེ་དག་ལ་རབ་ཏུ་འབྱུང་བའི་སྐབས་ཕྱེ་སྟེ། དེ་ནས་བཅོམ་ལྡན་འདས་ཀྱིས་
བྱང་ཆུབ་སེམས་དཔའ་བྱམས་པ་དང་། བྱང་ཆུབ་སེམས་དཔའ་སྤྱོད་པ་ཐམས་ཅད་
རྣམ་པར་དག་པ་ལ་འདི་སྐད་ཅེས་བཀའ་སྩལ་ཏོ། །སྐྱེས་བུ་དམ་པ་ཁྱེད་གཉིས་ཀྱིས་
ཁྱིམ་བདག་འདི་རྣམས་རབ་ཏུ་ཕྱུང་ལ་བསྙེན་པར་རྫོགས་པར་གྱིས་ཤིག་ཅེས་བཅོམ་
ལྡན་འདས་ཀྱིས་གནང་ནས་བྱང་ཆུབ་སེམས་དཔའ་བྱམས་པས་ཁྱིམ་བདག་དགུ་སྟོང་
རབ་ཏུ་ཕྱུང་ངོ་། །བྱང་ཆུབ་སེམས་དཔའ་སྤྱོད་པ་ཐམས་ཅད་རྣམ་པར་དག་པས་ནི་
ཁྱིམ་བདག་བདུན་སྟོང་རབ་ཏུ་ཕྱུང་ངོ་། །བྱང་ཆུབ་སེམས་དཔའ་ཁྱིམ་པ་རྣམས་ཀྱི་
བསླབ་པའི་རྒྱུན་བསྟན་པའི་ཆོས་ཀྱི་རྣམ་གྲངས་འདི་བཤད་པ་ན་སྲོག་ཆགས་སྟོང་དུ་
ཚང་བ་དག་བླ་ན་མེད་པ་ཡང་དག་པར་རྫོགས་པའི་བྱང་ཆུབ་ཏུ་སེམས་སྐྱེས་

སོ།། །།བམ་པོ་གསུམ་པ་སྟེ་ཐ་མ། དེ་ནས་བཅོམ་ལྡན་འདས་ལ་ཁྱིམ་བདག་དྲག་ཤུལ་ཅན་གྱིས་འདི་སྐད་ཅེས་གསོལ་ཏོ། །བཅོམ་ལྡན་འདས་ཀྱིས་བྱང་ཆུབ་སེམས་དཔའ་ཁྱིམ་པ་རྣམས་ཀྱི་ཁྱིམ་གྱིས་དང་། ཁྱིམ་ན་གནས་པའི་ནོངས་པ་དག་ནི་བཤད་ལགས་ན། བཅོམ་ལྡན་འདས་ཀྱིས་བྱང་ཆུབ་སེམས་དཔའ་རབ་ཏུ་བྱུང་བར་གཏོགས་པ་རྣམས་ཀྱི་རབ་ཏུ་བྱུང་བའི་སྒྲུབ་པ་དང་། ཚུལ་ཁྲིམས་དང་། ཐོས་པ་དང་། སྦྱངས་པའི་ཡོན་ཏན་དང་། ཡོ་བྱད་བསླུངས་པ་དང་། སྤྱོད་པ་དང་། ཚོ་ག་ཕུན་སུམ་ཚོགས་པ་དེ་ལེགས་པར་བཤད་དུ་གསོལ། བཅོམ་ལྡན་འདས་ཇི་ལྟར་ན་ལེགས་པར་བཤད་པའི་ཆོས་འདུལ་བ་ལ་བྱང་ཆུབ་སེམས་དཔའ་རབ་ཏུ་བྱུང་ནས་གུས་པར་སླ་བ་དང་། ཕྱག་འཚལ་བ་དང་། ལྡང་བ་དང་། ཐལ་མོ་སྦྱོར་བ་དང་། འདུད་པའི་ལས་དོན་མ་མཆིས་པར་མི་བགྱིད་པ་ལགས། དེ་སྐད་ཅེས་གསོལ་པ་དང་། བཅོམ་ལྡན་འདས་ཀྱིས་ཁྱིམ་བདག་དྲག་ཤུལ་ཅན་ལ་འདི་སྐད་ཅེས་བཀའ་སྩལ་ཏོ། །ཁྱིམ་བདག་ཁྱོད་གང་དེ་བཞིན་གཤེགས་པ་ལ་རབ་ཏུ་བྱུང་བའི་སྒྲུབ་པ་དང་། ཚུལ་ཁྲིམས་དང་། ཐོས་པ་དང་། སྦྱངས་པའི་ཡོན་ཏན་དང་། ཡོ་བྱད་བསླུངས་པ་དང་། སྤྱོད་པ་དང་། ཚོ་ག་ཕུན་སུམ་ཚོགས་པ་འདི་ཀུན་འདྲི་བ་ནི་ལེགས་སོ་ལེགས་སོ། །ཁྱིམ་བདག་དེའི་ཕྱིར་ལེགས་པར་རབ་ཏུ་ཉོན་ལ་ཡིད་ལ་ཟུང་ཤིག་དང་། བྱང་ཆུབ་སེམས་དཔའ་རབ་ཏུ་བྱུང་བར་གཏོགས་པས་ཇི་ལྟར་གནས་པར་བྱ་བ་དང་། ཇི་ལྟར་བསྒྲུབ་པར་བྱ་བ་ངས་ཁྱོད་ལ་བཤད་དོ། །བཅོམ་ལྡན་འདས་ལེགས་སོ་ཞེས་གསོལ་ནས་ཁྱིམ་བདག་དྲག་ཤུལ་ཅན་བཅོམ་ལྡན་འདས་ཀྱི་ལྟར་ཉན་པ་དང་། བཅོམ་ལྡན་འདས་ཀྱིས་དེ་ལ་འདི་སྐད་ཅེས་བཀའ་སྩལ་ཏོ། །ཁྱིམ་བདག་འདི་ལ་བྱང་ཆུབ་སེམས་དཔའ་རབ་ཏུ་བྱུང་བས་འདི་ལྟར་བདག་སུའི་ཆེད་ལ་ཁྱིམ་ནས་ཁྱིམ་མ་ཡིན་པར་རབ་ཏུ་བྱུང་སྙམ་དུ་གཞལ་བར་བྱ་སྟེ། དེས་མགོ་དང་གོས་ལ་མེ་འབར་བ་བཞིན་དུ་ཡེ་ཤེས་ཡོངས་སུ་བཙལ་བས་བརྩོན་འགྲུས་བརྩམ་པར་བྱའོ། །དེ་དེ་ལྟར་ཡོངས་སུ་འཇལ་བས་ཐོག་མ་ཉིད་དུ་འཕགས་པའི་རིགས་བཞི་པོ་དག་ལ་རབ་ཏུ་གནས་ཤིང་སྦྱངས་པའི་ཡོན་ཏན་དང་།

ཡོ་བྱད་བསྐུངས་པ་ལ་མངོན་པར་དགའ་བར་བྱའོ། །ཁྱིམ་བདག་ཇི་ལྟར་ན་བྱང་ཆུབ་སེམས་དཔའ་རབ་ཏུ་བྱུང་བ་འཕགས་པའི་རིགས་བཞི་པོ་དག་ལ་རབ་ཏུ་གནས་པ་ཡིན་ཞེ་ན། ཁྱིམ་བདག་འདི་ལ་བྱང་ཆུབ་སེམས་དཔའ་རབ་ཏུ་བྱུང་བ་ནི་ཆོས་གོས་ངན་ངོན་གྱིས་ཆོག་པར་འཛིན་པ་ཡིན། ཆོས་གོས་ངན་ངོན་གྱིས་ཆོག་པར་འཛིན་པའི་བསྔགས་པ་ཡང་བརྗོད་པ་ཡིན་ཏེ། དེ་ཆོས་གོས་ཀྱི་ཕྱིར་ཚུལ་དང་མི་འདྲ་བས་ཚོལ་བར་མི་བྱེད་དོ། །ཆོས་གོས་མ་རྙེད་ན་ཡང་ཡི་མི་འཆད་ཅིང་ཡོངས་སུ་གདུང་བ་མེད་དོ། །ཆོས་གོས་རྙེད་ན་ཡང་ཆགས་པ་མེད། རྨོངས་པ་མེད། དགའ་བ་མེད། ཞེན་པ་མེད་ཅིང་ཞེན་པར་མི་འགྱུར་ཏེ། ཉེས་དམིགས་མཐོང་ལ་འབྱུང་བ་རབ་ཏུ་ཤེས་ནས་ཆགས་པ་མེད་པར་སྤྱོད་དེ། ཆོས་གོས་ངན་ངོན་གྱིས་ཆོག་པར་འཛིན་པ་དེ་བདག་ལ་མི་སྟོད་ཅིང་གཞན་ལ་མི་སྨོད་དོ། །ཁྱིམ་བདག་གཞན་ཡང་བྱང་ཆུབ་སེམས་དཔའ་རབ་ཏུ་བྱུང་བ་ནི་བསོད་སྙོམས་ངན་ངོན་གྱིས་ཆོག་པར་འཛིན་པ་ཡིན། བསོད་སྙོམས་ངན་ངོན་གྱིས་ཆོག་པར་འཛིན་པའི་བསྔགས་པ་ཡང་རྗོད་པ་ཡིན་ཏེ། དེ་བསོད་སྙོམས་ཀྱི་ཕྱིར་ཚུལ་དང་མི་འདྲ་བས་ཚོལ་བར་མི་བྱེད་དོ། །བསོད་སྙོམས་མ་རྙེད་ན་ཡང་ཡི་མི་འཆད་ཅིང་ཡོངས་སུ་གདུང་བ་མེད་དོ། །བསོད་སྙོམས་རྙེད་ན་ཡང་ཆགས་པ་མེད། རྨོངས་པ་མེད། དགའ་བ་མེད། ཞེན་པ་མེད་ཅིང་ཞེན་པར་མི་འགྱུར་ཏེ། ཉེས་དམིགས་མཐོང་ལ་འབྱུང་བ་རབ་ཏུ་ཤེས་ནས་ཆགས་པ་མེད་པར་སྤྱོད་དེ། བསོད་སྙོམས་ངན་ངོན་གྱིས་ཆོག་པར་འཛིན་པ་དེ་བདག་ལ་མི་སྟོད་ཅིང་གཞན་ལ་མི་སྨོད་དོ། །ཁྱིམ་བདག་གཞན་ཡང་བྱང་ཆུབ་སེམས་དཔའ་རབ་ཏུ་བྱུང་བ་ནི་མལ་ཆ་ངན་ངོན་གྱིས་ཆོག་པར་འཛིན་པ་ཡིན། མལ་ཆ་ངན་ངོན་གྱིས་ཆོག་པར་འཛིན་པའི་བསྔགས་པ་ཡང་བརྗོད་པ་ཡིན་ཏེ། དེ་མལ་ཆའི་ཕྱིར་ཚུལ་དང་མི་འདྲ་བས་ཚོལ་བར་མི་བྱེད་དོ། །མལ་ཆ་མ་རྙེད་ན་ཡང་ཡི་མི་འཆད་ཅིང་ཡོངས་སུ་གདུང་བ་མེད་དོ། །མལ་ཆ་རྙེད་ན་ཡང་ཆགས་པ་མེད། རྨོངས་པ་མེད། དགའ་བ་མེད། ཞེན་པ་མེད་ཅིང་ཞེན་པར་མི་འགྱུར་ཏེ། ཉེས་དམིགས་མཐོང་ལ་འབྱུང་བ་རབ་ཏུ་ཤེས་ནས་ཆགས་པ་མེད་པར་སྤྱོད་དེ།

མལ་ཆ་ངན་ངོན་གྱིས་ཆོག་པར་འཛིན་པ་དེ་བདག་ལ་མི་སྟོད་ཅིང་གཞན་ལ་མི་སྨོད་དོ། །ཁྱིམ་བདག་གཞན་ཡང་བྱང་ཆུབ་སེམས་དཔའ་རབ་ཏུ་བྱུང་བ་ནི་ན་བའི་གསོས་སྨན་དང་། ཡོ་བྱད་ངན་ངོན་གྱིས་ཆོག་པར་འཛིན་པ་ཡིན། ན་བའི་གསོས་སྨན་དང་། ཡོ་བྱད་ངན་ངོན་གྱིས་ཆོག་པར་འཛིན་པའི་བསྟུགས་པ་ཡང་རྗོད་པ་ཡིན་ཏེ། དེ་ན་བའི་གསོས་སྨན་དང་། ཡོ་བྱད་ཀྱི་ཕྱིར་ཚུལ་དང་མི་འདྲ་བས་ཚོལ་བར་མི་བྱེད་དོ། །ན་བའི་གསོས་སྨན་དང་། ཡོ་བྱད་མ་རྙེད་ན་ཡང་ཡི་མི་འཆད་ཅིང་ཡོངས་སུ་གདུང་བ་མེད་དོ། །ན་བའི་གསོས་སྨན་དང་། ཡོ་བྱད་རྙེད་ན་ཡང་ཆགས་པ་མེད། རྨོངས་པ་མེད། དགའ་བ་མེད། ཞེན་པ་མེད་ཅིང་ཞེན་པར་མི་འགྱུར་ཏེ། ཉེས་དམིགས་མཐོང་ལ་འབྱུང་བ་རབ་ཏུ་ཤེས་ནས་ཆགས་པ་མེད་པར་སྤྱོད་དེ། ན་བའི་གསོས་སྨན་དང་། ཡོ་བྱད་ངན་ངོན་གྱིས་ཆོག་པར་འཛིན་པ་དེ་བདག་ལ་མི་སྟོད་ཅིང་གཞན་ལ་མི་སྨོད་དོ། །སྤོང་བ་ལ་དགའ་བ་ཡང་ཡིན་ཏེ། སྤོང་བ་ལ་མོས་ཤིང་སྤོང་བ་ལ་དགའ་བའི་སྦྱོར་བ་ལ་བརྩོན་ནོ། །དེ་སྡིག་པ་མི་དགེ་བའི་ཆོས་རྣམས་སྤངས་བས་དགའ་བར་འགྱུར་ཏེ། མ་སྤངས་པས་ནི་མ་ཡིན་ནོ། །དེ་བསྒོམ་པ་ལ་དགའ་བ་ཡིན་ཏེ། བསྒོམ་པ་ལ་དགའ་བའི་སྦྱོར་བ་ལ་བརྩོན་ནོ། །དགེ་བའི་ཆོས་བསྒོམས་པས་དགའ་བར་འགྱུར་ཏེ། མ་བསྒོམས་པས་ནི་མ་ཡིན་ཏེ། སྤོང་བ་ལ་དགའ་བ། སྤོང་བ་ལ་མོས་པ། སྤོང་བ་ལ་དགའ་བའི་སྦྱོར་བ་ལ་བརྩོན་པ། བསྒོམ་པ་ལ་དགའ་བ། བསྒོམ་པ་ལ་མོས་པ། བསྒོམ་པ་ལ་དགའ་བའི་སྦྱོར་བ་ལ་བརྩོན་པ་དེ་བདག་ལ་མི་སྟོད་ཅིང་གཞན་ལ་མི་སྨོད་དོ། །ཁྱིམ་བདག་དེ་ལྟར་ན་བྱང་ཆུབ་སེམས་དཔའ་རབ་ཏུ་བྱུང་བ་འཕགས་པའི་རིགས་བཞི་པོ་དག་ལ་གནས་པ་ཡིན་ནོ། །ཅིའི་ཕྱིར་འཕགས་པའི་རིགས་ཞེས་བྱ་ཞེ་ན། བྱང་ཆུབ་ཀྱི་ཕྱོགས་ཀྱི་ཆོས་ཐམས་ཅད་འདི་ལ་གནས་པས་དེའི་ཕྱིར་འཕགས་པའི་རིགས་ཞེས་བྱའོ། །ཁྱིམ་བདག་གཞན་ཡང་བྱང་ཆུབ་སེམས་དཔའ་རབ་ཏུ་བྱུང་བས་ཕན་ཡོན་ལ། དགའ་བ་བཅུས་ཆོས་གོས་ལུས་ལ་བཅད་པར་བྱ་སྟེ། བཅུ་གང་ཞེ་ན། འདི་ལྟ་སྟེ། ང་ཚ་ཤིང་འཛེམ་པས་དགྲི་བ་དང་། ཤ་སྦྲང་དང་། སྦྲང་བུ་དང་།

རླུང་དང་། ཉི་མ་དང་། སྡིག་སྦྲུལ་གྱིས་རེག་པར་འགྱུར་བ་གཡོགས་པ་དང་།
དགེ་སྦྱོང་གི་ཁ་དོག་དང་། རྟགས་བསྟན་པ་དང་། ངུར་སྨྲིག་དེ་དག་ནི་ལྷ་དང་།
མི་དང་། ལྷ་མ་ཡིན་དུ་བཅས་པའི་འཇིག་རྟེན་གྱི་མཆོད་རྟེན་ཡིན་ནོ་སྙམ་ནས་མཆོད་
རྟེན་གྱི་ཕྱིར་ཡང་དག་པར་གཟུང་བར་བྱ་བ་དང་། དེ་དག་ནི་ཡིད་འབྱུང་བ་དང་།
འདོད་ཆགས་དང་བྲལ་བས་ཁ་དོག་བསྒྱུར་བ་ཡིན་ཏེ། འདི་དག་ནི་འདོད་ཆགས་
ཀྱིས་ཁ་དོག་བསྒྱུར་བ་མ་ཡིན་པ་དང་། འདི་དག་ནི་ཉེ་བར་ཞི་བ་དང་འཐུན་པ་ཡིན་
གྱི། འདི་དག་ནི་ཉོན་མོངས་པ་འབར་བ་དང་འཐུན་པ་མ་ཡིན་པ་དང་། ངུར་
སྨྲིག་འདི་དག་གིས་དཀྲིས་ཤིང་གཡོགས་ནས་སྡིག་པ་ལས་ལྡོག་པར་བྱ་བ་དང་།
ལེགས་པར་བྱ་བའི་ལས་བྱ་བ་དང་། ཆོས་གོས་ཀྱིས་ཆ་བར་སྦྱོར་བ་ལ་བརྩོན་པ་མ་
ཡིན་པ་དང་། ངུར་སྨྲིག་འདི་དག་འཕགས་པའི་ལམ་གྱི་ཚོགས་དང་འཐུན་པ་ཡིན་
པར་ཤེས་ནས་ཅི་ནས་སྐད་ཅིག་གཅིག་ལ་ཡང་རྙོག་པ་དང་། འགྲོགས་པར་མི་བྱ་
བར་ངུར་སྨྲིག་རྣམས་བཅང་བར་བྱ་སྟེ། ཁྱིམ་བདག་བྱང་ཆུབ་སེམས་དཔའ་རབ་ཏུ་
བྱུང་བས་ཕན་ཡོན་ལ་དགའ་བ་བཅུ་པོ་དེ་དག་གིས་ཆོས་གོས་ལུས་ལ་བཅད་བར་
བྱའོ། །ཁྱིམ་བདག་གཞན་ཡང་བྱང་ཆུབ་སེམས་དཔའ་རབ་ཏུ་བྱུང་བས་ཕན་ཡོན་
བཅུ་མཐོང་ནས་ཇི་སྲིད་འཚོའི་བར་དུ་བསོད་སྙོམས་སྤྱོད་པ་གཏང་བར་མི་བྱ་སྟེ།
བཅུ་གང་ཞེ་ན། རང་དབང་དུ་གྱུར་པའི་ཚུལ་གྱིས་འཚོ་བར་བྱའི་གཞན་ལ་རག་
ལུས་པས་མ་ཡིན་པ་དང་། སེམས་ཅན་གང་དག་བདག་བསོད་སྙོམས་འདོད་པ་ལ་
བསོད་སྙོམས་བྱིན་པ་དེ་དག་ཀྱང་དཀོན་མཆོག་གསུམ་ལ་བཀོད་དེ་ཕྱིས་བསོད་སྙོམས་
བླང་བར་བྱ་བ་དང་། སེམས་ཅན་གང་དག་བདག་བསོད་སྙོམས་འདོད་པ་ལ་བསོད་
སྙོམས་མི་སྟེར་བ་དེ་དག་ལ་སྙིང་རྗེ་ཆེན་པོ་བསྐྱེད་ནས། སེམས་ཅན་དེ་དག་གཏོང་
བ་ལ་གཟུང་པའི་ཕྱིར་བརྩོན་འགྲུས་བརྩམ་པར་བྱ་བ་དང་། བྱ་བ་བྱས་ཏེ་བསོད་
སྙོམས་བཟའ་བ་དང་། བདག་གིས་དེ་བཞིན་གཤེགས་པའི་བཀའ་དང་འཐུན་པར་
བྱས་པར་འགྱུར་བ་དང་། ད་གང་སླ་ཞིང་གསོ་སླ་བར་བྱ་བའི་ཕྱིར་བདག་གིས་རྒྱུ་
བསྐྱེད་པར་འགྱུར་བ་དང་། བདག་གིས་ང་རྒྱལ་བཅག་པ་བསྟན་པར་འགྱུར་བ་དང་།

བདག་གི་སྤྱི་གཙུག་བལྟར་མི་མཐོང་བའི་དགེ་བའི་རྩ་བ་བསགས་པར་འགྱུར་བ་དང་།
བདག་མཐོང་ནས་དེ་བཞིན་དུ་སློབ་པར་འགྱུར་ཞིང་བདག་སྐྱེས་པ་དང་། བུད་མེད་
དང་། ཕྱེའུ་དང་། བུ་མོ་ལ་བསྟེན་པར་མི་འགྱུར་བ་དང་། བསོད་སྙོམས་
ཡང་དག་པར་བླང་བའི་སྤྱོད་པ་ཡང་བདག་སེམས་ཅན་ཐམས་ཅད་ལ་སེམས་སྙོམས་
པས་ཐམས་ཅད་མཁྱེན་པའི་ཡེ་ཤེས་ཀྱི་ཚོགས་སུ་འགྱུར་བ་སྟེ། ཁྱིམ་བདག་བྱང་
ཆུབ་སེམས་དཔའ་རབ་ཏུ་བྱུང་བས་ཕན་ཡོན་བཅུ་པོ་དེ་དག་མཐོང་ནས་ཇི་སྲིད་འཚོ་བའི་
མཐའི་བར་དུ་བསོད་སྙོམས་སྤྱོད་པ་མི་གཏང་བར་བྱའོ། །གལ་ཏེ་དེ་ལ་ལ་ཞིག་
གིས་འགྲོན་དུ་བོས་ན་དེས་ལྷག་པའི་བསམ་པ་དང་། དད་པ་དང་། དང་བ་
བསྐྱེད་པའི་ཕྱིར་འགྲོ་བར་བྱ་སྟེ། འདྲིད་པ་དང་། འཆོས་པས་ནི་མ་ཡིན་
ནོ། །གང་ལ་ལ་བསོད་སྙོམས་བླངས་ཏེ་བདག་དང་གཞན་གྱི་དོན་རྫོགས་པར་བྱེད་
ནུས་ན། ངས་བྱང་ཆུབ་སེམས་དཔའ་དེ་འགྲོན་དུ་འགྲོ་བར་གནང་ངོ་། །ཁྱིམ་
བདག་གཞན་ཡང་བྱང་ཆུབ་སེམས་དཔའ་རབ་ཏུ་བྱུང་བས་ཕན་ཡོན་བཅུ་མཐོང་ནས་ཇི་
སྲིད་འཚོ་བའི་བར་དུ་སྨན་བསྙུས་པས་ཚོག་ཤེས་པར་བྱ་སྟེ་བཅུ་གང་ཞེ་ན། དེ་
བཞིན་གཤེགས་པའི་བསྟན་པ་ལ་ཞུགས་པར་འགྱུར་བ་དང་། གཞན་གྱི་ངོར་ལྟ་བར་
མི་འགྱུར་བ་དང་། བདག་གིས་ནི་མི་སྡུག་པའི་འདུ་ཤེས་བསྟེན་པར་འགྱུར་བ་དང་།
བདག་མི་འཐུན་པའི་འདུ་ཤེས་སོ་སོར་ཉེ་བར་གནས་པར་འགྱུར་བ་དང་། རོ་བྲོ་བ་
ལ་ཆགས་པ་ཡང་བདག་གིས་ཚོགས་ཆུང་ངུས་སྤྱངས་པར་འགྱུར་བ་དང་། བྱིས་པ་
སོ་སོའི་སྐྱེ་བོ་ཐམས་ཅད་བདག་ལ་ཡིད་རྟོན་པར་འགྱུར་བ་དང་། བདག་ཁ་ཟས་
བསླུངས་པ་མངོན་དུ་གྱུར་པར་འགྱུར་བ་དང་། བདག་ལ་སྨན་ཡོངས་སུ་ཚོལ་བའི་
ཕོངས་པ་མེད་པར་འགྱུར་བ་དང་། བདག་གིས་སེམས་ལ་ཉོན་མོངས་པའི་ནད་ཀྱི་
གནོད་པ་མེད་པར་བྱས་པར་འགྱུར་བ་དང་དེ་ལྟར་ཞུགས་ན་མྱུར་དུ་ཉོན་མོངས་པའི་ནད་
དང་འབྲལ་བ་ཐོབ་པར་འགྱུར་བ་སྟེ། ཁྱིམ་བདག་བྱང་ཆུབ་སེམས་དཔའ་རབ་ཏུ་
བྱུང་བས་ཕན་ཡོན་བཅུ་པོ་དེ་དག་མཐོང་ནས་ཇི་སྲིད་འཚོའི་བར་དུ་སྨན་བསྙུས་པས་
ཚོག་ཤེས་པར་བྱའོ། །ཁྱིམ་བདག་གཞན་ཡང་བྱང་ཆུབ་སེམས་དཔའ་རབ་ཏུ་བྱུང་

བས་ཕན་ཡོན་བཅུ་མཐོང་ནས་ཇི་སྲིད་འཚོ་བའི་མཐའི་བར་དུ་དགོན་པ་ལ་གནས་པ་ཡོངས་སུ་མི་གཏང་བར་བྱ་སྟེ། བཅུ་གང་ཞེ་ན། བདག་གི་ཉམ་རངས་དང་། བདག་གི་དབང་དུ་འགྲོ་བ་དང་། ངའི་བ་མེད་ཅིང་ཡོངས་སུ་འཛིན་པ་མེད་པ་དང་། མལ་ཆ་ལྷུག་པར་གཏོང་བ་དང་། དགོན་པའི་གནས་ལ་དགའ་བ་དང་མ་བྲལ་བ་དང་། གནས་རྣམས་སུ་དོན་ཉུང་ཞིང་བྱེད་པ་ཉུང་བ་དང་། གཡོག་གི་ཚོགས་འདོར་ཞིང་ལུས་དང་སྲོག་ལ་མི་ལྟ་བ་དང་། དབེན་པར་དགའ་ཞིང་འདུ་འཛི་ཡོངས་སུ་སྤོང་བ་དང་། ལས་བྱས་པའི་ཡོན་ཏན་གྱི་ཕན་ཡོན་ཡོངས་སུ་གཏོང་བ་དང་། ཏིང་ངེ་འཛིན་དང་འཐུན་པའི་སེམས་རྩེ་གཅིག་པ་དང་། ཡིད་ལ་བྱེད་པ་བླ་གབ་མེད་པ་ཡིད་ལ་བྱེད་པའི་སྒྲིབ་པ་མེད་པ་སྟེ། ཁྱིམ་བདག་གཞན་ཡང་བྱང་ཆུབ་སེམས་དཔའ་རབ་ཏུ་བྱུང་བས་ཕན་ཡོན་བཅུ་པོ་དེ་དག་མཐོང་ནས་ཇི་སྲིད་འཚོ་བའི་མཐའི་བར་དུ་དགོན་པ་ལ་གནས་པ་ཡོངས་སུ་མི་གཏོང་བར་བྱའོ། །ཁྱིམ་བདག་གལ་ཏེ་བྱང་ཆུབ་སེམས་དཔའ་དགོན་པ་ལ་གནས་པ་ཆོས་ཉན་པར་འདོད་དམ། སློབ་དཔོན་དང་། མཁན་པོ་བལྟ་བར་འདོད་དམ། ན་བ་དྲི་བའི་ཕྱིར་གྲོང་གི་གནས་སུ་འོངས་ན། དེས་དགོངས་སུ་སླར་ལྡོག་པར་བྱ་བའི་ཕྱིར་འགྲོ་བའི་སེམས་བསྐྱེད་པར་བྱའོ། །དེ་གལ་ཏེ་ལུང་མནོད་པ་དང་། ཁ་ཏོན་བྱ་བ་གཞན་ལ་རག་ལས་ཏེ། གཙུག་ལག་ཁང་ན་གནས་ན་ཡང་དེས་དགོན་པ་ལ་གཞོལ་བའི་སེམས་ཀྱིས་གང་དངོས་པོ་ཐམས་ཅད་ལ་དགོན་པར་འདུ་ཤེས་པ་དང་། ཆོས་ཚོལ་བས་མི་ངོམས་པ་དེ་ཉིད་དགོན་པ་ལ་གནས་པ་ཡིན་ནོ་སྙམ་དུ་བསམ་མོ། །ཁྱིམ་བདག་གཞན་ཡང་བྱང་ཆུབ་སེམས་དཔའ་རབ་ཏུ་བྱུང་བ་དགོན་པ་ལ་གནས་པས་འདི་ལྟར་བདག་ཅིའི་ཕྱིར་དགོན་པ་ལ་གནས། དགོན་པ་ལ་གནས་པ་འབའ་ཞིག་ནི་དགེ་སྦྱོང་མ་ཡིན་ཏེ། འདི་ན་ནི་མ་བྱང་བ། མ་སྡམས་པ། མ་ཞི་བ། མ་དུལ་བ། མི་འབྲུས་པ། རབ་ཏུ་མི་བརྩོན་པ་འདི་ལྟ་སྟེ། རི་དགས་དང་། སྤྲེའུ་དང་། བྱ་མང་པོ་དང་། ཆོམ་རྐུན་དང་། གདོལ་པ་དག་ཀྱང་མང་དུ་གནས་ཏེ། དེ་དག་ཀྱང་དགེ་སྦྱོང་གི་ཡོན་ཏན་དང་ལྡན་པ་མ་ཡིན་བས་གང་གི་ཕྱིར་བདག་དགོན་པ་ལ་གནས་པ་འདི་ལྟ་སྟེ།

དགེ་སྦྱོང་གི་དོན་དེ་ཡོངས་སུ་རྫོགས་པར་བྱའོ་སློམ་དུ་བརྟག་པར་བྱའོ། །ཁྲིམ་བདག་བྱང་ཆུབ་སེམས་དཔའ་རབ་ཏུ་བྱུང་བའི་དགེ་སྦྱོང་གི་དོན་གང་ཞེ་ན། འདི་ལྟ་སྟེ་དྲན་པ་དང་། ཤེས་བཞིན་དང་། མི་གཡེང་བ་དང་། གཟུངས་རབ་ཏུ་ཐོབ་པ་དང་། བྱམས་པ་བསྐྱེད་པ་དང་། སྙིང་རྗེ་བསྐྱེད་པ་དང་། མངོན་པར་ཤེས་པ་རྣམས་ལ་དབང་བསྒྱུར་བ་དང་། ཕ་རོལ་དུ་ཕྱིན་པ་དྲུག་བསྒོམ་པ་ཡོངས་སུ་རྫོགས་པར་བྱ་བ་དང་། ཐམས་ཅད་མཁྱེན་པ་ཉིད་ཀྱི་སེམས་ཡོངས་སུ་མི་གཏོང་བ་དང་། ཐབས་མཁས་པའི་ཡེ་ཤེས་བསྒོམ་པ་དང་། སེམས་ཅན་བསྡུ་བ་དང་། སེམས་ཅན་ཡོངས་སུ་སྨིན་པར་བྱ་བ་དང་། བསྡུ་བའི་དངོས་པོ་བཞི་ཡོངས་སུ་མི་གཏང་བ་དང་། རྗེས་སུ་དྲན་པ་དྲུག་རྗེས་སུ་དྲན་པ་དང་། ཐོས་པ་དང་། བརྩོན་འགྲུས་མི་འདོར་བ་དང་། ཚུལ་བཞིན་དུ་ཆོས་རབ་ཏུ་རྣམ་པར་འབྱེད་པ་དང་། ཡང་དག་པར་རྣམ་པར་གྲོལ་བའི་ཕྱིར་བརྩོན་པ་དང་། འབྲས་བུ་ཐོབ་པ་རྣམས་ཤེས་པ་དང་། སྐྱོན་མེད་པ་ལ་འཇུག་པར་གནས་པ་དང་། དམ་པའི་ཆོས་བསྲུང་བ་དང་། ལས་ཀྱི་རྣམ་པར་སྨིན་པ་ལ་ཡིད་ཆེས་པས་ཡང་དག་པར་ལྟ་བ་དང་། རྟོག་པ་དང་། རྣམ་པར་རྟོག་པ་ཐམས་ཅད་རབ་ཏུ་ཆད་པས་ཡང་དག་པའི་རྟོག་པ་དང་། མོས་པ་ཇི་ལྟ་བ་བཞིན་དུ་ཆོས་སྟོན་པས་ཡང་དག་པའི་ངག་དང་། ལས་ཟད་པ་ཡོངས་སུ་རྫོགས་པས་ཡང་དག་པའི་ལས་ཀྱི་མཐའ་དང་། བག་ཆགས་ཀྱི་མཚམས་སྦྱོར་བ་ཡང་དག་པར་བཅོམ་པས་ཡང་དག་པའི་འཚོ་བ་དང་། རྫོགས་པའི་བྱང་ཆུབ་ཁོང་དུ་ཆུད་པས་ཡང་དག་པའི་རྩོལ་བ་དང་། བརྗེད་པ་མེད་པའི་ཆོས་ཉིད་ཀྱིས་ཡང་དག་པའི་དྲན་པ་དང་། ཐམས་ཅད་མཁྱེན་པའི་ཡེ་ཤེས་ཡོངས་སུ་ཐོབ་པས་ཡང་དག་པའི་ཏིང་ངེ་འཛིན་དང་། སྟོང་པ་ཉིད་ཀྱིས་མི་སྐྲག་པ་དང་། མཚན་མ་མེད་པ་ལ་མི་ཞུམ་པ་དང་། སྨོན་པ་མེད་པ་ལ་མི་འགོང་བ་དང་། བསམས་བཞིན་དུ་ཡེ་ཤེས་ཀྱིས་སྲིད་པ་ཡོངས་སུ་འཛིན་པ་དང་། དོན་ལ་རྟོན་གྱི་ཡི་གེ་ལ་མི་རྟོན་པ་དང་། ཡེ་ཤེས་ལ་རྟོན་གྱི་རྣམ་པར་ཤེས་པ་ལ་མི་རྟོན་པ་དང་། ཆོས་ལ་རྟོན་གྱི་གང་ཟག་ལ་མི་རྟོན་པ་དང་། ངེས་པའི་དོན་གྱི་མདོ་སྡེ་ལ་རྟོན་གྱི་དྲང་

བའི་མདོ་སྡེ་ལ་མི་རྟོན་པ་དང་། ཐོག་མ་ནས་མ་བྱུང་ཞིང་མི་འཇིག་པའི་ཚུལ་གྱིས་
ཆོས་ཀྱི་ངོ་བོ་ཉིད་ལ་མི་རྟོག་པ་དེ་ནི་ཁྱིམ་བདག་བྱང་ཆུབ་སེམས་དཔའ་རབ་ཏུ་བྱུང་བའི་
དགེ་སྦྱོང་གི་དོན་ཅེས་བྱའོ། །ཁྱིམ་བདག་ཡང་བྱང་ཆུབ་སེམས་དཔའ་རབ་ཏུ་བྱུང་
བས་འགྲོགས་པ་མེད་པ་མང་དུ་བྱའོ། །དེས་འདི་ལྟར་ཡང་བདག་ནི་སེམས་ཅན་
དང་འདྲེ་བར་མི་བྱ་སྟེ། བདག་གིས་སེམས་ཅན་གཅིག་གི་དགེ་བའི་རྩ་བ་བསྐྱེད་
པར་མི་བྱའི། བདག་གིས་སེམས་ཅན་ཐམས་ཅད་ཀྱི་དགེ་བའི་རྩ་བ་བསྐྱེད་པར་བྱའོ་
སྙམ་དུ་བརྟག་པར་བྱའོ། །དེ་ལྟ་མོད་ཀྱི་ཁྱིམ་བདག་བྱང་ཆུབ་སེམས་དཔའ་རབ་ཏུ་
བྱུང་བའི་འགྲོགས་པ་བཞི་པོ་འདི་དག་ནི་དེ་བཞིན་གཤེགས་པས་གནང་སྟེ། བཞི་
གང་ཞེ་ན། ཆོས་མཉན་པའི་ཕྱིར་འགྲོགས་པ་དང་། སེམས་ཅན་ཡོངས་སུ་སྨིན་
པར་བྱ་བའི་ཕྱིར་འགྲོགས་པ་དང་། དེ་བཞིན་གཤེགས་པ་ལ་མཆོད་པ་དང་།
རིམ་གྲོ་བྱ་བའི་ཕྱིར་འགྲོགས་པ་དང་། ཐམས་ཅད་མཁྱེན་པ་ཉིད་ཀྱི་སེམས་འདྲེས་
པ་མེད་པ་དང་འགྲོགས་པ་སྟེ། ཁྱིམ་བདག་བྱང་ཆུབ་སེམས་དཔའ་རབ་ཏུ་བྱུང་བའི་
འགྲོགས་པ་བཞི་པོ་དེ་དག་ནི་དེ་བཞིན་གཤེགས་པས་གནང་བའོ། །ཁྱིམ་བདག་དེ་
བས་ན་བྱང་ཆུབ་སེམས་དཔའ་རབ་ཏུ་བྱུང་བས་འགྲོགས་པ་ལས་རྣམ་པར་གྲོལ་བར་
བྱའོ། །ཁྱིམ་བདག་གཞན་ཡང་བྱང་ཆུབ་སེམས་དཔའ་རབ་ཏུ་བྱུང་བ་དགོན་པ་ན་
གནས་པས་བདག་ཅིའི་ཕྱིར་དགོན་པར་འོངས་སྙམ་དུ་བརྟག་པར་བྱ་སྟེ། དེས་ཡང་
འདི་ལྟར་བདག་ནི་འཇིགས་ཤིང་སྐྲག་པའི་ཕྱིར་དགོན་པར་འོངས་སོ། །ཅི་ཞིག་གིས་
འཇིགས་ཤིང་སྐྲག་ཅེ་ན། འདུ་འཛིས་འཇིགས་ཤིང་སྐྲག་གོ །འགྲོགས་པས་
འཇིགས་ཤིང་སྐྲག་གོ །འདོད་ཆགས་དང་། ཞེ་སྡང་དང་། གཏི་མུག་གིས་
འཇིགས་ཤིང་སྐྲག་གོ །ང་རྒྱལ་དང་། རྒྱགས་པ་དང་། འཆབ་པས་འཇིགས་
ཤིང་སྐྲག་གོ །ཆགས་པ་དང་། ཕྲག་དོག་དང་། སེར་སྣས་འཇིགས་ཤིང་
སྐྲག་གོ །གཟུགས་དང་། སྒྲ་དང་། དྲི་དང་། རོ་དང་། རེག་བྱས་
འཇིགས་ཤིང་སྐྲག་གོ །ཕུང་པོའི་བདུད་ཀྱིས་འཇིགས་ཤིང་སྐྲག་གོ །ཉོན་མོངས་
པའི་བདུད་ཀྱིས་འཇིགས་ཤིང་སྐྲག་གོ །འཆི་བདག་གི་བདུད་ཀྱིས་འཇིགས་ཤིང་

སྐྲག་གོ ། ལྷའི་བུའི་བདུད་ཀྱིས་འཇིགས་ཤིང་སྐྲག་གོ ། མི་རྟག་པ་ལ་རྟག་པར་ཕྱིན་ཅི་ལོག་པས་འཇིགས་ཤིང་སྐྲག་གོ ། སྡུག་བསྔལ་ལ་བདེ་བར་ཕྱིན་ཅི་ལོག་པས་འཇིགས་ཤིང་སྐྲག་གོ ། བདག་མེད་པ་ལ་བདག་ཏུ་ཕྱིན་ཅི་ལོག་པས་འཇིགས་ཤིང་སྐྲག་གོ ། མི་གཙང་བ་ལ་གཙང་བར་ཕྱིན་ཅི་ལོག་པས་འཇིགས་ཤིང་སྐྲག་གོ ། སེམས་དང་ཡིད་དང་རྣམ་པར་ཤེས་པས་འཇིགས་ཤིང་སྐྲག་གོ ། སྲིད་པས་འཇིགས་ཤིང་སྐྲག་གོ ། འཁོར་བས་འཇིགས་ཤིང་སྐྲག་གོ ། སྒྲིབ་པ་དང་ཚོད་པ་དང་ཀུན་ནས་ལྡང་བས་འཇིགས་ཤིང་སྐྲག་གོ ། འཇིག་ཚོགས་ལ་ལྟ་བས་འཇིགས་ཤིང་སྐྲག་གོ ། བདག་ཏུ་འཛིན་པ་དང་། བདག་གིར་འཛིན་པས་འཇིགས་ཤིང་སྐྲག་གོ ། རྒོད་པས་འཇིགས་ཤིང་སྐྲག་གོ ། འགྱོད་པ་དང་ཐེ་ཚོམ་གྱིས་འཇིགས་ཤིང་སྐྲག་གོ ། སྡིག་པའི་གྲོགས་པོས་འཇིགས་ཤིང་སྐྲག་གོ ། རྙེད་པ་དང་བཀུར་སྟིས་འཇིགས་ཤིང་སྐྲག་གོ ། མི་དགེ་བའི་བཤེས་གཉེན་གྱིས་འཇིགས་ཤིང་སྐྲག་གོ ། མ་མཐོང་བར་མཐོང་ངོ་སྙམ་དུ་འཛིན་པས་འཇིགས་ཤིང་སྐྲག་གོ ། མ་ཐོས་པར་ཐོས་སོ་སྙམ་དུ་འཛིན་པས་འཇིགས་ཤིང་སྐྲག་གོ ། མ་དྲན་པར་དྲན་ནོ་སྙམ་དུ་འཛིན་པས་འཇིགས་ཤིང་སྐྲག་གོ ། བྱེ་བྲག་མ་ཕྱེད་པར་བྱེ་བྲག་ཕྱེད་དོ་སྙམ་དུ་འཛིན་པས་འཇིགས་ཤིང་སྐྲག་གོ ། མི་ཤེས་པར་ཤེས་སོ་སྙམ་དུ་འཛིན་པས་འཇིགས་ཤིང་སྐྲག་གོ ། དགེ་སྦྱོང་གི་དྲི་མས་འཇིགས་ཤིང་སྐྲག་གོ ། གཅིག་ལ་གཅིག་གནོད་པར་སེམས་པས་འཇིགས་ཤིང་སྐྲག་གོ ། འདོད་པའི་ཁམས་དང་། གཟུགས་ཀྱི་ཁམས་དང་། གཟུགས་མེད་པའི་ཁམས་ཀྱིས་འཇིགས་ཤིང་སྐྲག་གོ ། སྲིད་པའི་འགྲོ་བ་ཐམས་ཅད་དུ་འཆི་འཕོ་བ་དང་སྐྱེ་བས་འཇིགས་ཤིང་སྐྲག་གོ ། སེམས་ཅན་དམྱལ་བ་དང་། དུད་འགྲོའི་སྐྱེ་གནས་དང་། ཡི་དགས་ཀྱི་ཡུལ་དུ་འགྲོ་བས་འཇིགས་ཤིང་སྐྲག་གོ ། མི་ཁོམ་པས་འཇིགས་ཤིང་སྐྲག་གོ ། མདོར་ན་མི་དགེ་བའི་ཆོས་ཐམས་ཅད་ཡིད་ལ་བྱེད་པས་འཇིགས་ཤིང་སྐྲག་སྟེ། བདག་དེ་ལྟ་བུས་འཇིགས་ཤིང་སྐྲག་པ་དེ་དག་གིས་འཇིགས་ནས་དགོན་པར་འོངས་ཏེ། ཁྱིམ་ན་གནས་པ་དང་། འདུ་འཛིས་གནས་པ་དང་། མི་འགྲུས་ཤིང་རྣལ་འབྱོར་ལ་མི་

བརྩོན་པ་དང་། ཚུལ་བཞིན་མ་ཡིན་པའི་ཡིད་ལ་བྱེད་པས་གནས་པ་ནི་འདི་ལྟ་བུའི་
འཇིགས་སྐྲག་པ་དེ་དག་ལས་ཡོངས་སུ་ཐར་བར་མི་ནུས་ཏེ། གང་དག་འདས་པའི་
དུས་ན་བྱུང་བའི་བྱང་ཆུབ་སེམས་དཔའ་སེམས་དཔའ་ཆེན་པོ་དེ་དག་ཐམས་ཅད་ཀྱང་
དགོན་པ་ལ་གནས་ནས་འཇིགས་པ་ཐམས་ཅད་ལས་རྣམ་པར་གྲོལ་ཏེ། འདི་ལྟ་སྟེ།
བླ་ན་མེད་པ་ཡང་དག་པར་རྫོགས་པའི་བྱང་ཆུབ་འཇིགས་པ་མེད་པ་ཐོབ་བོ། །གང་
དག་མ་འོངས་པའི་དུས་ན་འབྱུང་བའི་བྱང་ཆུབ་སེམས་དཔའ་སེམས་དཔའ་ཆེན་པོ་དེ་
དག་ཐམས་ཅད་ཀྱང་དགོན་པ་ལ་གནས་ནས་འཇིགས་པ་ཐམས་ཅད་ལས་རྣམ་པར་
གྲོལ་ཏེ། འདི་ལྟ་སྟེ། བླ་ན་མེད་པ་ཡང་དག་པར་རྫོགས་པའི་བྱང་ཆུབ་འཇིགས་
པ་མེད་པ་ཐོབ་པར་འགྱུར་རོ། །གང་དག་ད་ལྟར་བྱུང་བའི་དུས་ཀྱི་བྱང་ཆུབ་སེམས་
དཔའ་སེམས་དཔའ་ཆེན་པོ་བླ་ན་མེད་པ་ཡང་དག་པར་རྫོགས་པའི་བྱང་ཆུབ་ཐོབ་པ།
དེ་དག་ཐམས་ཅད་ཀྱང་དགོན་པ་ལ་གནས་ནས་འཇིགས་པ་ཐམས་ཅད་ལས་རྣམ་པར་
གྲོལ་ཏེ། འདི་ལྟ་སྟེ། བླ་ན་མེད་པ་ཡང་དག་པར་རྫོགས་པའི་བྱང་ཆུབ་འཇིགས་
པ་མེད་པ་ཐོབ་བོ། །དེ་བས་ན་བདག་ཀྱང་འདི་ལ་འཇིགས་ཤིང་སྐྲག་སྟེ།
འཇིགས་པ་ཐམས་ཅད་ལས་ནི་ཤིན་ཏུ་འདའ་བར་འདོད། མི་འཇིགས་པ་ནི་རྗེས་སུ་
ཐོབ་པར་འདོད་པས་དགོན་པ་ལ་གནས་པར་བྱའོ་སྙམ་དུ་ཡོངས་སུ་དཔྱད་པར་
བྱའོ། །ཁྱིམ་བདག་གཞན་ཡང་བྱང་ཆུབ་སེམས་དཔའ་རབ་ཏུ་བྱུང་བ་འཇིགས་ཤིང་
སྐྲག་ནས་དགོན་པའི་གནས་ལ་གནས་པས་འདི་ལ་ཅུང་ཟད་འཇིགས་པ་སྐྱེས་པ་དེ་དག
ཐམས་ཅད་ནི་བདག་ཏུ་འཛིན་པ་ལས་སྐྱེས་སོ། །བདག་ཏུ་མངོན་པར་ཆགས་པ་
དང་། བདག་ཏུ་ཡོངས་སུ་འཛིན་པ་དང་། བདག་གི་གཞི་དང་། བདག་སྲེད་
པ་དང་། བདག་འདུ་ཤེས་པ་དང་། བདག་ཏུ་སྨྲ་བ་ཉེ་བར་ལེན་པ་དང་།
བདག་ཏུ་ལྟ་བ་དང་། བདག་གི་གནས་དང་། བདག་ཏུ་ཡོངས་སུ་རྟོག་པ་དང་།
བདག་བསྲུང་པ་ལས་སྐྱེས་ཏེ། གལ་ཏེ་བདག་དགོན་པ་ལ་གནས་ལ་བདག་ཏུ་འཛིན་
པ་ཡོངས་སུ་མ་སྤངས། བདག་ཏུ་མངོན་པར་ཆགས་པ་དང་། བདག་ཏུ་ཡོངས་
སུ་འཛིན་པ་དང་། བདག་གི་གཞི་དང་། བདག་ལ་སྲེད་པ་དང་། བདག་ཏུ་

འདུ་ཤེས་པ་དང་། བདག་ཏུ་སྨྲ་བ་ཉེ་བར་ལེན་པ་དང་། བདག་ཏུ་ལྟ་བ་དང་། བདག་གི་གནས་དང་། བདག་ཏུ་ཡོངས་སུ་རྟོག་པ་དང་། བདག་སྲུང་བ་ཡོངས་སུ་མ་སྤངས་ན་ནི་བདག་དགོན་པ་ལ་གནས་པ་དོན་མེད་པར་འགྱུར་རོ་སླམ་དུ་བསླབ་པར་བྱ་སྟེ། བདག་ཏུ་འདུ་ཤེས་པ་ལ་ནི་དགོན་པ་ལ་གནས་པ་མེད་དོ། །གཞན་དུ་འདུ་ཤེས་པ་ལ་ཡང་མེད་དོ། །ངར་འཛིན་པ་དང་། ང་ཡིར་འཛིན་པ་ལ་མངོན་པར་ཞེན་པ་ལ་ནི་དགོན་པ་ལ་གནས་པ་མེད་དོ། །དམིགས་པར་ལྟ་བ་ལ་ནི་དགོན་པ་ལ་གནས་པ་མེད་དོ། །ཕྱིན་ཅི་ལོག་ཏུ་ལྟ་བ་ལ་ནི་དགོན་པ་ལ་གནས་པ་མེད་དོ། །ཁྱིམ་བདག་མྱ་ངན་ལས་འདས་པར་འདུ་ཤེས་པ་ལ་ཡང་དགོན་པ་ལ་གནས་པ་མེད་ན་ཉོན་མོངས་པ་ཐམས་ཅད་ཀྱི་འདུ་ཤེས་ཅན་ལ་ལྟ་ཅི་སྨོས། ཁྱིམ་བདག་དགོན་པ་ལ་གནས་པ་ཞེས་བྱ་བ་ནི་ཆོས་ཐམས་ཅད་ལ་མི་རྟེན་པར་གནས་པའོ། །ཆོས་ཐམས་ཅད་ལ་མི་འཛིན་པར་གནས་པའོ། །མཚན་མ་ཐམས་ཅད་ལ་མི་ཆགས་པར་གནས་པའོ། །གཟུགས་ཐམས་ཅད་ལ་མི་རྟེན་པར་གནས་པའོ། །སྒྲ་དང་དང་། དྲི་དང་། རོ་དང་། རེག་བྱ་ཐམས་ཅད་ལ་མི་རྟེན་པར་གནས་པའོ། །ཆོས་ཐམས་ཅད་མཉམ་པ་ཉིད་དང་མི་འགལ་བར་གནས་པའོ། །སེམས་ཤིན་ཏུ་ཞི་བས་ཤིན་ཏུ་སྦྱངས་པར་གནས་པའོ། །འཇིགས་པ་ཐམས་ཅད་སྤངས་པས་མི་འཇིགས་པར་གནས་པའོ། །ཉོན་མོངས་པ་ཐམས་ཅད་ལས་རྣམ་པར་གྲོལ་བས་ཆུ་བོ་ལས་རྒལ་བར་གནས་པའོ། །བརྟན་པར་གནས་པའོ། །ངན་ངོན་གྱིས་ཆོག་ཤེས་པར་འཛིན་ཅིང་འདོད་པ་ཆུང་བས་འཕགས་པའི་རིགས་རྣམས་ལ་རབ་ཏུ་དགའ་བར་གནས་པའོ། །དེ་གང་སླ་ཞིང་གསོ་སླ་བས་ཆོག་པར་འཛིན་པར་གནས་པའོ། །ཤེས་རབ་ཀྱི་ཕྱིར་ཚུལ་བཞིན་ལ་སྦྱོར་བས་ཐོས་པ་ལ་གནས་པའོ། །རྣམ་པར་ཐར་པའི་སྒོ་སྟོང་པ་ཉིད་དང་། མཚན་མ་མེད་པ་དང་། སྨོན་པ་མེད་པ་ལ་སོ་སོར་རྟོག་པས་ཐར་པར་གནས་པའོ། །བཅིངས་པ་བཅད་པས་རྣམ་པར་གྲོལ་བར་གནས་པའོ། །རྟེན་ཅིང་འབྲེལ་པར་འབྱུང་བ་དང་འཐུན་པས་མ་དུལ་བ་རྣམས་ཉེ་བར་ཞི་བར་གནས་པའོ། །ཤིན་ཏུ་རྣམ་པར་དག་པས་བྱ་བ་བྱས་པར་གནས་པའོ། །ཁྱིམ་བདག་འདི་

ལྷ་སྟེ་དཔེར་ན་དགོན་པ་ལ་རྩ་དང་། ཤིང་གེལ་པ་དང་། ནགས་ཚལ་གནས་ཀྱང་འཛིགས་པ་མེད་ཅིང་སྐྲག་པར་མི་འགྱུར་རོ། །ཁྱིམ་བདག་དེ་བཞིན་དུ་བྱང་ཆུབ་སེམས་དཔའ་རབ་ཏུ་བྱུང་བ་དགོན་པ་ལ་གནས་ཀྱང་ལུས་ལ་རྩ་དང་། ཤིང་གེལ་པ་དང་། སྨན་དང་། རྩིག་པ་དང་། ཤིང་དང་། མིག་ཡོར་ལྟ་བུ་དང་། སྒྱུ་མ་དང་མཚུངས་པའི་འདུ་ཤེས་བསྐྱེད་པར་བྱ་སྟེ། འདི་ལ་སུ་ཞིག་འཛིགས་པར་འགྱུར། འདི་ལ་སུ་ཞིག་སྐྲག་པར་འགྱུར་སྙམ་པའི་སེམས་བསྐྱེད་པར་བྱའོ། །དེ་འཛིགས་ཤིང་སྐྲག་པ་ལྟ་ན། འདི་ལྟར་ལུས་འདི་ལ་ནི་བདག་གམ། སེམས་ཅན་ནམ། སྲོག་གམ། སྐྱེ་བ་པོ་འམ། གསོ་བ་འམ། སྐྱེས་བུ་འམ། གང་ཟག་གམ། ཤེད་ལས་སྐྱེས་སམ། ཤེད་བུ་མེད་དེ། འདི་ལྟར་འཛིགས་པ་ཞེས་བྱ་བ་འདི་ནི་ཡང་དག་པ་མ་ཡིན་པ་ཀུན་བརྟགས་པ་ཡིན་གྱིས་བདག་གིས་ནི་ཡང་དག་པ་མ་ཡིན་པ་ཀུན་བརྟགས་པ་དེ་ལ་བརྟག་པར་མི་བྱའོ་སྙམ་དུ་ལུས་ལ་ཚུལ་བཞིན་བརྟག་པར་བྱའོ། །དེས་ཇི་ལྟར་དགོན་པ་ལ་རྩ་དང་། ཤིང་གེལ་པ་དང་། སྨན་དང་། ནགས་ཚལ་གནས་པ་རྣམས་ངའི་བ་མེད་པ། ཡོངས་སུ་འཛིན་པ་མེད་པ་དེ་བཞིན་དུ་བྱང་ཆུབ་སེམས་དཔའ་ཡང་ངའི་བ་མེད་པ། ཡོངས་སུ་འཛིན་པ་མེད་པས་ཆོས་ཐམས་ཅད་དགོན་པ་ཉིད་དོ་སྙམ་དུ་ཤེས་ནས་ཉེ་བར་བསྒྲུབས་ཏེ་གནས་པར་བྱའོ། །དེ་ཅིའི་ཕྱིར་ཞེ་ན། དགོན་པ་ལ་གནས་པ་ནི་ཉོན་མོངས་པ་གཅོད་པ་སྟེ། ངའི་བ་མེད་པ། ཡོངས་སུ་འཛིན་པ་མེད་པའོ། །ཁྱིམ་བདག་གཞན་ཡང་བྱང་ཆུབ་སེམས་དཔའ་རབ་ཏུ་བྱུང་བ་དགོན་པ་ལ་གནས་པས་འདི་ལ་དགོན་པ་ལ་གནས་པ་ནི་ཚུལ་ཁྲིམས་ཀྱི་ཕུང་པོ་དང་འཐུན་པའོ། །དགོན་པ་ལ་གནས་པ་ནི་ཏིང་ངེ་འཛིན་གྱི་ཕུང་པོ་ལ་གཞོལ་བའོ། །དགོན་པ་ལ་གནས་པ་ནི་ཤེས་རབ་ཀྱི་ཕུང་པོ་ཚོགས་པའོ། །དགོན་པ་ལ་གནས་པ་ནི་རྣམ་པར་གྲོལ་བའི་ཕུང་པོ་འགྲུབ་པའོ། །དགོན་པ་ལ་གནས་པ་ནི་རྣམ་པར་གྲོལ་བའི་ཡེ་ཤེས་མཐོང་བའི་ཕུང་པོ་སྐྱེ་བའོ། །དགོན་པ་ལ་གནས་པ་ནི་བྱང་ཆུབ་ཀྱི་ཕྱོགས་ཀྱི་ཆོས་རྣམས་རབ་ཏུ་སྟེན་པའོ། །དགོན་པ་ལ་གནས་པ་ནི་སྦྱངས་པའི་ཡོན་ཏན་བཅུ་གཉིས་པོ་དག་སྤྱོད་པའོ། །དགོན་

པ་ལ་གནས་པ་ནི་བདེན་པ་རྣམས་རྟོགས་པའོ། །དགོན་པ་ལ་གནས་པ་ནི་ཕུང་པོ་
རྣམས་ཡོངས་སུ་ཤེས་པའོ། །དགོན་པ་ལ་གནས་པ་ནི་ཁམས་རྣམས་ཆོས་ཀྱི་
དབྱིངས་དང་མཉམ་པར་འཇལ་བའོ། །དགོན་པ་ལ་གནས་པ་ནི་སྐྱེ་མཆེད་རྣམས་
སེལ་བའོ། །དགོན་པ་ལ་གནས་པ་ནི་བྱང་ཆུབ་ཀྱི་སེམས་མི་བརྗེད་པའོ། །
དགོན་པ་ལ་གནས་པ་ནི་སྟོང་པ་ཉིད་ལ་སོ་སོར་རྟོག་པས་སྐྲག་པ་མེད་པའོ། །དགོན་
པ་ལ་གནས་པ་ནི་ཆོས་ཀུན་ཏུ་འཛིན་པའོ། །དགོན་པ་ལ་གནས་པ་ནི་དགེ་བའི་རྩ་བ་
ཐམས་ཅད་ཆུད་མི་གཟོན་པའོ། །དགོན་པ་ལ་གནས་པ་ནི་སངས་རྒྱས་རྣམས་ཀྱིས་
བསྔགས་པའོ། །དགོན་པ་ལ་གནས་པ་ནི་བྱང་ཆུབ་སེམས་དཔའ་རྣམས་ཀྱིས་བསྟོད་
པའོ། །དགོན་པ་ལ་གནས་པ་ནི་འཕགས་པ་རྣམས་ཀྱིས་བཀུར་བའོ། །དགོན་པ་
ལ་གནས་པ་ནི་ཐར་པ་འདོད་པ་རྣམས་ཀྱིས་བསྟེན་པའོ། །དགོན་པ་ལ་གནས་པ་ནི་
ཐམས་ཅད་མཁྱེན་པའི་ཡེ་ཤེས་ཁོང་དུ་ཆུད་པར་བྱ་བའི་ཕྱིར་བསྟེན་པའོ་སྙམ་དུ་བསླབ་
པར་བྱའོ། །ཁྱིམ་བདག་གཞན་ཡང་བྱང་ཆུབ་སེམས་དཔའ་རབ་ཏུ་བྱུང་བ་དགོན་པ་
ལ་གནས་པ་ནི་ཚེགས་ཆུང་ངུས་ཕ་རོལ་ཏུ་ཕྱིན་པ་དྲུག་བསྒོམ་པ་ཡོངས་སུ་རྫོགས་པར་
འགྱུར་རོ། །དེ་ཅིའི་ཕྱིར་ཞེ་ན། གང་དགོན་པ་ལ་གནས་པའི་བྱང་ཆུབ་སེམས་
དཔའ་ནི་ལུས་དང་སྲོག་ལ་ཡང་མི་ལྟ་བ་ཡིན་ཏེ། དེ་ལྟར་དགོན་པ་ལ་གནས་པ་དེའི་
སྦྱིན་པའི་ཕ་རོལ་ཏུ་ཕྱིན་པ་བསྒོམ་པ་ཡོངས་སུ་རྫོགས་པར་འགྱུར་རོ། །ཁྱིམ་བདག་
ཇི་ལྟར་ན་བྱང་ཆུབ་སེམས་དཔའ་རབ་ཏུ་བྱུང་བ་དགོན་པ་ལ་གནས་པའི་ཚུལ་ཁྲིམས་ཀྱི་
ཕ་རོལ་ཏུ་ཕྱིན་པ་བསྒོམ་པ་ཡོངས་སུ་རྫོགས་པར་འགྱུར་ཞེ་ན། ཁྱིམ་བདག་གང་
བྱང་ཆུབ་སེམས་དཔའ་རབ་ཏུ་བྱུང་བ་དགོན་པ་ལ་གནས་པ་ནི་སྦྱངས་པའི་ཡོན་ཏན་
དང་། ཡོ་བྱད་བསྙུངས་པ་ལ་རབ་ཏུ་གནས་ནས་སྡོམ་པ་གསུམ་གྱིས་ཡང་དག་པར་
སྒྲུབ་སྟེ། དེ་ལྟར་དགོན་པ་ལ་གནས་པ་དེའི་ཚུལ་ཁྲིམས་ཀྱི་ཕ་རོལ་ཏུ་ཕྱིན་པ་བསྒོམ་
པ་ཡོངས་སུ་རྫོགས་པར་འགྱུར་རོ། །ཁྱིམ་བདག་ཇི་ལྟར་ན་བྱང་ཆུབ་སེམས་དཔའ་
རབ་ཏུ་བྱུང་བ་དགོན་པ་ལ་གནས་པའི་བཟོད་པའི་ཕ་རོལ་ཏུ་ཕྱིན་པ་བསྒོམ་པ་ཡོངས་སུ་
རྫོགས་པར་འགྱུར་ཞེ་ན། ཁྱིམ་བདག་གང་བྱང་ཆུབ་སེམས་དཔའ་རབ་ཏུ་བྱུང་བ་

དགོན་པ་ལ་གནས་པ་ནི་སེམས་ལ་གནོད་སེམས་མེད་ཅིང་སེམས་ཅན་ཐམས་ཅད་ལ་བྱམས་པར་བྱེད། དེ་ཐམས་ཅད་མཁྱེན་པ་ཉིད་ལ་ཡང་བཟོད་པ་ཡིན་ཏེ། དེ་ལྟར་དགོན་པ་ལ་གནས་པ་དེའི་བཟོད་པའི་ཕ་རོལ་ཏུ་ཕྱིན་པ་བསྒོམ་པ་ཡོངས་སུ་རྫོགས་པར་འགྱུར་རོ། །ཁྱིམ་བདག་ཇི་ལྟར་ན་བྱང་ཆུབ་སེམས་དཔའ་རབ་ཏུ་བྱུང་བ་དགོན་པ་ལ་གནས་པའི་བརྩོན་འགྲུས་ཀྱི་ཕ་རོལ་ཏུ་ཕྱིན་པ་བསྒོམ་པ་ཡོངས་སུ་རྫོགས་པར་འགྱུར་ཞེ་ན། ཁྱིམ་བདག་འདི་ལ་བྱང་ཆུབ་སེམས་དཔའ་རབ་ཏུ་བྱུང་བ་ནི་མི་སྐྱེ་བ་ལ་བཟོད་པ་རབ་ཏུ་ཐོབ་པར་བྱ་བའི་ཕྱིར་བདག་དགོན་པ་འདི་ལས་ལྡོག་པར་མི་བྱའོ་སྙམ་དུ་སློབ་སྟེ། དེ་ལྟར་དགོན་པ་ལ་གནས་པ་དེའི་བརྩོན་འགྲུས་ཀྱི་ཕ་རོལ་ཏུ་ཕྱིན་པ་བསྒོམ་པ་ཡོངས་སུ་རྫོགས་པར་འགྱུར་རོ། །ཁྱིམ་བདག་ཇི་ལྟར་ན་བྱང་ཆུབ་སེམས་དཔའ་རབ་ཏུ་བྱུང་བ་དགོན་པ་ལ་གནས་པའི་བསམ་གཏན་གྱི་ཕ་རོལ་ཏུ་ཕྱིན་པ་བསྒོམ་པ་ཡོངས་སུ་རྫོགས་པར་འགྱུར་ཞེ་ན། ཁྱིམ་བདག་གང་བྱང་ཆུབ་སེམས་དཔའ་རབ་ཏུ་བྱུང་བ་དགོན་པ་ལ་གནས་པ་ནི་བསམ་གཏན་གྱི་ཕ་རོལ་ཏུ་ཕྱིན་པ་རབ་ཏུ་འཐོབ་སྟེ། སེམས་ཅན་ཡོངས་སུ་སྨིན་པར་བྱེད་པ་ཡང་ཡལ་བར་མི་འདོར་ལ། འདི་ལྟར་དགེ་བའི་རྩ་བ་ཡང་སོགས་པར་འདོད་པ་ཡིན་ཏེ། དེ་ལྟར་དགོན་པ་ལ་གནས་པ་དེའི་བསམ་གཏན་གྱི་ཕ་རོལ་ཏུ་ཕྱིན་པ་བསྒོམ་པ་ཡོངས་སུ་རྫོགས་པར་འགྱུར་རོ། །ཁྱིམ་བདག་ཇི་ལྟར་ན་བྱང་ཆུབ་སེམས་དཔའ་རབ་ཏུ་བྱུང་བ་དགོན་པ་ལ་གནས་པའི་ཤེས་རབ་ཀྱི་ཕ་རོལ་ཏུ་ཕྱིན་པ་བསྒོམ་པ་ཡོངས་སུ་རྫོགས་པར་འགྱུར་ཞེ་ན། ཁྱིམ་བདག་གང་བྱང་ཆུབ་སེམས་དཔའ་རབ་ཏུ་བྱུང་བ་ནི་འདི་ལ་ལུས་ཇི་ལྟ་བ་དགོན་པ་ཡང་དེ་བཞིན་ནོ། །ལུས་ཇི་ལྟ་བ་བྱང་ཆུབ་ཀྱང་དེ་བཞིན་ནོ་སྙམ་དུ་སློབ་ཅིང་དེ་བཞིན་ཉིད་ཀྱིས་མི་རྟོག་རྣམ་པར་མི་རྟོག་སྟེ། དེ་ལྟར་དགོན་པ་ལ་གནས་པ་དེའི་ཤེས་རབ་ཀྱི་ཕ་རོལ་ཏུ་ཕྱིན་པ་བསྒོམ་པ་ཡོངས་སུ་རྫོགས་པར་འགྱུར་རོ། །ཁྱིམ་བདག་དེ་ལྟར་ན་བྱང་ཆུབ་སེམས་དཔའ་རབ་ཏུ་བྱུང་བ་དགོན་པ་ལ་གནས་པ་ཚོགས་ཆུང་ངུས་ཕ་རོལ་ཏུ་ཕྱིན་པ་དྲུག་བསྒོམ་པ་ཡོངས་སུ་རྫོགས་པར་འགྱུར་རོ། །ཁྱིམ་བདག་བྱང་ཆུབ་སེམས་དཔའ་རབ་ཏུ་བྱུང་བ་ཆོས་བཞི་དང་ལྡན་ན་དགོན་པ་ལ་གནས་

པར་གནང་བ་ཡིན་ནོ། །བཞི་གང་ཞེ་ན། ཁྱིམ་བདག་འདི་ལ་བྱང་ཆུབ་སེམས་དཔའ་རབ་ཏུ་བྱུང་བ་མང་དུ་ཐོས་པ་ཡིན་ཏེ། ཐོས་པ་འཛིན་པ། ཆོས་རྣམ་པར་ངེས་པ་ལ་མཁས་པ། ཚུལ་བཞིན་ཡིད་ལ་བྱེད་པ་ལ་བརྩོན་ཞིང་། ཆོས་དང་ཆོས་ཀྱི་རྗེས་སུ་འཐུན་པ་སྒྲུབ་པ་དེས་དགོན་པ་ལ་གནས་པར་བྱའོ། །ཁྱིམ་བདག་གཞན་ཡང་བྱང་ཆུབ་སེམས་དཔའ་རབ་ཏུ་བྱུང་བ་ཉོན་མོངས་པའི་ཤས་ཆེ་ན་དེས་ཉོན་མོངས་པ་རྣམས་ཞི་བར་བྱ་བའི་ཕྱིར་འགྲོགས་པ་མེད་པར་དགོན་པ་ལ་གནས་པར་བྱ་སྟེ། དེས་ཉོན་མོངས་པ་ཚར་གཅད་པར་བྱའོ། །ཁྱིམ་བདག་གཞན་ཡང་བྱང་ཆུབ་སེམས་དཔའ་རབ་ཏུ་བྱུང་བ་ནི་མངོན་པར་ཤེས་པ་ལྔ་པོ་དག་ཐོབ་པ་ཡིན་ཏེ། དེས་ལྷ་དང་། ཀླུ་དང་། གནོད་སྦྱིན་དང་། དྲི་ཟ་རྣམས་ཡོངས་སུ་སྨིན་པར་བྱ་བའི་ཕྱིར་དགོན་པ་ལ་གནས་པར་བྱའོ། །ཁྱིམ་བདག་གཞན་ཡང་བྱང་ཆུབ་སེམས་དཔའ་རབ་ཏུ་བྱུང་བས་སངས་རྒྱས་ཀྱིས་དགོན་པ་ལ་གནས་པར་གནང་བར་བཀའ་སྩལ་བར་ཤེས་ནས་དགོན་པ་ལ་གནས་པར་བྱ་སྟེ། དེར་དགེ་བའི་ཆོས་ཐམས་ཅད་ཡོངས་སུ་རྫོགས་པར་འགྱུར་རོ། །དགེ་བའི་རྩ་བས་ཉེ་བར་བརྟན་ནས་ཕྱིས་གྲོང་དང་། གྲོང་ཁྱེར་དང་། གྲོང་རྡལ་དང་། ལྗོངས་དང་། ཡུལ་འཁོར་དང་། ཕོ་བྲང་འཁོར་དག་ཏུ་ཞུགས་ཏེ་ཆོས་བསྟན་པར་བྱའོ། །ཁྱིམ་བདག་བྱང་ཆུབ་སེམས་དཔའ་རབ་ཏུ་བྱུང་བ་ཆོས་བཞི་པོ་དེ་དག་དང་ལྡན་ན་དགོན་པ་ལ་གནས་པར་གནང་ངོ་། །ཁྱིམ་བདག་གལ་ཏེ་བྱང་ཆུབ་སེམས་དཔའ་རབ་ཏུ་བྱུང་བ་ལུང་དང་ཁ་ཏོན་མནོད་པའི་ཕྱིར་ཚོགས་ཀྱི་ནང་དུ་འཇུག་ན་ཡང་དེས་དེར་གུས་པ་དང་བཅས་པར་བྱ་སྟེ། སློབ་དཔོན་དང་། མཁན་པོ་རྣམས་དང་། གནས་བརྟན་དང་། བར་མ་དང་། དགེ་སློང་གསར་བུ་རྣམས་ལ་ཞེ་ས་དང་བཅས་པར་བྱ། ཚུལ་མཁས་པར་བྱའོ། །སྙོམ་ལས་མེད་པར་རང་གིས་བྱ་བ་དང་། གཞན་ལ་གདུང་བ་མེད་པར་བྱའོ། །དེས་བསྙེན་བཀུར་ལ་གདུ་བར་མི་བྱའོ། །དེས་འདི་ལྟར་དེ་བཞིན་གཤེགས་པ་དགྲ་བཅོམ་པ་ཡང་དག་པར་རྫོགས་པའི་སངས་རྒྱས་ལྷ་དང་བཅས་པའི་འཇིག་རྟེན་དང་། བདུད་དང་བཅས་པ་དང་། ཚངས་པ་དང་བཅས་པ་དང་། དགེ་སྦྱོང་དང་།

བྲམ་ཟེའི་སྐྱེ་དགུ་དང་བཅས་པ་དང་། ལྷ་དང་། མི་དང་། ལྷ་མ་ཡིན་དུ་བཅས་པས་མཆོད་པ་སྦྱིན་གནས་སུ་གྱུར་པ་དེ་ཡང་སེམས་ཅན་ཐམས་ཅད་ལ་གང་ལས་ཀྱང་རིམ་གྲོར་བྱ་བ་བདག་གིར་མི་མཛད་ན། བདག་ཅག་མ་བསླབས་པ་སློབ་འདོད་པ་རྣམས་ལྟ་ཅི་སྨོས་ཏེ། བདག་གིས་ནི་སེམས་ཅན་ཐམས་ཅད་ལ་བསྙེན་བཀུར་བྱའི། གང་ལས་ཀྱང་བསྙེན་བཀུར་བྱ་བ་བདག་གིར་མི་བྱའོ་སྙམ་དུ་བརྟག་པར་བྱའོ། །དེ་ཅིའི་ཕྱིར་ཞེ་ན། ཁྱིམ་བདག་དགེ་སློང་བསྙེན་བཀུར་ལ་གདུ་བ་ནི་ཡོན་ཏན་གྱི་ཆོས་རྗེས་སུ་བཟུང་བ་ཆུད་གཟོན་པ་ཡིན་ཏེ། དེས་གང་དག་སྤྱོད་པ་དེ་དག་ཀྱང་འདི་སྙམ་དུ་སེམས་ཏེ། བདག་ཅག་ནི་བསྙེན་བཀུར་གྱི་ཕྱིར་སྤྱོད་ཀྱི། ཆོས་ཀྱི་ཕྱིར་ནི་མ་ཡིན་ནོ་སྙམ་སྟེ། དེ་བདག་ཉིད་ཀྱི་དད་པ་ཆུད་གསོན་ཏོ། ། གང་དག་དེ་ལ་བསྙེན་བཀུར་བྱེད་པ་འཇིག་རྟེན་གྱི་ཟང་ཟིང་དང་ལྡན་པ་དེ་དག་གི་ཡང་དོན་ཆེན་པོར་མི་འགྱུར་རོ། །འབྲས་བུ་ཆེན་པོར་མི་འགྱུར་རོ། །དེ་སློབ་དཔོན་དང་། མཁན་པོའི་གནས་དུ་འགྲོ་ན་ཡང་སློབ་དཔོན་དང་། མཁན་པོས་མ་དད་པའི་བག་གང་ཡང་རུང་བ་ཞིག་ལས་བརྟགས་ནས་བདག་ལ་ལུང་འབོག་པ་དང་། ཁ་ཏོན་བྱ་བ་དང་། རྗེས་སུ་བསྟེན་པས་ཕན་འདོགས་པར་མི་འགྱུར་དུ་འོང་ཞེས་ལུས་དང་སེམས་ལས་སུ་རུང་བ་དང་། སེམས་ཅང་ཤེས་པས་འགྲོ་བར་བྱའོ། ། དེ་ལུང་མནོད་པ་དང་། ཁ་ཏོན་གྱི་ཕྱིར་ལུས་དང་སྲོག་ལ་ཡང་མི་བལྟ་བར་བྱའོ། །ཆོས་འདོད་པས་སློབ་དཔོན་དང་། མཁན་པོ་རྣམས་ཀྱི་བསམ་པ་ཡོངས་སུ་རྫོགས་པར་བྱའོ། །ཡོན་ཏན་དོན་དུ་གཉེར་བས་རླེད་པ་དང་། བཀུར་སྟི་དང་། ཚིགས་སུ་བཅད་པ་ཐམས་ཅད་དོན་དུ་མི་གཉེར་བར་བྱའོ། །ཁྱིམ་བདག་གལ་ཏེ་བྱང་ཆུབ་སེམས་དཔའ་ལུང་མནོད་པ་དང་། ཁ་ཏོན་བྱ་བ་དོན་དུ་གཉེར་བས་གཞན་དག་ལས་ཚིགས་བཞི་པའི་ཚིགས་སུ་བཅད་པ་ཙམ་འམ། སྦྱིན་པ་དང་། ཚུལ་ཁྲིམས་དང་། བཟོད་པ་དང་། བརྩོན་འགྲུས་དང་། བསམ་གཏན་དང་། ཤེས་རབ་དང་ལྡན་པ་འམ། བྱང་ཆུབ་སེམས་དཔའི་ལམ་གྱི་ཚོགས་སོགས་པ་དང་ལྡན་པའི་ཚིགས་བཞི་པའི་ཚིགས་སུ་བཅད་པ་སུ་ལས་མཉན་ཏམ། ལུང་མནོས་སམ།

བཟུང་ན་ངེས་སློབ་དཔོན་དེ་ལ་ཆོས་ཀྱི་ཕྱིར་གུས་པར་བྱའོ། །མིང་དང་། ཚིག་དང་། ཡི་གེ་ཇི་སྙེད་ཀྱིས་ཚིགས་སུ་བཅད་པ་བསྟན་པ་དེ་སྙེད་ཀྱི་བསྐལ་པར་གལ་ཏེ་སློབ་དཔོན་དེ་ལ་གཡོ་མེད་པས་བསྙེན་བཀུར་དང་། གཡོག་བྱས་ཤིང་རྙེད་པ་དང་། བཀུར་སྟི་ཐམས་ཅད་ཀྱིས་མཆོད་པ་བྱས་སུ་ཟིན་ཀྱང་། ཁྱིམ་བདག་ད་དུང་དུ་ངེས་སློབ་དཔོན་ལ་སློབ་དཔོན་དུ་རི་མོ་བྱ་བ་རྫོགས་པར་མི་འགྱུར་ན་ཆོས་མ་ཡིན་པའི་གུས་པས་ལྟ་ཅི་སྨོས། ཁྱིམ་བདག་དད་པས་མཉན་ཅིང་བསྒོམ་པ་དང་། ཁ་ཏོན་ལ་འཇུག་པ་དེའི་སེམས་དང་། སེམས་ལས་བྱུང་བ་དགེ་བ་དང་ལྡན་པ་འམ། སངས་རྒྱས་དང་ལྡན་པ་འམ། ཆོས་དང་ལྡན་པ་འམ། དགེ་འདུན་དང་ལྡན་པ་འམ། སྐྱོ་ཞིང་འདོད་ཆགས་དང་བྲལ་བ་དང་ལྡན་པ་འམ། བྱང་བ་དང་། དུལ་བ་དང་། ཞི་བ་དང་ལྡན་པའི་འཇུག་པ་ཇི་སྙེད་པ་གལ་ཏེ་དེ་སྙེད་ཀྱི་བསྐལ་པར་སློབ་དཔོན་ལ་བསྙེན་བཀུར་བྱས་སུ་ཟིན་ཀྱང་། ཁྱིམ་བདག་ད་དུང་དུ་སློབ་དཔོན་ལ་སློབ་དཔོན་དུ་རི་མོ་བྱ་བ་རྫོགས་པ་མ་ཡིན་ནོ། །ཁྱིམ་བདག་རྣམ་གྲངས་འདིས་ཀྱང་ཇི་ལྟར་རྣམ་པར་སྨིན་པའི་ཆོས་ཚད་མེད་ཅིང་ཡེ་ཤེས་ཁོང་དུ་ཆུད་པ་ཚད་མེད་པ་དེ་ལྟར་རིག་པར་བྱའོ། །ཁྱིམ་བདག་དེ་ལྟ་བས་ན་རྣམ་པར་སྨིན་པའི་ཆོས་ཚད་མེད་པ་དང་། ཡེ་ཤེས་ཁོང་དུ་ཆུད་པ་ཚད་མེད་པ་དྲིས་པས་བདག་གི་སློབ་དཔོན་ཡང་ཚད་མེད་དོ་སྙམ་ནས་བྱང་ཆུབ་སེམས་དཔའ་ཆོས་ལ་རི་མོ་ཚད་མེད་པར་བྱའོ། །ཁྱིམ་བདག་གཞན་ཡང་བྱང་ཆུབ་སེམས་དཔའ་རབ་ཏུ་བྱུང་བས། རབ་ཏུ་བྱུང་བའི་སྒྲུབ་པ་ལ་གནས་པར་བྱའོ། །ཁྱིམ་བདག་ཇི་ལྟར་ན་བྱང་ཆུབ་སེམས་དཔའ་རབ་ཏུ་བྱུང་བ་རབ་ཏུ་བྱུང་བའི་སྒྲུབ་པ་ལ་གནས་པ་ཡིན་ཞེ་ན། ཁྱིམ་བདག་འདི་ལ་བྱང་ཆུབ་སེམས་དཔའ་རབ་ཏུ་བྱུང་བ་ཚུལ་ཁྲིམས་ཡོངས་སུ་དག་པ་ཐོས་ན་དེ་ལ་སློབ་སྟེ། བཞི་པོ་འདི་དག་ནི་ཚུལ་ཁྲིམས་ཡོངས་སུ་དག་པའོ། །བཞི་གང་ཞེ་ན། འཕགས་པའི་རིགས་རྣམས་ལ་གནས་པ་དང་། སྦྱངས་པའི་ཡོན་ཏན་དང་ཡོ་བྱད་བསྙུངས་པ་ལ་མངོན་པར་དགའ་བ་དང་། ཁྱིམ་ན་གནས་པ་དང་། རབ་ཏུ་བྱུང་བ་རྣམས་དང་མི་འདྲེ་བ་དང་། ཚུལ་འཆོས་པ་མེད་པར་དགོན་པ་ལ་གནས་པ་སྟེ། བཞི་པོ་དེ་དག་ནི་

ཚུལ་ཁྲིམས་ཡོངས་སུ་དག་པའོ། །ཁྱིམ་བདག་གཞན་ཡང་ཚུལ་ཁྲིམས་ཡོངས་སུ་དག་པ་བཞི་སྟེ། བཞི་གང་ཞེ་ན། ལུས་བསྡམས་པས་ལུས་མི་དམིགས་པ་དང་། ངག་བསྡམས་པས་ངག་མི་དམིགས་པ་དང་། ཡིད་བསྡམས་པས་ཡིད་མི་དམིགས་པ་དང་། ལྟ་བ་དང་བྲལ་བས་ཐམས་ཅད་མཁྱེན་པར་སེམས་བསྐྱེད་པ་སྟེ། བཞི་པོ་དེ་དག་ནི་ཚུལ་ཁྲིམས་ཡོངས་སུ་དག་པའོ། །ཁྱིམ་བདག་གཞན་ཡང་ཚུལ་ཁྲིམས་ཡོངས་སུ་དག་པ་བཞི་སྟེ། བཞི་གང་ཞེ་ན། ངར་འཛིན་པ་སྤངས་པ་དང་། ང་ཡིར་འཛིན་པ་བོར་བ་དང་། ཆད་པ་དང་། རྟག་པ་དང་བྲལ་བ་དང་། རྟེན་པའི་ཆོས་ལ་འཇུག་པ་སྟེ། བཞི་པོ་དེ་དག་ནི་ཚུལ་ཁྲིམས་ཡོངས་སུ་དག་པའོ། །ཁྱིམ་བདག་གཞན་ཡང་ཚུལ་ཁྲིམས་ཡོངས་སུ་དག་པ་བཞི་སྟེ། བཞི་གང་ཞེ་ན། ཕུང་པོ་རྣམས་ལ་འབྱུང་བ་དང་འཇིག་པར་རྟོག་པ་དང་། ཁམས་རྣམས་ལ་ཆོས་ཀྱི་དབྱིངས་སུ་ཡོངས་སུ་འཇལ་བ་དང་། སྐྱེ་མཆེད་རྣམས་ལ་གྲོང་སྟོང་པར་འདུ་ཤེས་པ་དང་། ཐ་སྙད་བཏགས་པ་རྣམས་ལ་མངོན་པར་མ་ཞེན་པ་སྟེ། བཞི་པོ་དེ་དག་ནི་ཚུལ་ཁྲིམས་ཡོངས་སུ་དག་པའོ། །ཁྱིམ་བདག་གཞན་ཡང་ཚུལ་ཁྲིམས་ཡོངས་སུ་དག་པ་བཞི་སྟེ། བཞི་གང་ཞེ་ན། བདག་ལ་བདག་མེད་པར་འདུ་ཤེས་པས་བདག་ལ་མི་སྟོད་པ་དང་། གཞན་མི་དམིགས་པས་གཞན་ལ་མི་སྨོད་པ་དང་། སེམས་ཤིན་ཏུ་སྦྱངས་པས་རློམ་སེམས་མེད་པ་དང་། ཆོས་ཐམས་ཅད་མཉམ་པ་ཉིད་པས་གཡོ་བ་མེད་པ་སྟེ། བཞི་པོ་དེ་དག་ནི་ཚུལ་ཁྲིམས་ཡོངས་སུ་དག་པའོ། །ཁྱིམ་བདག་གཞན་ཡང་ཚུལ་ཁྲིམས་ཡོངས་སུ་དག་པ་བཞི་སྟེ། བཞི་གང་ཞེ་ན། སྟོང་པ་ཉིད་ལ་མོས་པ་དང་། མཚན་མ་མེད་པས་མི་སྐྲག་པ་དང་། སེམས་ཅན་ཐམས་ཅད་ལ་ཆེར་སྙིང་རྗེ་བ་དང་། བདག་མེད་པ་ལ་བཟོད་པ་སྟེ། བཞི་པོ་དེ་དག་ནི་ཚུལ་ཁྲིམས་ཡོངས་སུ་དག་པའོ། །ཁྱིམ་བདག་གཞན་ཡང་བྱང་ཆུབ་སེམས་དཔའ་རབ་ཏུ་བྱུང་བ་ཏིང་ངེ་འཛིན་ཡོངས་སུ་དག་པ་ཐོས་ན་དེ་ལ་སློབ་སྟེ། ཏིང་ངེ་འཛིན་ཡོངས་སུ་དག་པ་གང་ཞེ་ན། གང་ཆོས་ཐམས་ཅད་ལ་རྩོལ་བ་མེད་པ་དང་། ཆོས་ཐམས་ཅད་མཉམ་པ་ཉིད་པས་གཉིས་སུ་དབྱེར་མེད་པ་དང་།

སེམས་ལས་སུ་རུང་བ་དང་། སེམས་རྩེ་གཅིག་པ་དང་། སེམས་ངེས་པར་བྱུང་བ་དང་། སེམས་མི་འཕྲོ་བ་དང་། སེམས་ཀུན་ཏུ་མི་རྒྱུག་པ་དང་། སེམས་མི་གནས་པ་དང་། སེམས་ངེས་པར་སེམས་པར་བྱིན་གྱིས་རློབ་པ་དང་། སེམས་ལ་དབང་སྒྱུར་བ་དང་། སེམས་འདོད་པའི་ཡོན་ཏན་རྣམས་ལ་མི་ཆགས་པ་དང་། སེམས་ཆོས་ལ་སྒྱུ་མར་སོ་སོར་རྟོག་པ་དང་། ཇི་ལྟར་ཆོས་ཀྱི་དབྱིངས་མངོན་པར་འདུ་མི་བྱེད་པ་དང་། ཇི་ལྟར་མི་སྐྱེ་མི་འབྱུང་ཞིང་མཉམ་པ་ཉིད་པ་དེ་ལྟར་ཁྱིམ་བདག་བྱང་ཆུབ་སེམས་དཔའ་རབ་ཏུ་བྱུང་བ་ཏིང་ངེ་འཛིན་ཡོངས་སུ་དག་པ་ལ་སོ་སོར་རྟོག་གོ །ཁྱིམ་བདག་གཞན་ཡང་བྱང་ཆུབ་སེམས་དཔའ་རབ་ཏུ་བྱུང་བ་ཤེས་རབ་ཀྱི་ཕ་རོལ་ཏུ་ཕྱིན་པ་ཡོངས་སུ་དག་པ་ཐོས་ན་དེ་ལ་སློབ་སྟེ། ཤེས་རབ་ཡོངས་སུ་དག་པ་དེ་གང་ཞེ་ན། དེ་འདི་ལྟར་སོ་སོར་རྟོག་སྟེ། ཆོས་ཐམས་ཅད་མངོན་སུམ་དུ་ཤེས་པ་དང་། ཚིག་རབ་ཏུ་དབྱེ་བ་ཤེས་པ་དང་། སོ་སོ་ཡང་དག་པར་རིག་པ་འཇུག་པ་ཤེས་པ་དང་། སེམས་ཅན་གཞན་དག་ལ་ཆོས་གོ་བར་བྱེད་པ་ཤེས་པ་སྟེ། ཁྱིམ་བདག་དེ་ལྟར་བྱང་ཆུབ་སེམས་དཔའ་རབ་ཏུ་བྱུང་བ་ཤེས་རབ་ཡོངས་སུ་དག་པ་ལ་སོ་སོར་རྟོག་གོ །ཁྱིམ་བདག་གཞན་ཡང་བྱང་ཆུབ་སེམས་དཔའ་རབ་ཏུ་བྱུང་བ་འདི་ལ་ཤེས་རབ་འདི་ནི་ལུས་མེད་པས་ཐོགས་པ་མེད་པའི་མཚན་ཉིད་དོ། །རྒྱུ་བ་མེད་པས་གཟུང་བ་མེད་པའི་མཚན་ཉིད་དོ། །སྐྱེ་བ་མེད་པས་གནས་པ་མེད་པའི་མཚན་ཉིད་དོ། །ནམ་མཁའ་ལྟར་ངོ་བོ་ཉིད་མེད་པས་མངོན་པར་འདུ་མི་བྱེད་པའི་མཚན་ཉིད་དོ་སྙམ་དུ་རབ་ཏུ་སློབ་བོ། །ཁྱིམ་བདག་དེ་ལྟར་ན་གང་འདི་ལྟར་ཆོས་ལ་སོ་སོར་རྟོག་པ་འདི་ནི་བྱང་ཆུབ་སེམས་དཔའ་རབ་ཏུ་བྱུང་བའི་སྒྲུབ་པའོ། །བཅོམ་ལྡན་འདས་ཀྱིས་ཆོས་ཀྱི་རྣམ་གྲངས་འདི་བཤད་པ་ན་སྲོག་ཆགས་བརྒྱ་སྟོང་གིས་ནི་བླ་ན་མེད་པ་ཡང་དག་པར་རྫོགས་པའི་བྱང་ཆུབ་ཏུ་སེམས་བསྐྱེད་དོ། །ཁྱིམ་བདག་དེ་དག་ཐམས་ཅད་ལས་ཕལ་ཆེར་ནི་མི་སྐྱེ་བའི་ཆོས་ལ་བཟོད་པ་རབ་ཏུ་ཐོབ་བོ། །སྲོག་ཆགས་སུམ་ཁྲི་ཉིས་སྟོང་ནི་ཆོས་རྣམས་ལ་ཆོས་ཀྱི་མིག་རྡུལ་དང་བྲལ་ཞིང་དྲི་མ་མེད་པ་རྣམ་པར་དག་གོ །དེ་ནས་ཁྱིམ་བདག་དྲག་ཤུལ་ཅན་

དགའ་ལ་ཡི་རངས་ཏེ། རབ་ཏུ་དགའ་ནས་མགུ་བ་དང་ཡིད་བདེ་བ་སྐྱེས་ཏེ། བརྒྱ་སྟོང་རི་བའི་རས་བཅོས་བུའི་ཟླུང་བཅོམ་ལྡན་འདས་ཀྱི་སྐུ་ལ་གསོལ་ནས་འདི་སྐད་ཅེས་གསོལ་ཏོ། །བཅོམ་ལྡན་འདས་བདག་གི་དགེ་བའི་རྩ་བ་འདི་སེམས་ཅན་རྣམས་ལ་སྩལ་ཏོ། །བདག་གི་དགེ་བའི་རྩ་བ་འདིས་བྱང་ཆུབ་སེམས་དཔའ་ཁྱིམ་པ་རྣམས་ཀྱི་བསླབ་པ་ཇི་ལྟར་བཅས་པ་དེ་ལྟར་བྱང་ཆུབ་སེམས་དཔའ་ཁྱིམ་པ་གང་ལགས་པ་དེ་དག་གི་ཆོས་ཡོངས་སུ་རྫོགས་པར་གྱུར་ཅིག །བཅོམ་ལྡན་འདས་ཀྱིས་ཇི་ལྟར་བྱང་ཆུབ་སེམས་དཔའ་རབ་ཏུ་བྱུང་བ་རྣམས་ཀྱི་བསླབ་པ་བཅས་པ་ཡང་དེ་ལྟར་བྱང་ཆུབ་སེམས་དཔའ་རབ་ཏུ་བྱུང་བ་གང་དག་ལགས་པ་དེ་དག་གི་ཆོས་ཡོངས་སུ་རྫོགས་པར་གྱུར་ཅིག །བཅོམ་ལྡན་འདས་ལ་ཡང་ཞུ་བར་འཚལ་ཏེ། བཅོམ་ལྡན་འདས་བྱང་ཆུབ་སེམས་དཔའ་ཁྱིམ་པ་ཁྱིམ་ན་གནས་པ་ཆོས་དུ་ཞིག་དང་ལྡན་ན་རབ་ཏུ་བྱུང་བའི་བསླབ་པ་ལ་སློབ་པ་ལགས། དེ་སྐད་ཅེས་གསོལ་པ་དང་། བཅོམ་ལྡན་འདས་ཀྱིས་ཁྱིམ་བདག་དྲག་ཤུལ་ཅན་ལ་འདི་སྐད་ཅེས་བཀའ་སྩལ་ཏོ། །ཁྱིམ་བདག་འདི་ལ་བྱང་ཆུབ་སེམས་དཔའ་ཁྱིམ་པ་ཁྱིམ་ན་གནས་པ་ཆོས་ལྔ་དང་ལྡན་ན་རབ་ཏུ་བྱུང་བའི་བསླབ་པ་ལ་སློབ་པ་ཡིན་ཏེ། ལྔ་གང་ཞེ་ན། ཁྱིམ་བདག་འདི་ལ་བྱང་ཆུབ་སེམས་དཔའ་ཁྱིམ་པ་ཁྱིམ་ན་གནས་པ་མི་ལྟ་བར་དངོས་པོ་ཐམས་ཅད་ཡོངས་སུ་གཏོང་བ་ཡིན་ཏེ། ཐམས་ཅད་མཁྱེན་པ་ཉིད་ཀྱི་ཡེ་ཤེས་དང་ལྡན་པས་རྣམ་པར་སྨིན་པ་ལ་རེ་བ་མེད་པ་དང་། ཁྱིམ་བདག་གཞན་ཡང་བྱང་ཆུབ་སེམས་དཔའ་ཁྱིམ་པ་ཁྱིམ་ན་གནས་པ་ཚངས་པར་སྤྱོད་ཅིང་གཙང་མ་ཡིན་ཏེ། ཡིད་ཀྱི་མགུ་ལ་ཡང་འདོད་པ་མི་སྐྱེད་ན་མཚན་གཉིས་སྤྱོད་པ་འམ། ཡན་ལག་མ་ཡིན་པར་འཇུག་པ་ལྟ་ཅི་སྨོས་པ་དང་། ཁྱིམ་བདག་གཞན་ཡང་བྱང་ཆུབ་སེམས་དཔའ་ཁྱིམ་པ་ཁྱིམ་ན་གནས་པ་ཡང་དག་པར་སྐྱོན་མེད་པ་ལ་མི་རེག་ཅིང་ཁྱིམ་སྟོང་པར་ཞུགས་ནས་ཐབས་ཀྱིས་མངོན་པར་བསྒྲུབས་པ་བསམ་གཏན་བཞི་པོ་དག་ལ་སྙོམས་པར་འཇུག་པ་དང་། ཁྱིམ་བདག་གཞན་ཡང་བྱང་ཆུབ་སེམས་དཔའ་ཁྱིམ་པ་ཁྱིམ་ན་གནས་པ་སེམས་ཅན་ཐམས་ཅད་བདེ་བར་བྱེད་པ་ལ་བརྩོན་པ་ཤེས་རབ་ཀྱི་ཕ་རོལ་ཏུ་ཕྱིན་པས་ངེས་པར་འབྱུང་བར་

བརྗོད་འགྲུས་རྩོམ་པ་དང་། ཁྱིམ་བདག་གཞན་ཡང་བྱང་ཆུབ་སེམས་དཔའ་ཁྱིམ་པ་ཁྱིམ་ན་གནས་པ་དག་ཀྱང་དམ་པའི་ཆོས་ཡོངས་སུ་འཛིན་ཅིང་གཞན་ཡང་ཡང་དག་པའི་ཆོས་ལ་སྦྱོར་བར་བྱེད་པ་སྟེ། ཁྱིམ་བདག་བྱང་ཆུབ་སེམས་དཔའ་ཁྱིམ་པ་ཁྱིམ་ན་གནས་པ་ཆོས་ལྔ་པོ་དེ་དག་དང་ལྡན་ན་རབ་ཏུ་བྱུང་བའི་བསླབ་པ་ལ་སློབ་པ་ཡིན་ནོ། །དེ་ནས་བཅོམ་ལྡན་འདས་ལ་ཁྱིམ་བདག་དྲག་ཤུལ་ཅན་གྱིས་འདི་སྐད་ཅེས་གསོལ་ཏོ། །བཅོམ་ལྡན་འདས་བདག་དེ་བཞིན་གཤེགས་པ་རྣམས་ཀྱི་བཀའ་བཞིན་དུ་བགྱི་བར་འཚལ་ལོ། །རབ་ཏུ་བྱུང་བའི་བསླབ་པ་ལ་བསླབ་བོ། །ཆོས་མཉམ་པ་ཉིད་འདི་ལྟ་བུ་ལ་ཡང་འཇུག་པར་བགྱིའོ། །དེ་ནས་དེའི་ཚེ་བཅོམ་ལྡན་འདས་འཛུམ་པ་མཛད་དོ། །འདི་ནི་སངས་རྒྱས་བཅོམ་ལྡན་འདས་རྣམས་གང་གི་ཚེ་འཛུམ་པ་མཛད་པའི་ཆོས་ཉིད་དེ། དེའི་ཚེ་བཅོམ་ལྡན་འདས་ཀྱི་ཞལ་གྱི་སྒོ་ནས་འོད་འཕྲོ་བ་ཁ་དོག་དུ་མ་ཁ་དོག་སྣ་ཚོགས་བྱུང་བ་འདི་ལྟ་སྟེ། སྔོན་པོ་དང་། སེར་པོ་དང་། དམར་པོ་དང་། དཀར་པོ་དང་། ལི་བཀྲན་དང་། ཤེལ་དང་། དངུལ་གྱི་ཁ་དོག་ལྟ་བུ་སྟེ། དེ་དག་གིས་འཇིག་རྟེན་གྱི་ཁམས་མཐའ་ཡས་མུ་མེད་པ་རྣམས་སུ་འོད་ཀྱིས་སྣང་བས་ཁྱབ་པར་བྱས་ནས་ཚངས་པའི་འཇིག་རྟེན་གྱི་བར་དུ་མངོན་པར་འཕགས་ཏེ། སླར་ལོག་ནས་བཅོམ་ལྡན་འདས་ལ་ལན་གསུམ་བསྐོར་བ་བྱས་ཏེ་བཅོམ་ལྡན་འདས་ཀྱི་དབུའི་གཙུག་ཏུ་ནུབ་པར་གྱུར་ཏོ། །དེ་ནས་ཚེ་དང་ལྡན་པ་ཀུན་དགའ་བོ་སངས་རྒྱས་ཀྱི་མཐུས་སྟན་ལས་ལངས་ནས་བླ་གོས་ཕྲག་པ་གཅིག་ཏུ་གཟར་ཏེ་པུས་མོ་གཡས་པའི་ལྷ་ང་ས་ལ་བཙུགས་ནས། བཅོམ་ལྡན་འདས་ག་ལ་བ་དེ་ལོགས་སུ་ཐལ་མོ་སྦྱར་བ་བཏུད་དེ་བཅོམ་ལྡན་འདས་ལ་འདི་སྐད་ཅེས་གསོལ་ཏོ། །བཅོམ་ལྡན་འདས་རྒྱུ་མ་མཆིས་རྐྱེན་མ་མཆིས་པར་ནི་དེ་བཞིན་གཤེགས་པ་འཛུམ་པ་མི་མཛད་ན་འཛུམ་པ་མཛད་པའི་རྒྱུ་གང་ལགས། རྐྱེན་གང་ལགས། དེ་སྐད་ཅེས་གསོལ་པ་དང་། བཅོམ་ལྡན་འདས་ཀྱིས་ཚེ་དང་ལྡན་པ་ཀུན་དགའ་བོ་ལ་འདི་སྐད་ཅེས་བཀའ་སྩལ་ཏོ། །ཀུན་དགའ་བོ་ཁྱོད་ཀྱིས་ཁྱིམ་བདག་དྲག་ཤུལ་ཅན་འདིས་དེ་བཞིན་གཤེགས་པ་ལ་མཆོད་པ་བྱས་ཏེ་ཆོས་བསྒྲུབ་པའི་ཕྱིར་སེང་གེའི་སྒྲ་བསྒྲགས་པ་

མཐོང་ངམ། གསོལ་པ། བཅོམ་ལྡན་འདས་མཐོང་ལགས་སོ། །བདེ་བར་གཤེགས་པ་མཐོང་ལགས་སོ། །བཅོམ་ལྡན་འདས་ཀྱིས་བཀའ་སྩལ་པ། ཀུན་དགའ་བོ་ཁྱིམ་བདག་དྲག་ཤུལ་ཅན་འདི་ནི་གང་དག་བསྐལ་པ་བཟང་པོ་འདི་ལ་འབྱུང་བའི་དེ་བཞིན་གཤེགས་པ་དེ་དག་ཐམས་ཅད་ལ་རིམ་གྲོ་བྱེད་པར་འགྱུར་རོ། །བསྟི་སྟང་དང་། མཆོད་པ་ཐམས་ཅད་ཀྱིས་མཆོད་པར་འགྱུར་རོ། །དམ་པའི་ཆོས་ཀྱང་འཛིན་པར་འགྱུར་རོ། །རྟག་ཏུ་ཡང་ཁྱིམ་བདག་ཏུ་གྱུར་ནས་རབ་ཏུ་བྱུང་བའི་བསླབ་པ་ལ་གནས་སོ། །དེ་བཞིན་གཤེགས་པའི་བྱང་ཆུབ་དེ་ཡང་རྒྱས་པར་བྱེད་པར་འགྱུར་རོ། །དེ་ནས་ཚེ་དང་ལྡན་པ་ཀུན་དགའ་བོས་ཁྱིམ་བདག་དྲག་ཤུལ་ཅན་ལ་འདི་སྐད་ཅེས་སྨྲས་སོ། །ཁྱིམ་བདག་རྒྱུ་གང་དང་རྐྱེན་གང་གིས་གང་ཁྱིམ་ན་གནས་ཤིང་རྫུལ་ལ་གནས་པ་ལ་དགའ་བར་བྱེད། དྲག་ཤུལ་ཅན་གྱིས་སྨྲས་པ། བཙུན་པ་ཀུན་དགའ་བོ་རྫུལ་ལ་ནི་རྫུལ་ཙུང་ཟད་ཀྱང་མེད་དོ། །སྙིང་རྗེ་ཆེན་པོ་དང་ལྡན་པས་བདག་བདེ་བ་ལ་མི་རེ་བ་ཡིན་ནོ། །བཙུན་པ་ཀུན་དགའ་བོ་བྱང་ཆུབ་སེམས་དཔའ་ནི་སྡུག་བསྔལ་ཐམས་ཅད་ཀྱིས་གཟིར་ཀྱང་བཟོད་དེ། སེམས་ཅན་རྣམས་ཡོངས་སུ་མི་གཏོང་ངོ་། །དེ་སྐད་ཅེས་སྨྲས་པ་དང་། བཅོམ་ལྡན་འདས་ཀྱིས་ཚེ་དང་ལྡན་པ་ཀུན་དགའ་བོ་ལ་འདི་སྐད་ཅེས་བཀའ་སྩལ་ཏོ། །ཀུན་དགའ་བོ་ཁྱིམ་བདག་དྲག་ཤུལ་ཅན་འདི་ཁྱིམ་གྱི་ས་ལ་གནས་ནས་བསྐལ་པ་བཟང་པོ་འདི་ལ་སེམས་ཅན་རབ་ཏུ་མང་པོ་ཡོངས་སུ་སྨིན་པར་བྱེད་པར་འགྱུར་ཏེ། རབ་ཏུ་བྱུང་བའི་བྱང་ཆུབ་སེམས་དཔས་ནི་བསྐལ་པ་སྟོང་ངམ། བསྐལ་པ་བརྒྱ་སྟོང་དུ་མར་ཡང་དེ་ལྟར་མི་ནུས་སོ། །དེ་ཅིའི་ཕྱིར་ཞེ་ན། ཀུན་དགའ་བོ་འདི་ལྟར་ཁྱིམ་བདག་འདི་ལ་ཡོད་པའི་ཡོན་ཏན་རྣམས་ནི་རབ་ཏུ་བྱུང་བའི་བྱང་ཆུབ་སེམས་དཔའ་སྟོང་ལ་ཡང་མེད་དོ། །དེ་ནས་བཅོམ་ལྡན་འདས་ལ་ཚེ་དང་ལྡན་པ་ཀུན་དགའ་བོས་འདི་སྐད་ཅེས་གསོལ་ཏོ། །བཅོམ་ལྡན་འདས་ཆོས་ཀྱི་རྣམ་གྲངས་འདིའི་མིང་ཅི་ལགས། འདི་ཇི་ལྟར་གཟུང་བར་བགྱི། བཅོམ་ལྡན་འདས་ཀྱིས་བཀའ་སྩལ་པ། ཀུན་དགའ་བོ་དེའི་ཕྱིར་ཆོས་ཀྱི་རྣམ་གྲངས་འདི་དྲག་ཤུལ་ཅན་གྱིས་ཞུས་པ་ཞེས་བྱ་བར་ཟུང་

ཤིག  །ཁྱིམ་པ་དང་རབ་ཏུ་བྱུང་བའི་བསླབ་པ་སྒྲུབ་པ་ཞེས་བྱ་བར་ཡང་ཟུང་
ཤིག  །ལྷག་པའི་བསམ་པས་བླ་མ་ལ་བསྙེན་བཀུར་བྱ་བའི་ལེའུ་ཞེས་བྱ་བར་ཡང་
ཟུང་ཤིག  །ཀུན་དགའ་བོ་ཆོས་ཀྱི་རྣམ་གྲངས་འདི་ཐོས་མ་ཐག་ཏུ་བྱང་ཆུབ་སེམས་
དཔའི་ཡོན་ཏན་དང་།  བརྩོན་འགྲུས་དང་།  ཆོས་མང་པོ་རབ་ཏུ་འཐོབ་སྟེ།
བརྩོན་འགྲུས་ཞན་པས་བསྐལ་པ་བརྒྱར་ཚངས་པར་སྤྱོད་པ་ལ་གནས་པས་ནི་དེ་ལྟ་མ་
ཡིན་ནོ།  །ཀུན་དགའ་བོ་དེ་བས་ན་བདག་ཀྱང་འདི་ལ་བརྩོན་འགྲུས་བསྐྱེད་པར་
འདོད་པ་དང་།  གཞན་ཡང་བརྩོན་འགྲུས་ལ་གཟུད་པར་འདོད་པ་དང་།  བདག་
ཀྱང་ཡོན་ཏན་གྱི་ཆོས་མཉམ་པ་ཉིད་ཐམས་ཅད་ལ་གནས་པར་འདོད་པ་དང་།
གཞན་ཡང་ཡོན་ཏན་གྱི་ཆོས་མཉམ་པ་ཉིད་ཐམས་ཅད་ལ་དགོད་པར་འདོད་པས་ཆོས་ཀྱི་
རྣམ་གྲངས་འདི་མཉན་པར་བྱ།  ཀུན་ཆུབ་པར་བྱ།  བཀླག་པར་བྱ།  གཞན་
དག་ལ་ཡང་རྒྱ་ཆེར་ཡང་དག་པར་རབ་ཏུ་བསྟན་པར་བྱའོ།  །ཀུན་དགའ་བོ་ངས་
ཆོས་ཀྱི་རྣམ་གྲངས་འདི་ཡང་དང་ཡང་རྒྱ་ཆེར་ཡང་དག་པར་རབ་ཏུ་བསྟན་པར་བྱ་བའི་
ཕྱིར་ཁྱོད་ལ་ཡོངས་སུ་གཏད་དོ།  །དེ་ཅིའི་ཕྱིར་ཞེ་ན།  ཆོས་ཀྱི་རྣམ་གྲངས་འདིའི་
ནང་དུ་ཡོན་ཏན་ཐམས་ཅད་འདུས་པར་དེ་བཞིན་གཤེགས་པས་བཤད་པའི་ཕྱིར་རོ།  །
ཀུན་དགའ་བོ་བྱང་ཆུབ་སེམས་དཔའ་གང་ཆོས་ཀྱི་རྣམ་གྲངས་འདི་དང་མི་འབྲལ་བར་
གནས་པ་དེ་སངས་རྒྱས་འབྱུང་བ་དང་མི་འབྲལ་ལོ།  །ཀུན་དགའ་བོ་བྱང་ཆུབ་
སེམས་དཔའ་གང་ཆོས་ཀྱི་རྣམ་གྲངས་འདི་ཉན་ཏམ།  འཛིན་ཏམ།  ཀློག་པ་དང་
མི་འབྲལ་བ་དེ་སངས་རྒྱས་འབྱུང་བ་དང་།  སངས་རྒྱས་ཐམས་ཅད་མཐོང་བ་དང་
མི་འབྲལ་ལོ།  །དེ་ཅིའི་ཕྱིར་ཞེ་ན།  ཀུན་དགའ་བོ་ཆོས་ཀྱི་རྣམ་གྲངས་འདིའི་ནང་
དུ་ཡོན་ཏན་ཐམས་ཅད་འདུས་ཤིང་ཆོས་ཀྱི་རྣམ་གྲངས་འདིའི་ནང་དུ་བསླབ་པ་བསྒྲུབ་
པའི་ལམ་གྱི་ཡོན་ཏན་ཐམས་ཅད་འདུས་པར་དེ་བཞིན་གཤེགས་པས་ཡང་དག་པར་རབ་
ཏུ་བཤད་པའི་ཕྱིར་རོ།  །ཀུན་དགའ་བོ་རིགས་ཀྱི་བུ་འམ་རིགས་ཀྱི་བུ་མོ་ཡང་དག་
པར་རྫོགས་པའི་བྱང་ཆུབ་དོན་དུ་གཉེར་བ་དག་གིས་སྟོང་གསུམ་གྱི་སྟོང་ཆེན་པོའི་
འཇིག་རྟེན་གྱི་ཁམས་མེས་རབ་ཏུ་གང་བ་ཡང་འབོགས་ཏེ།  ཆོས་ཀྱི་རྣམ་གྲངས་

འདི་མཉན་པར་བྱ། ཀུན་ཆུབ་པར་བྱའོ། །ཀུན་དགའ་བོ་སྟོང་གསུམ་གྱི་སྟོང་ཆེན་པོའི་འཇིག་རྟེན་གྱི་ཁམས་རིན་པོ་ཆེ་སྣ་བདུན་གྱིས་རབ་ཏུ་གང་བ་ཙམ་ཡང་རི་མོར་བྱས་ཏེ་སློབ་དཔོན་ལ་ཕུལ་ནས་ཆོས་ཀྱི་རྣམ་གྲངས་འདི་མཉན་པར་བྱའོ། །ཀུན་ཆུབ་པར་བྱའོ། ཀུན་དགའ་བོ་བྱང་ཆུབ་སེམས་དཔའ་གང་གིས་འདས་པའི་སངས་རྒྱས་བཅོམ་ལྡན་འདས་རྣམས་ཀྱི་མཆོད་རྟེན་རིན་པོ་ཆེ་ལས་སོ་སོར་བྱས་ཏེ་མཆོད་པ་ཐམས་ཅད་ཀྱིས་མཆོད་ལ། དེ་བཞིན་དུ་ད་ལྟར་བྱུང་བའི་སངས་རྒྱས་བཅོམ་ལྡན་འདས་ཉན་ཐོས་ཀྱི་དགེ་འདུན་དང་བཅས་པ་རྣམས་ལ་ཇི་སྲིད་འཚོའི་བར་དུ་བདེ་བའི་ཡོ་བྱད་ཐམས་ཅད་ཀྱིས་བསྙེན་བཀུར་བྱེད་ཅིང་། གང་མ་འོངས་པའི་སངས་རྒྱས་བཅོམ་ལྡན་འདས་རྣམས་དང་། བྱང་ཆུབ་སེམས་དཔའ་རྣམས་ཀྱི་བྲན་དང་། སློབ་མར་ཁས་བླངས་ཏེ་བསྙེན་བཀུར་བྱས་སུ་ཟིན་ཀྱང་ཆོས་ཀྱི་རྣམ་གྲངས་འདི་མི་འཛིན། མི་འཆང་། མི་ཀློག །ཀུན་ཆུབ་པར་མི་བྱེད། འཇུག་པར་མི་བྱེད་ཅིང་སྒྲུབ་པ་འདི་ལ་མི་གནས་ན། ཀུན་དགའ་བོ་བྱང་ཆུབ་སེམས་དཔའ་དེས་འདས་པ་དང་། མ་འོངས་པ་དང་། ད་ལྟར་བྱུང་བའི་དེ་བཞིན་གཤེགས་པ་རྣམས་ལ་མཆོད་པ་བྱས་པར་མི་འགྱུར་རོ། །ཀུན་དགའ་བོ་བྱང་ཆུབ་སེམས་དཔའ་གང་ཆོས་ཀྱི་རྣམ་གྲངས་འདི་ཉན་ཅིང་ཀུན་ཆུབ་པར་བྱེད་ལ་དམ་པའི་ཆོས་ཡུན་རིང་དུ་གནས་པར་བྱ་བ་དང་། སངས་རྒྱས་ཀྱི་རིགས་རྒྱུན་མི་འཆད་པར་བྱ་བའི་ཕྱིར་གཞན་དག་ལ་ཡང་རྒྱ་ཆེར་ཡང་དག་པར་རབ་ཏུ་སྟོན་ཅིང་སྒྲུབ་པ་འདི་ལ་ཡང་གནས་ན་ཀུན་དགའ་བོ་བྱང་ཆུབ་སེམས་དཔའ་དེས་འདས་པ་དང་། མ་འོངས་པ་དང་། ད་ལྟར་བྱུང་བའི་སངས་རྒྱས་བཅོམ་ལྡན་འདས་རྣམས་ལ་མཆོད་པ་བྱས་པར་འགྱུར་རོ། །གུས་པ་དང་བཅས་པས་བསྙེན་བཀུར་བྱས་པར་ཡང་འགྱུར་རོ། །བཅོམ་ལྡན་འདས་ཀྱིས་དེ་སྐད་ཅེས་བཀའ་སྩལ་ནས། ཚེ་དང་ལྡན་པ་ཀུན་དགའ་བོ་དང་། ཁྱིམ་བདག་དྲག་ཤུལ་ཅན་དང་། དགེ་སློང་དེ་དག་དང་། བྱང་ཆུབ་སེམས་དཔའ་དེ་དག་དང་། ལྷ་དང་། མི་དང་། ལྷ་མ་ཡིན་དང་། དྲི་ཟར་བཅས་པའི་འཇིག་རྟེན་ཡི་རངས་ཏེ། བཅོམ་ལྡན་འདས་ཀྱིས་གསུངས་པ་ལ་མངོན་པར་བསྟོད

རོ༎ ༎འཕགས་པ་དཀོན་མཆོག་བརྩེགས་པ་ཆེན་པོའི་ཆོས་ཀྱི་རྣམ་གྲངས་ལེའུ་སྟོང་ཕྲག་བརྒྱ་པ་ལས། འཕགས་པ་དྲག་ཤུལ་ཅན་གྱིས་ཞུས་པ་ཞེས་བྱ་བ་སྟེ་ལེའུ་བཅུ་དགུ་པ་རྫོགས་སོ༎ ༎རྒྱ་གར་གྱི་མཁན་པོ་སུ་རེནདྲ་བོ་དྷི་དང་། ཞུ་ཆེན་གྱི་ལོ་ཙྪ་བ་བན་དེ་ཡེ་ཤེས་སྡེས་བསྒྱུར་ཅིང་ཞུས་ཏེ་གཏན་ལ་ཕབ་པ༎ ༎

# INDEX


a great possession . . . . . . . . . . 30
about the *Noble Great Stack of Jewels* . . . . . . . . . . . . . . . . iii, v
absence of self . . . . . . . . . 10, 84
act of giving . . . . . . . . . . . 19, 20
action of a bodhisatva . . . . . . 20
actions of a bad being . . . 12, 17
actions of a holy being . . . 12, 17
adventitious . . . . . . . . . . . 28, 93
affliction . . 18, 30, 46, 47, 50, 52, 57, 79, 93
aggregate . . . . . . . . . . 26, 66, 76
aggregates, dhātus, and āyatanas . . . . . . . . . . . . . . . . . . . 34, 105
alcohol . . . . . . . . . . . . . . 17, 19
alertness . 19, 20, 23, 68, 94, 102
all phenomena . xix, 6, 74, 78, 97
all sentient beings . . 5, 9, 13, 15, 18, 21, 41-43, 66, 70, 78, 80, 84, 86, 95, 98
all-knowing mind . . . . . . . xvi, 11
all-knowing mind of a buddha xvi
all-knowing wisdom . . . . . i, xviii, xix, 6, 16, 26, 31, 34, 42, 46, 66, 69, 70, 77, 81, 86
all-knowing wisdom of a buddha . . . . . . . . . . . . . . . . xviii, xix, 26
Ānanda . . vii, ix, xiv, 3, 48, 87-92
Anāthapiṇḍada . . . . . . . . . . . 2-4
Apāyajaha . . . . . . . . . . . . . . . . . 3
approach completion . . . . 59, 60
appropriation . . . . . . . 43, 73, 94
arhat . . . . . . 4, 10, 45, 46, 80, 98
armour of all-knowingness . . 23
armour of the strength of patience . . . . . . . . . . . . . . . 21
*Ārya Mahāratnakūṭa* . . . . . . . . . v
ascetic training's good qualities . . . . . . . . . . . . . . 61, 62, 77, 83
attend . . . . vii, 14, 18, 45, 66, 76, 77, 94
authentic statement . . . viii, 4, 94
authoritative statement . . iii, vii, viii, 4, 5, 67, 68, 80-82, 94, 95
Avalokiteśhvara . . . . . . . . . . . . 3
avarice . . . . . . 17, 22, 31, 56, 71
bad migrations . . . 24, 26, 49, 51
bases of training . . . . . 17, 20, 26
Becoming . . . xv, xvi, 6, 7, 10, 19, 20, 24, 25, 30, 37, 46, 48, 51, 60, 69, 72, 81, 88, 95
being content with the worst kind

..................... 62-64
benefit and ease ........... 21
bhagavan ... 2-8, 45, 46, 59-62, 85-89, 92
bhagavan gave a smile ...... 87
bhagavan tathāgata arhat truly complete buddha ..... 45, 46
bodhichitta .......... ix, 95, 98
bodhisatva ... ix-xv, xvii-xix, 1-4, 6-14, 17, 19-21, 23, 24, 29-33, 35-43, 45, 47, 48, 54, 55, 57, 58, 60-70, 72, 73, 75-80, 82-87, 89-92, 95, 96, 98, 104
bodhisatva householders .. xii, 6, 8, 60, 86
bodhisatva mahāsattva .... 3, 72, 95, 96
Brahmans ....... 22, 25, 45, 80
buddha is not to be sought elsewhere .............. xxiv
buddha is the deity ........ 21
buddha-mind ............. xxii
Buddhist sūtras ............. v
bundle ............. 1, 33, 60
cause of wisdom's occurrence xxiv
child as specially attractive .. 41
clinging .. 15, 18, 33, 49, 62-64, 73, 84, 96
come forth ... xi, 6, 7, 47, 48, 50
command of the tathāgatas ... 6, 58, 87
commitments .......... 11, 14
complete purification ...... 46
complete purity ..... 46, 75, 96
conceived effort ........ 84, 96
concept tokens ...... 74, 96, 97
conduct of begging for alms ................... 65, 66
confusion .... xx, 19-21, 97, 104
consciousness .... 47, 70, 71, 74, 94, 97, 105
content with massage medicinals .................... 66, 67
covetous mind ............ 21
craving ...... 27, 29, 42, 71, 73
cyclic existence .. xxi, 96-99, 102
daughters of the family ... xii, 5, 6, 91
deeds for myself ........... 14
deeds for others ........... 14
definitive meaning ..... xxiii, 70, 102
dharma .. iii, v, vi, viii-xii, xv, xvi, xviii, xx-xxii, 1, 3, 6-15, 17, 19, 20, 22, 23, 25, 27-29, 33-35, 42-45, 50, 51, 53-65, 67-70, 72-77, 79-92, 94, 97, 103, 104, 109
dharma enumeration of the three heaps .................. 45
dharma enumerations iii, vi, 1, 92
dharma practices ........... 8
dharma robes for the body 64, 65
dharmadhātu .... 76, 84, 85, 97
dharmas of the side of enlightenment ....... 6, 7, 58
dhyāna .................. 98
diminished articles 61, 62, 77, 83
direct perception .. xxi, xxii, xxiv, 85
direct transmission ... xvii, xxiv
direct transmission of wisdom ...................... xxiv
discursive thought ... 28, 69, 98
distribute possessions to the poor ...................... 14
distributions of generosity .. 17
Dzogchen ...... x, xviii, xxii, 21

eight worldly dharmas . . . 33-35
eightfold path of the noble ones . . . . . . . . . . . . . . . . . . . . . . xviii
elemental spirit . . . . . . . . . . . 17
embarrassment and shame . . . 44
emptiness . iii, x, xi, xix-xxi, xxvi, 15, 47, 69, 74, 77, 84, 90, 98, 109, 110
emptiness, signlessness, and wishlessness . . . . . . . . . . . . . xxi
enclosure of Anāthapiṇḍada 2-4
enlightenment mind . ix, 11, 12, 20, 32, 33, 44, 52, 58, 66, 76, 95, 98, 105
entirely without weariness . . . 13
entity . . . . . . . . . . . . 28, 99, 105
equality . . . . . . . . . . . . . . . 42, 76
equalness . . . xix, 33, 34, 42, 74, 76, 84, 85, 87, 90
equalness of all dharmas . . . . 34, 74, 84
equalness of dharmas . . . . 42, 87
equanimity . . . . . . . . xviii, 32, 47
evil karmic actions . . . . . . . . . 34
examination of the mind itself . . . . . . . . . . . . . . . . . . . . . . xxiv
experts . . . . 26, 33, 77, 104, 105
extremes of action . . . . . . 15, 69
fame and infamy . . . . . . . . 13, 57
familiarization . . . . . . . . . . . . 25
faults of medicines . . . . . . . . . 56
faults of staying in a household . . . . . . . . . . . . . . . . 24, 29, 59
faults of the begging bowl . . . 56
faults of the dharma robes . . . 56
first bundle . . . . . . . . . . . . . . . 1
five aggregates . . . 13, 26, 53, 54, 65, 76
five bases of training . . . . 17, 20
five paths . . . . . . . . . . . . . . . . 99
five thousand bodhisatvas . . . . 3
five types of migrator . . . . . . . 42
five vows of a layman . . . . 17, 20
forty-nine chapters . . . . . . vi, vii
four companions of an ordained bodhisatva . . . . . . . . . . . . . . 70
four families of noble ones . . 62
four totally pure disciplines 83, 84
friendly or unfriendly . . . . . . 42
full-ripening 31, 33, 35, 69, 83, 86
gain and loss . . . . . . . xviii, 13, 57
gentle speech . . . . . . . . . . . . . 20
gift of dharma . . . . . . . . 9, 11, 53
gone for refuge to the buddha . . . . . . . . . . . . . . . . . . 9, 11, 12
gone for refuge to the dharma . . . . . . . . . . . . . . . . . . . . 9-12
gone for refuge to the saṅgha . . . . . . . . . . . . . . . . . . . . 10-12
gone forth . . . . . . . . . . . . . . . 6, 7
gossip . . . . . . . . . . . . . . . . . . . 20
great compassion . . xxiii, 11, 23, 46, 89
great monk community . . . . . . 2
*Great Stages of the Path to Enlightenment* . . . . . . . . . . . 94
Great Vehicle . . iv-vi, xx, xxiv, 2, 4-7, 9, 10, 43, 98-101, 105, 109, 110
Great Vehicle sūtra . iv, v, 2, 109
*Great Vehicle Unravelling the Intent Sūtra* . . . . . . . . . . . . . . xx
grove of prince Jetṛi . . . . . . . 2-4
habituation . . . . . . . . . . . . . . 100
happiness and suffering . . 13, 57
happy with instructions given . . . . . . . . . . . . . . . . . . . 10, 44
Hindu tradition . . . . . . . . . . . 22

homosexual activities . . . . . . . 18
honourable task . . . . . . . . . . . 13
household . . . . xi-xiv, xix, 6-8, 12, 13, 15, 16, 24, 27-30, 33, 35, 41, 43, 45, 47-53, 58-60, 72, 83, 86-89
householder . . i, iii-v, ix-xv, xvii-xix, xxiii, xxiv, 1-5, 7-14, 16, 17, 19-21, 23, 24, 29-33, 35-43, 45, 47-49, 54, 55, 58-63, 65-67, 70, 73, 75, 77-83, 85-89, 92
householder bodhisatva . . . ix-xv, xvii-xix, 35
householder Uncouth . . i, iii, iv, ix, xiv, xvii, xxiii, xxiv, 1, 3-5, 8, 59-62, 86-89, 92
hundred thousand chapters . . iii, vi, 1, 92
if a bodhisatva householder sees a requester . . . . . . . . . . . . . 30-33
*Illuminator Tibetan-English Dictionary* . . . . . . . . . . 108, 112
ill-will . . . . 20-22, 27, 32, 37, 47, 52, 78
impermanence xxi, 12, 27, 28, 35
in accord with how it actually is . . . . . . . . . . . . . . . . . . . . . . 41
in regard to his wife . . . . . . 35-40
Indian Buddhist texts . . . . . . . . 1
individualized being . . . . . . . 10
internal comprehension of all-knowingness . . . . . . . . . . . 42
irreversibility of a bodhisatva's progress . . . . . . . . . . . . . . . . 7
joining the palms . . . . . . . . . . 16
joy and sorrow . . . . . . . . . . . . 7
joy in abandoning . . . . . . . . . 64
kalpa . . . . . . xiv, 5, 53, 82, 88-90
karmic actions . xviii, 15, 16, 34, 35, 44, 100
karmic allotment . . . . . . . . . . 34
Kimpāka fruit . . . . . . . . . . . . . 51
latency . . . . . . . . . . . 31, 69, 100
lay aside . . . . . . . . . . . . . 45, 100
layman . . . . xi, 17, 20, 26, 27, 89
laypeople . . . . . . . . . . . . . 27, 45
Lesser Vehicle sūtra . . . . . . . . . . v
list of features of the dharma . . 3
livelihood through right means 12
living being . . . . . . . . . . . 17, 75
logical analysis . . . . . . . . . . . . xxi
loving kindness . . 15, 18, 32, 41, 44, 47, 52, 68, 78
Mahāmudrā . x, xviii, xxii, 21, 98
mahāsattva . . . 3, 72, 95, 96, 104
Mahāsthāma-prāpta . . . . . . . . . 3
mahāyāna . . . . . . . . . . . . . . 1, 99
Maitreya . . . vii, viii, xx, xxii, xxiii, 3, 22, 60, 109
make the effort to rise . . . . . . 10
making thorough dedications 43
manifest complete buddha . . 10, 23, 48
Mañjuśhrī . . . . . . . . . . . . . . . . . 3
māra . . 30, 31, 38, 50, 53, 71, 80, 101
measureless veneration for the dharma . . . . . . . . . . . . . . . 83
meditation . . xxii-xxv, 12, 15, 25, 44, 98, 100, 105, 106, 110
meditation on impermanence 12
mental veneration . . . . . . . . . . 9
mentation . . . . . . . . . 57, 79, 101
migrator . . . . . . . . . . . . . 42, 101
mind . . . . . v, ix, xii, xiv, xvi, xviii, xix, xxi-xxv, 5, 6, 8, 9, 11-14, 17-21, 26, 28, 32, 33, 37, 38, 41-45, 47, 48, 52, 54, 55, 57,

58, 60-62, 66-72, 74-76, 78, 81, 83-86, 93-103, 105, 106
mindfulness . . 19, 20, 23, 68, 69, 94, 96, 102
mindfulness and alertness . . . 19, 20, 23
mistakes made by bodhisatva householders . . . . . . . . . . . 60
mistakes of staying in a household . . . . . . . . . . . . . . . . . . . . . . . 60
monk . . xi-xiv, 1, 2, 6, 10, 45-47, 55-59, 61, 80, 81, 89, 107
much hearing . . . . 14, 15, 22, 55, 56, 79
Nāgaśhrī . . . . . . . . . . . . . . . . . . 3
name of this enumeration of dharma . . . . . . . . . . . . . . . . 89
Nandaka . . . . . . . . . . . . . . . . . . 3
noble beings . . . . . 10, 15, 24, 53
*Noble Great Stack of Jewels* . . iii, v
noble one . . . iii, vi, xxiv, 1, 2, 10, 92, 102, 109, 110
non-regressing bodhisatvas . . 12
non-returner . . . . . . . . . . . . 10
non-spiritual friends . . . . . . . 71
non-virtue . . . 24, 25, 28, 35, 40
not slip back at all . . . . . . . . . . 7
on hearing this dharma enumeration . . . . . . . . . . . . 90
one-time returner . . . . . . . . . 10
ordained . . . ix, xi-xv, 6-8, 16, 24, 45, 48, 50, 52, 54, 59-68, 70, 73, 75-80, 83-89, 107
ordained life . . . . . . . . . . . xiii-xv
ordained monk . . . . . . . . . . xi, 45
ordained ones . . . . . . . . . . . . . . 8
ordinary beings . . . . xxi, 10, 102
Other Emptiness . . . iii, xx, xxvi, 90, 98, 109, 110
Other Emptiness and this sutra . . . . . . . . . . . . . . . . . . . . . iii, xx
ownership . 15, 29, 31, 48, 75, 76
pāramitā . . xxi, 9, 19, 32, 33, 57, 69, 77-79, 87, 99
pāramitā of absorption . . . 33, 78
pāramitā of discipline . . . . 32, 77
pāramitā of generosity 19, 32, 77
pāramitā of patience . . . . . 32, 78
pāramitā of perseverance . 32, 78
pāramitā of prajñā . . . . . . 33, 78
parinirvāṇa . . . . . . . . . . . . . 5, 55
patience . . 21, 22, 32, 34, 78, 82
perceiving of a self . . . . . . . . . 73
perform the approach completion . . . . . . . . . . . . . . . . . . . . . . 59
petitioners . . . . . . . . . . . . . . viii
physical respect . . . 9, 10, 44, 47
physical respect and verbal respect . . . . . . . . . . . . . . . . . 10
poṣhada . . . . . . . . . . . . . . . . . 47
practising at the highest level . . . . . . . . . . . . . . . . . . xi, xviii
praise and blame . . . . . . . 13, 57
prajñā . xix, xxi, 9, 23, 26, 33, 37, 45, 51, 57, 74, 76, 78, 82, 85, 87, 99, 102
Prajñāpāramitā . . . . xxi, 9, 57, 99
Prajñāpāramitāsūtra . . . . . . . . 57
Pratyekabuddha Vehicle . . . . 10
profound meditation system of Maitreya . . . . . . . . . . . . . . xxiii
prostrating . . . . . . . . . . . . 16, 61
provisional and definitive meaning . . . . . . . . . . . . . . . 102
provisional meaning . . . . xxiii, 70
purpose of training in virtue . 68
rational mind . . . . . . 13, 97, 103
realization . . . xix, xx, xxii, 14, 95,

103, 104
recollection of the buddha 12, 44
recollection of the dharma .. 12
*Recollection of the Noble Three Jewels* .... viii, 2, 3, 44, 54, 105
reference and referencing .. 103
refuge ... 5, 8-12, 21, 23, 34, 39, 52, 66, 103, 104
remote monastery ... 48, 55, 57, 67, 68, 70, 72, 73, 75-80, 83
respect of body, speech, and mind ........................ 9
retinue ............. xvi, 3, 4
right accomplishment .... 5, 13
right view ............ 21, 69
rituals of respect .......... 22
roots of virtue .. 4, 9, 11, 16, 20, 24, 25, 41, 43, 44, 65, 70, 77, 78, 80
rough speech ............ 20
saṅgha of the non-regressing bodhisatvas ............ 12
saṅgha of the śhrāvakas ..... 12
saffron .......... 8, 45, 64, 65
saffron garments ....... 45, 65
saṃsāra .. xviii, xix, xxi-xxiii, 5, 6, 10, 16, 25, 43, 50, 53, 69, 71, 72, 75, 93, 95-97, 101, 103, 104
saṃsāric confusion ......... 20
saṃsāric mind .... xvi, xviii, xxi, xxii, xxiv, 26, 71, 97
Samāptaḥ ................ 3
sameness ................ 74
satva and sattva ....... 95, 104
Satyānanda ............... 3
second bundle ........... 33
second turning of the wheel .. x, xxi, xxiii, xxiv, 74
see his own faults ......... 45
seek armour .............. 5
sentient beings .... xiv, xxi, 5, 9, 13, 15, 16, 18, 21-24, 39, 41-43, 50, 55, 56, 65, 66, 69, 70, 72, 78, 80, 84-86, 89, 95, 98, 100, 101, 104, 106
serve and attend ........... 45
serve and honour ....... 45, 81
serve, attend, and serve and honour ................. 45
serving and honouring .. 10, 77, 80, 81
sexual misconduct ...... 18, 20
sexual penetration ......... 18
siblings ......... 13, 16, 27, 33
signlessness .. xxi, 47, 69, 74, 84
six pāramitās . 32, 33, 57, 69, 77, 79
skilful means ...... 57, 69, 103
skilled jeweller ............. xx
slight fears .............. 73
sons of the family ...... 5, 6, 91
special intentions .... 44, 52, 66
*Stack of Jewels* .. iii, v-vii, 92, 109
*Standard Grammar Volume I* . 82
staying in a household .. xii, xiii, 6-8, 12, 24, 27-29, 33, 35, 41, 43, 45, 48-53, 58-60, 72, 86-88
staying in a remote monastery ... 67, 68, 70, 72, 73, 75-79, 83
story of dharma ........... 22
stream-enterer ............ 10
sublime .................... v
subtle armour of all-knowingness ...................... 23
Sudhana .................. 3
sugata ............ 59, 88, 105
superfice, superficies ...... 105
system for translating texts ... 2

take authoritative statement or do recitation . . . . . . . . . . . . . . . 67
taking up the burden . . . . . . . 13
tathāgata . . . xxiii, 4-7, 12, 17, 19, 24, 31, 45-47, 55, 58, 61, 65, 66, 70, 80, 87, 88, 90, 91
tathāgata arhat truly complete buddha . . . . . . . . . . . 45, 46, 80
teacher of another religious tradition . . . . . . . . . . . . . . . . 21
ten joys at the benefits involved . . . . . . . . . . . . . . . . . . . . . . . 64
ten non-virtues . . . . . . . . . . . . 20
ten non-virtuous actions . . . xviii
ten specific activities . . . . . . . 22
the Buddha . . . i, v-xxv, 1, 3, 7-9, 11, 12, 14-18, 20-22, 26, 27, 41, 44-48, 50, 53, 54, 66, 67, 77, 79, 81, 87, 88, 90-95, 98-102, 106
the excellent speech of a teacher . . . . . . . . . . . . . . . . . . . . . . . 43
The Five Dharmas of Maitreya . . . . . . . . . . . . . . . . . . . . . . . xxii
the four things of gathering 31, 69
the great burden . . . . . . . . . . . . 5
*The Great Stack of Jewels* . . . . . vi, vii, 92, 109
The main themes of the sutra . . . . . . . . . . . . . . . . . . . . . . iii, ix
the particulars . . . . . . . . . . 7, 58
*The Point of Passage Wisdom Sūtra* . . . . . . . . . . . . . . . . . . . . . . . xxiv
*The Sūtra of the Three Heaps* . . 45
*The Sūtra Petitioned by King Dharaṇeśhvara* . . . . . . . . . . . . xx
*The Sūtra Petitioned by the Householder Uncouth* . . . . . iii, ix
the use of equalness . . . . . . . . 74
the word dharma . . . . . . . . . . 11
theme of ownership . . . . . . . . 29
third and last bundle . . . . . . . 60
third order thousandfold world system, . . . . . . . . . . . . . . . . 105
thirty-two marks of a great being . . . . . . . . . . . . . . . . . . . . . 9, 45
thoroughly dedicating . . . . . . 32
Three Jewels . . viii, 2, 3, 44, 54, 65, 104, 105
three perceptions . . . . 30-32, 35-41, 55
three perceptions in regard to his wife . . . . . . . . . . . . . . . 35-40
three things which bring total understanding . . . . . . . . . . . 43
three turnings . . . . . . . . . xx, 103
three turnings of the wheel of dharma . . . . . . . . . . . . . . xx, 103
three types of censure . . . . . . 41
Tibetan Buddhist schools . . xxii
total affliction . . . . . . . . . . 46, 50
totally pure discipline . . . 83, 84
totally pure Prajñāparamita . . 85
trainees in virtue . . . . 22, 25, 45, 58, 80
trainings of the ordained . 86-88
transmission of wisdom . . . . xvii, xix, xxiv
truly complete enlightenment . . 4, 5, 9-12, 16, 17, 20, 23, 32, 33, 48, 55, 58, 60, 72, 85, 91, 95, 96, 99, 100
Tsongkhapa . . . . . . . xx, 94, 110
twelve ascetic trainings . . . . . 61
two major types of beings . . . 10
Ugraḥ . . . . . . . . . . . . . . . . . . . 1
Śhākyamuni Buddha . . . . xvii, 4
śhamatha . . . . 14, 57, 72, 74, 81, 94, 102, 105, 106

Śhilānanda . . . . . . . . . . . . . . . . 3
śhrāvaka monks . . . . . . . . . . . . 7
Śhrāvaka Vehicle . . . . . . . 10, 11
Śhrāvastī . . . . . . . . . . . . . . . . . 2-4
ultimate meditation . . . . . . . . xxv
ultimate view . . . . . . . . . xxv, 110
Uncouth . . . . . . i, iii, iv, ix, xi-xix, xxiii, xxiv, 1, 3-5, 7, 8, 17, 48, 59-62, 86-89, 92
undertakes perseverance 9, 13, 87
*Unending Auspiciousness* . . . . viii, 2, 3, 54, 105
unmentionable actions 7, 52, 58
unsurpassed truly complete enlightenment . . . 4, 10-12, 16, 17, 20, 23, 32, 33, 48, 55, 58, 60, 72, 85
Vajrapāṇi . . . . . . . . . . . . . . . . 3
view of appropriation . . . . . . 43
vihāra . . . . . . . . . . 47, 55, 56, 68
Vinaya . 7, 26, 54, 55, 57, 59, 61
Vinaya dharma . . . . . . 54, 59, 61
Vinaya dharma which has been well explained . . . . . . . . . . . 61
vipaśhyanā . . . . 57, 72, 105, 106
virtuous behaviours . . . . . . . . . 8
Vitality-filled . . . . . . . . 87-89, 92
vows of a layperson . . . . . . . xviii
well explained . . . . . . . . . 59, 61
Western Buddhists . . . . . . . . xiv
what has been given . . . . . 29, 30
what has been placed in the household . . . . . . . . . . . 29, 30
what is frightening and scaring 70
what is not a branch . . . . . 18, 86
wisdom . . . i, iii, x, xi, xvi-xx, xxii-xxiv, 5, 6, 16, 26, 31, 34, 42, 46, 47, 52, 62, 66, 69, 70, 74, 76, 77, 81, 83, 86, 90, 97, 98, 101-103, 106, 110
wisdom-mind of a buddha . . . xxii
wisdom-mind of a buddha exists . . . . . . . . . . . . . . . . . . . . . . . xxii
wishlessness . . . . . xxi, 47, 69, 74
without observing their confused conduct . . . . . . . . . . . . . . . 45
workability . . . . . . . . . . . 74, 105
world with gods, men, and asuras . . . . . . . . . . . . . . . . . . . . . . . 6
world with gods, men, asuras, and gandharvas . . . . . . . . . . . . . 92
worldly dharmas . . . . . 13, 33-35
Yaśhodatta . . . . . . . . . . . . . . . . 3
Yaśhokāmaḥ . . . . . . . . . . . . . . 3

www.ingramcontent.com/pod-product-compliance
Lightning Source LLC
Chambersburg PA
CBHW022007160426
43197CB00007B/323
* 9 7 8 9 9 3 7 5 7 2 5 6 9 *